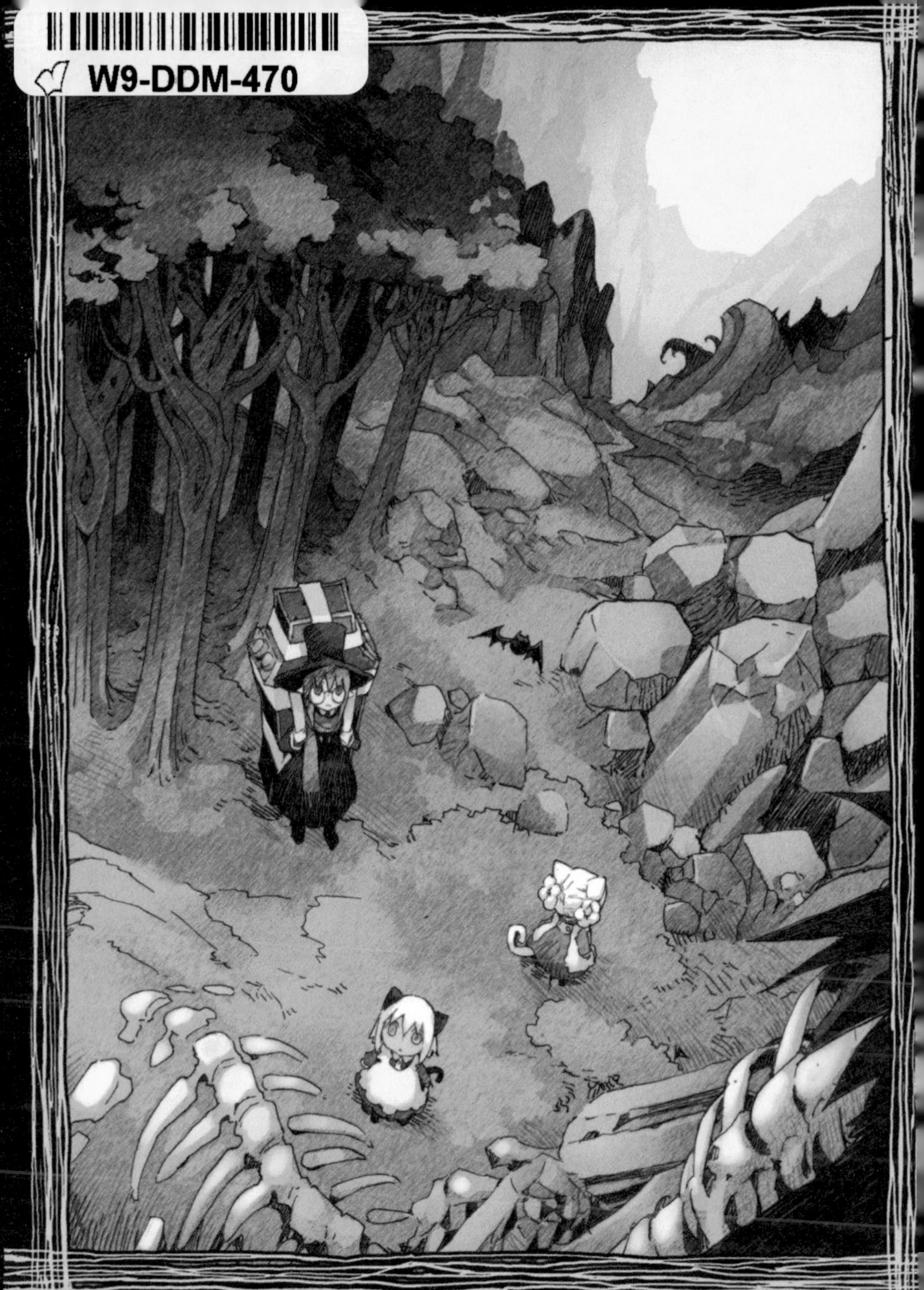

Through confused conversation, Kuro and company finally realized that each of them was looking at something different in the valley.

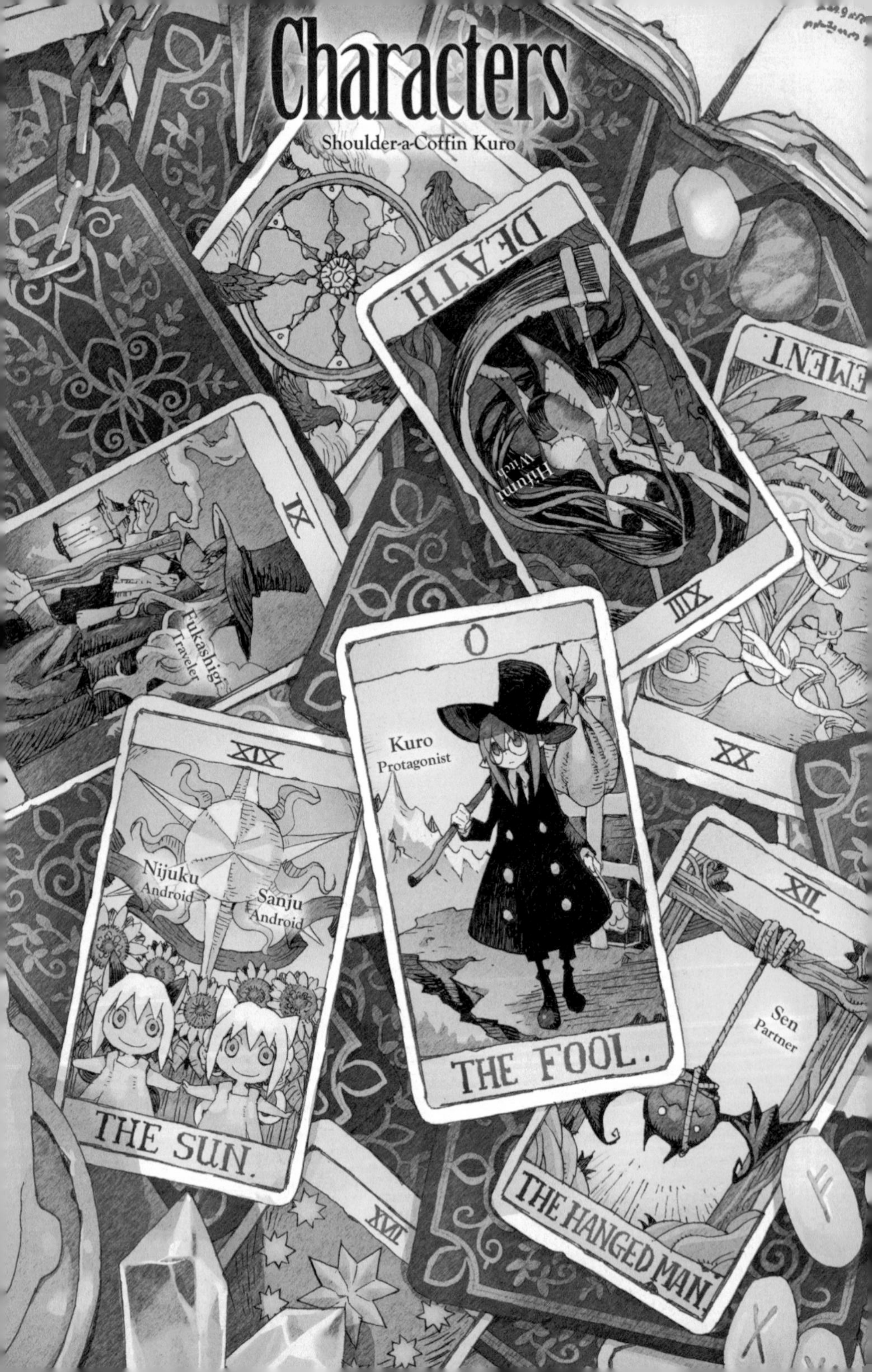
Characters
Shoulder-a-Coffin Kuro
DEATH
XIII
Hifumi
Witch
IX
Fukashigi
Traveler
0
Kuro
Protagonist
THE FOOL.
XX
XIX
Nijuku
Android
Sanju
Android
THE SUN.
XII
Sen
Partner
THE HANGED MAN
XVI

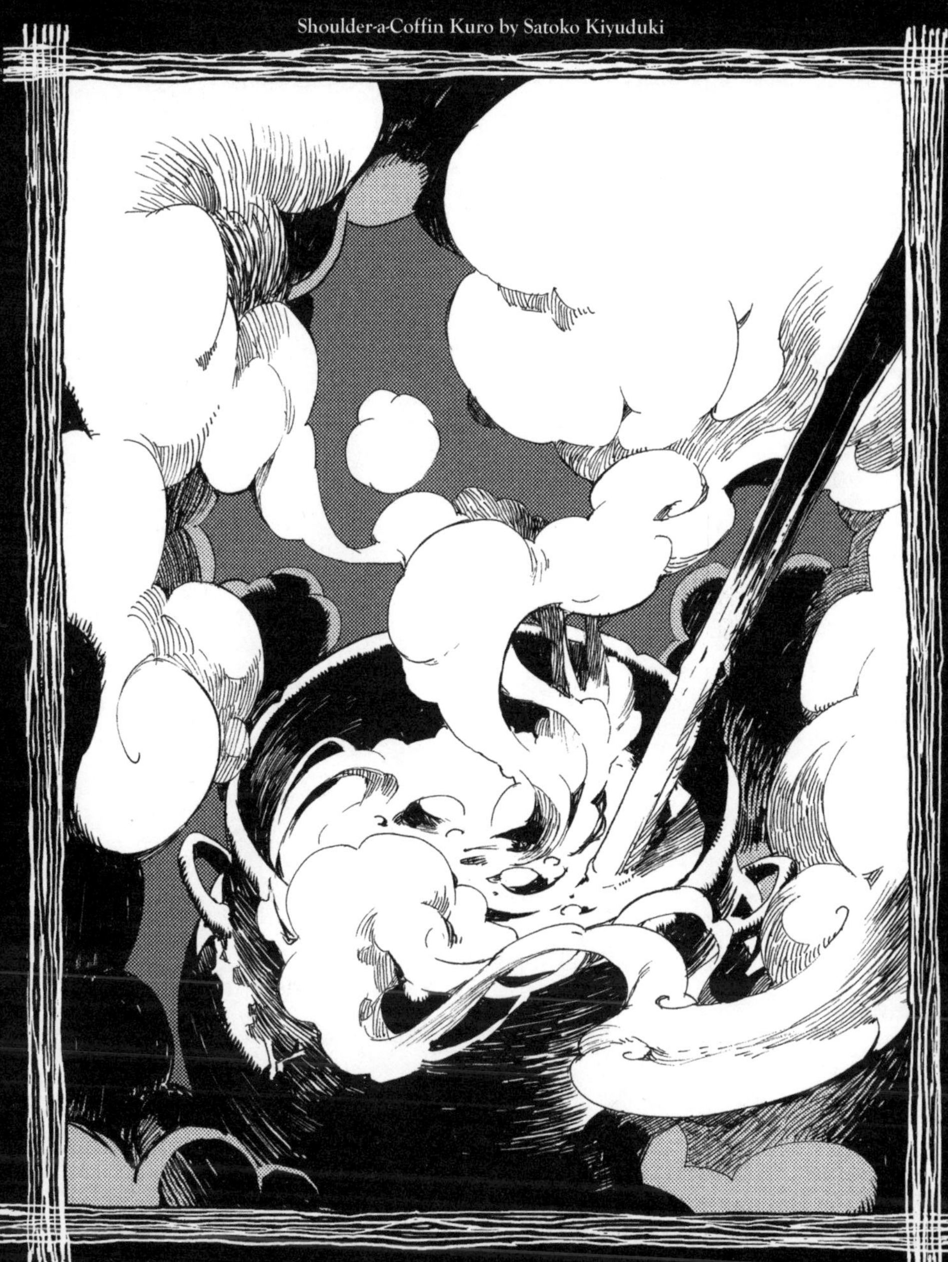

What are witches made of?
What kinds of things are witches made of?

Look in the cauldron.
You see, there are three ingredients simmering.

SHOULDER-A-COFFIN KURO

...ABOUT THREE WOMEN.

THIS IS A STORY...

...WAS A LIAR.

AND THE THIRD WOMAN...

THE FIRST WOMAN...

...WAS SOLITARY.

THIS STORY ENDS...

...WITH THE THREE WOMEN DYING.

THE SECOND WOMAN...

...WAS PROUD.

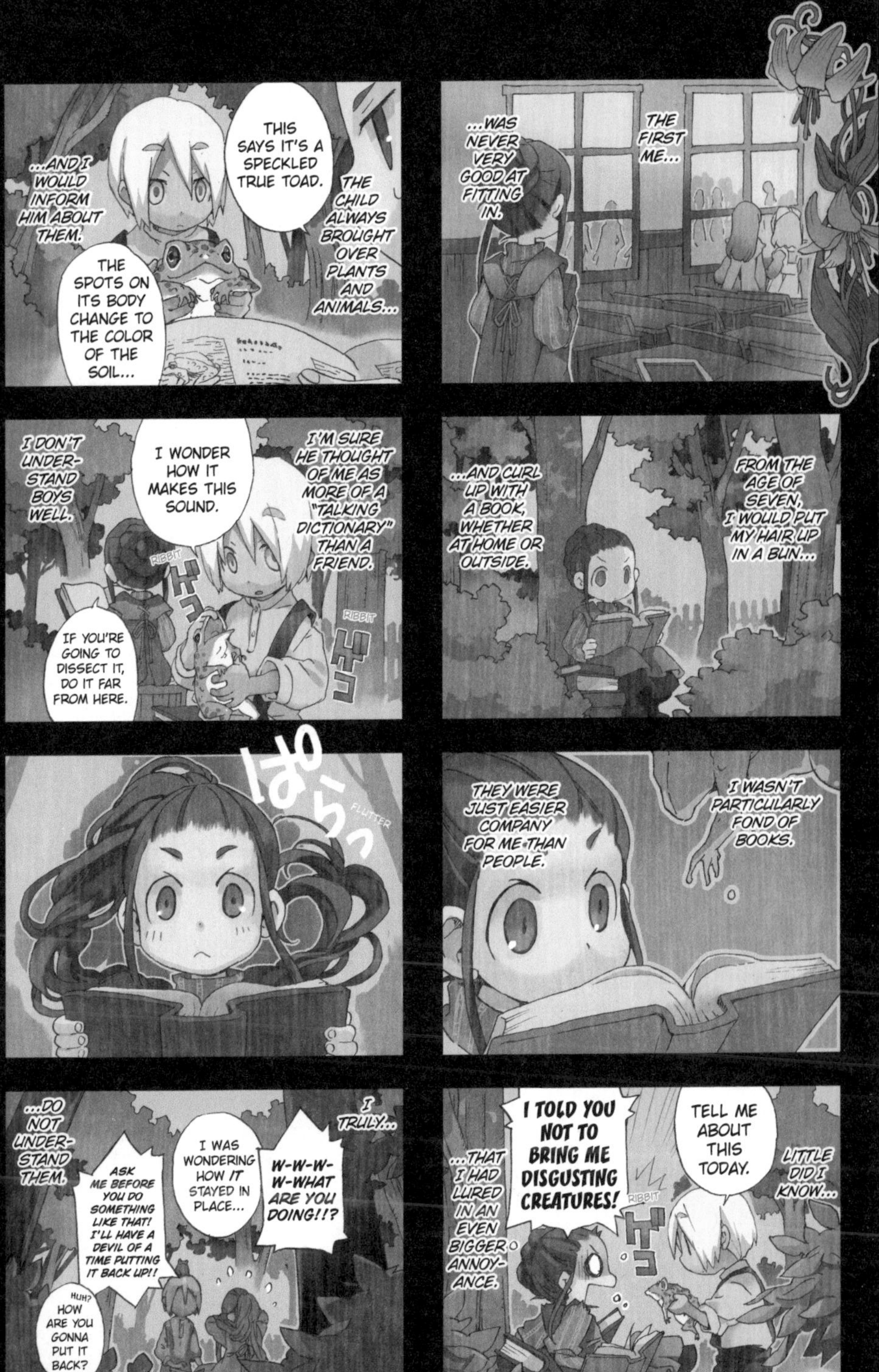
THE FIRST ME...
...WAS NEVER VERY GOOD AT FITTING IN.
THE CHILD ALWAYS BROUGHT OVER PLANTS AND ANIMALS...
THIS SAYS IT'S A SPECKLED TRUE TOAD.
...AND I WOULD INFORM HIM ABOUT THEM.
THE SPOTS ON ITS BODY CHANGE TO THE COLOR OF THE SOIL...
FROM THE AGE OF SEVEN, I WOULD PUT MY HAIR UP IN A BUN...
...AND CURL UP WITH A BOOK, WHETHER AT HOME OR OUTSIDE.
I'M SURE HE THOUGHT OF ME AS MORE OF A "TALKING DICTIONARY" THAN A FRIEND.
I WONDER HOW IT MAKES THIS SOUND.
I DON'T UNDER-STAND BOYS WELL.
RIBBIT
RIBBIT
IF YOU'RE GOING TO DISSECT IT, DO IT FAR FROM HERE.
I WASN'T PARTICULARLY FOND OF BOOKS.
THEY WERE JUST EASIER COMPANY FOR ME THAN PEOPLE.
FLUTTER
LITTLE DID I KNOW...
TELL ME ABOUT THIS TODAY.
I TOLD YOU NOT TO BRING ME DISGUSTING CREATURES!
...THAT I HAD LURED IN AN EVEN BIGGER ANNOY-ANCE.
RIBBIT
I TRULY...
W-W-W-W-WHAT ARE YOU DOING!!?
I WAS WONDERING HOW IT STAYED IN PLACE...
...DO NOT UNDER-STAND THEM.
ASK ME BEFORE YOU DO SOMETHING LIKE THAT! I'LL HAVE A DEVIL OF A TIME PUTTING IT BACK UP!!
HUH? HOW ARE YOU GONNA PUT IT BACK?

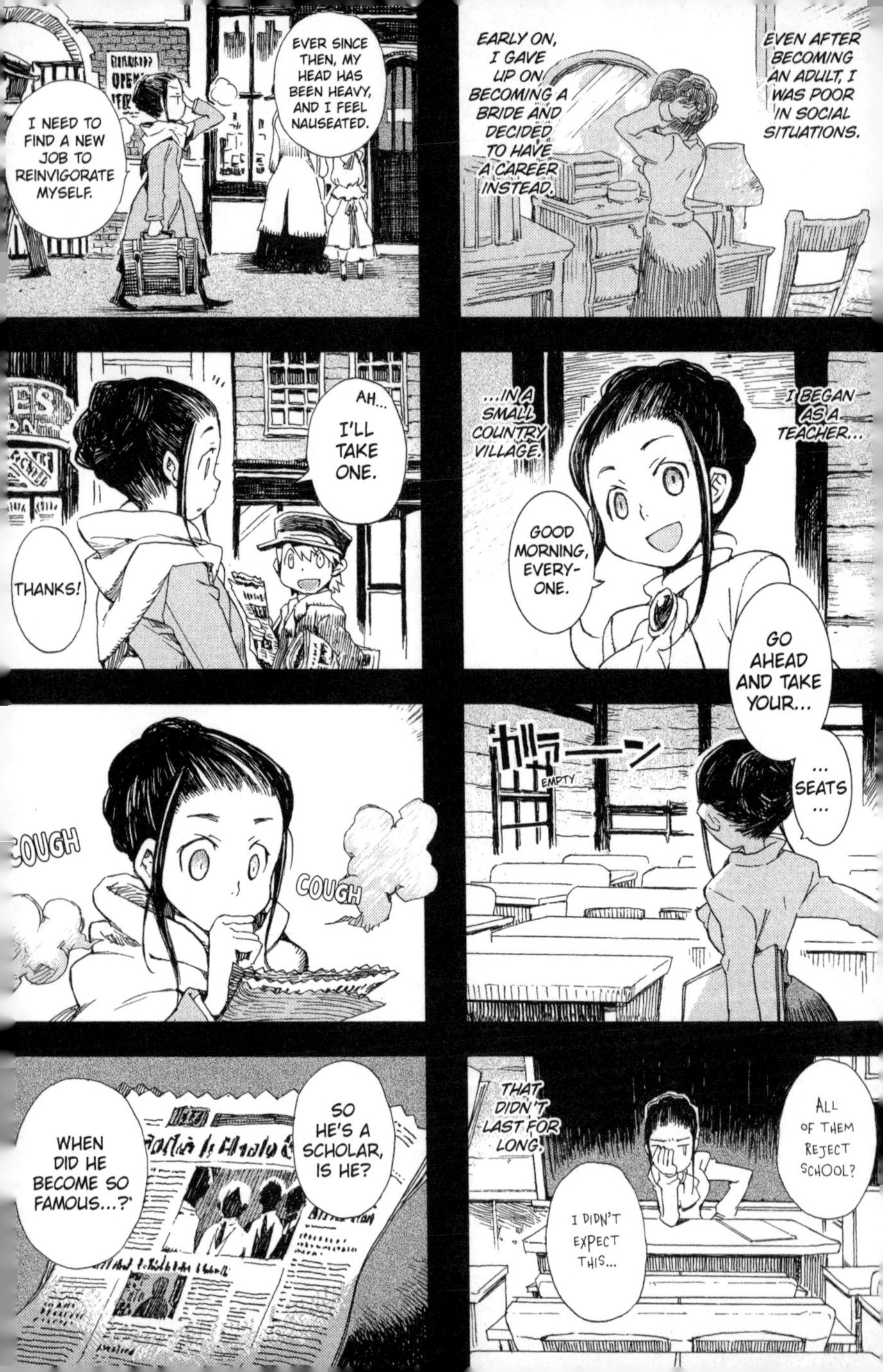
EVEN AFTER BECOMING AN ADULT, I WAS POOR IN SOCIAL SITUATIONS.
EARLY ON, I GAVE UP ON BECOMING A BRIDE AND DECIDED TO HAVE A CAREER INSTEAD.
EVER SINCE THEN, MY HEAD HAS BEEN HEAVY, AND I FEEL NAUSEATED.
I NEED TO FIND A NEW JOB TO REINVIGORATE MYSELF.
I BEGAN AS A TEACHER...
...IN A SMALL COUNTRY VILLAGE.
GOOD MORNING, EVERY-ONE.
AH... I'LL TAKE ONE.
THANKS!
GO AHEAD AND TAKE YOUR...
... SEATS ...
ガラーン
EMPTY
COUGH
COUGH
ALL OF THEM REJECT SCHOOL?
THAT DIDN'T LAST FOR LONG.
I DIDN'T EXPECT THIS...
SO HE'S A SCHOLAR, IS HE?
WHEN DID HE BECOME SO FAMOUS...?

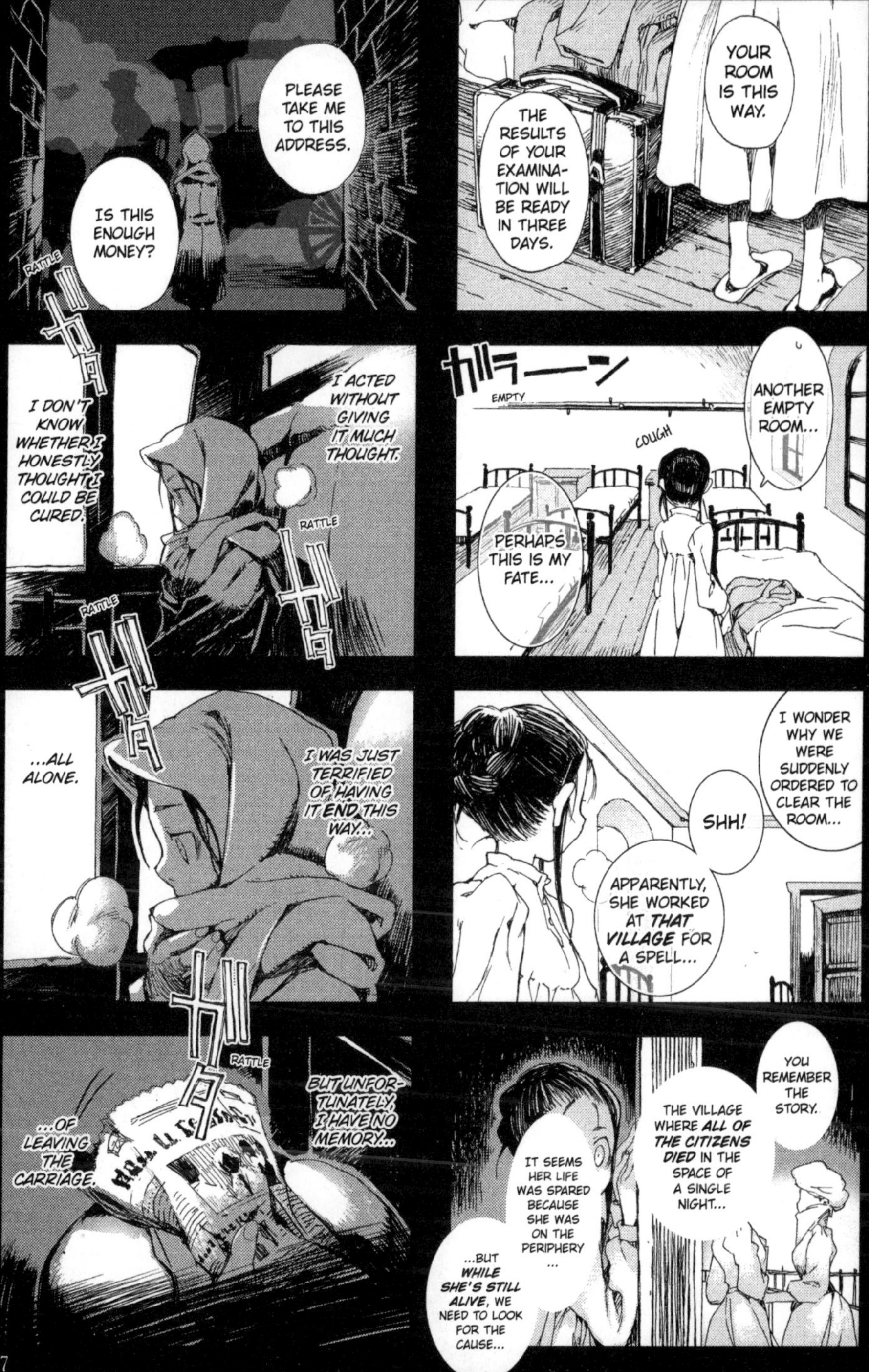

YOUR ROOM IS THIS WAY.
THE RESULTS OF YOUR EXAMINATION WILL BE READY IN THREE DAYS.
PLEASE TAKE ME TO THIS ADDRESS.
IS THIS ENOUGH MONEY?
RATTLE
ガラーン
EMPTY
ANOTHER EMPTY ROOM...
COUGH
PERHAPS THIS IS MY FATE...
I ACTED WITHOUT GIVING IT MUCH THOUGHT.
I DON'T KNOW WHETHER I HONESTLY THOUGHT I COULD BE CURED.
RATTLE
RATTLE
I WONDER WHY WE WERE SUDDENLY ORDERED TO CLEAR THE ROOM...
SHH!
APPARENTLY, SHE WORKED AT THAT VILLAGE FOR A SPELL...
I WAS JUST TERRIFIED OF HAVING IT END THIS WAY...
...ALL ALONE.
YOU REMEMBER THE STORY.
THE VILLAGE WHERE ALL OF THE CITIZENS DIED IN THE SPACE OF A SINGLE NIGHT...
IT SEEMS HER LIFE WAS SPARED BECAUSE SHE WAS ON THE PERIPHERY...
...BUT WHILE SHE'S STILL ALIVE, WE NEED TO LOOK FOR THE CAUSE...
RATTLE
BUT UNFORTUNATELY, I HAVE NO MEMORY...
...OF LEAVING THE CARRIAGE.

LOOK.

SOMETHING BAD IS COMING SOON.

YOU SHOULD BE CAREFUL, "RED ROSE."

...WAS A NATURAL BORN STAR.

THE SECOND ME...

YOU HAVE NO SELF-AWARENESS.

DO YOU KNOW HOW MANY PEOPLE BEAR A GRUDGE AGAINST YOU?

YOU SHUFFLED IN SEVERAL OF THE SAME CARD, SO WHAT ARE YOU TALKING ABOUT...

..."BLACK ROSE"?

HER SINGING VOICE WAS LIKE WINE.

SHE STOOD ON A STAGE THAT GLOWED AS IF LIT BY A FULL MOON.

DON'T DO IT. BLACK ROSE-SAN'S FORTUNES ARE USUALLY SPOT ON!

OH?

THEN SHALL WE MAKE A WAGER?

RIDICULOUS. THE ONLY CARDS I TRUST ARE INSIDE THE WALLETS OF THE NOBILITY.

THOSE OR PLAYING CARDS.

...FALL INTO HER PALM.

PEOPLE SAID THAT A SINGLE CARESS FROM HER HAND WOULD MAKE GENTLEMEN, JEWELS, AND POWER...

WHAT KIND OF FORTUNE-TELLER IS SHE?

ANOTHER WAS PRESSED INTO DUTY. ONE PERSON WON THE LOTTERY...

SHE HAS A REPUTATION! ONE PERSON SHE READ FOR GOT AN UPSET STOMACH FROM EATING SPOILED FOOD...

IT DIDN'T REALLY HAVE ANYTHING TO DO WITH THE CARDS...

SOUNDS MORE LIKE SHE CURSES PEOPLE...

...WERE "RESPECT" AND "TRUE FRIENDS."

ABOUT THE ONLY THINGS SHE COULDN'T OBTAIN...

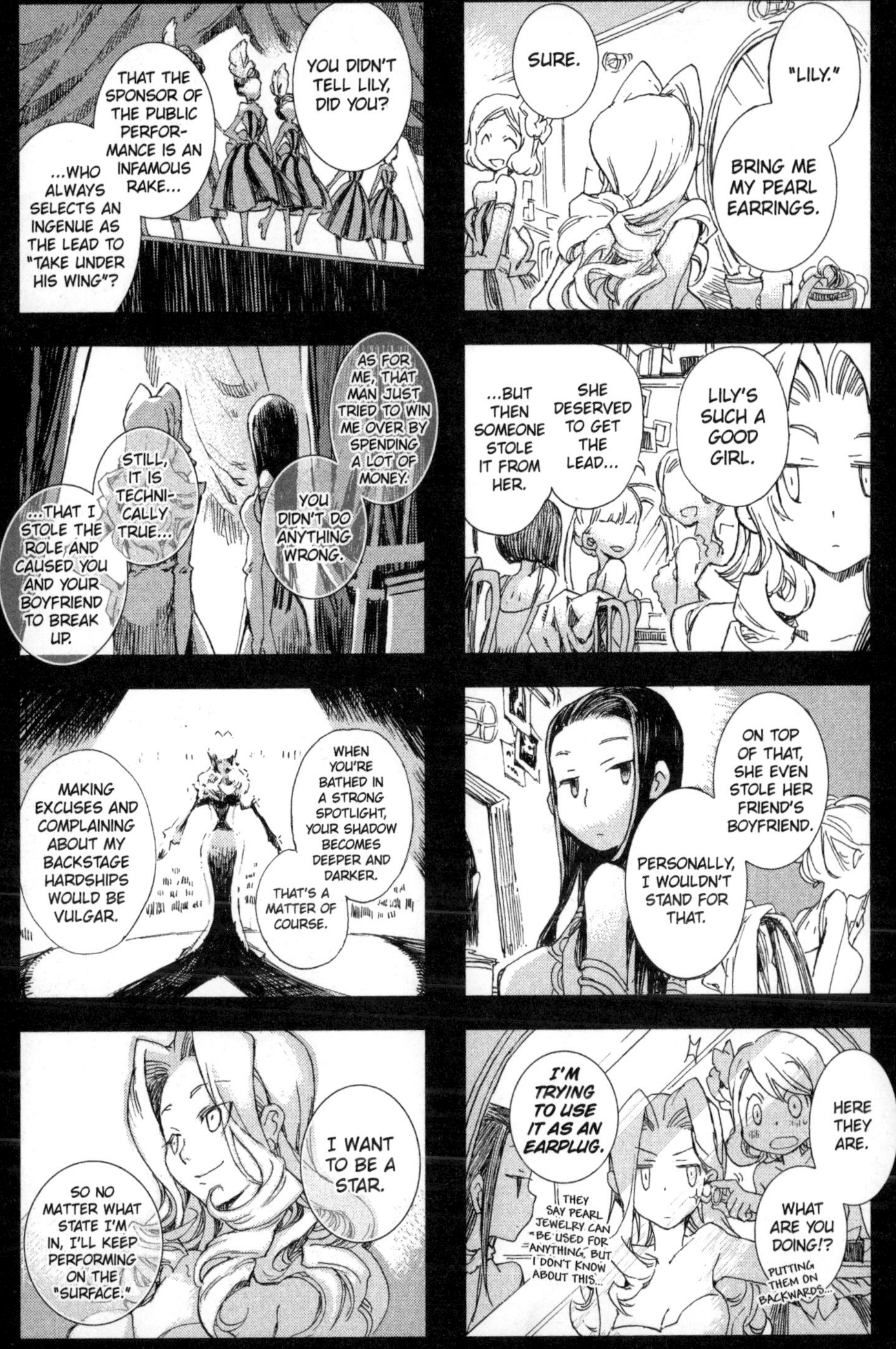
"LILY."
BRING ME MY PEARL EARRINGS.
SURE.
YOU DIDN'T TELL LILY, DID YOU?
THAT THE SPONSOR OF THE PUBLIC PERFOR-MANCE IS AN INFAMOUS RAKE...
...WHO ALWAYS SELECTS AN INGENUE AS THE LEAD TO "TAKE UNDER HIS WING"?
LILY'S SUCH A GOOD GIRL.
SHE DESERVED TO GET THE LEAD...
...BUT THEN SOMEONE STOLE IT FROM HER.
AS FOR ME, THAT MAN JUST TRIED TO WIN ME OVER BY SPENDING A LOT OF MONEY.
YOU DIDN'T DO ANYTHING WRONG.
STILL, IT IS TECHNI-CALLY TRUE...
...THAT I STOLE THE ROLE AND CAUSED YOU AND YOUR BOYFRIEND TO BREAK UP.
ON TOP OF THAT, SHE EVEN STOLE HER FRIEND'S BOYFRIEND.
PERSONALLY, I WOULDN'T STAND FOR THAT.
WHEN YOU'RE BATHED IN A STRONG SPOTLIGHT, YOUR SHADOW BECOMES DEEPER AND DARKER.
THAT'S A MATTER OF COURSE.
MAKING EXCUSES AND COMPLAINING ABOUT MY BACKSTAGE HARDSHIPS WOULD BE VULGAR.
HERE THEY ARE.
I'M TRYING TO USE IT AS AN EARPLUG.
WHAT ARE YOU DOING!?
PUTTING THEM ON BACKWARDS...
THEY SAY PEARL JEWELRY CAN BE USED FOR ANYTHING, BUT I DON'T KNOW ABOUT THIS...
I WANT TO BE A STAR.
SO NO MATTER WHAT STATE I'M IN, I'LL KEEP PERFORMING ON THE "SURFACE."

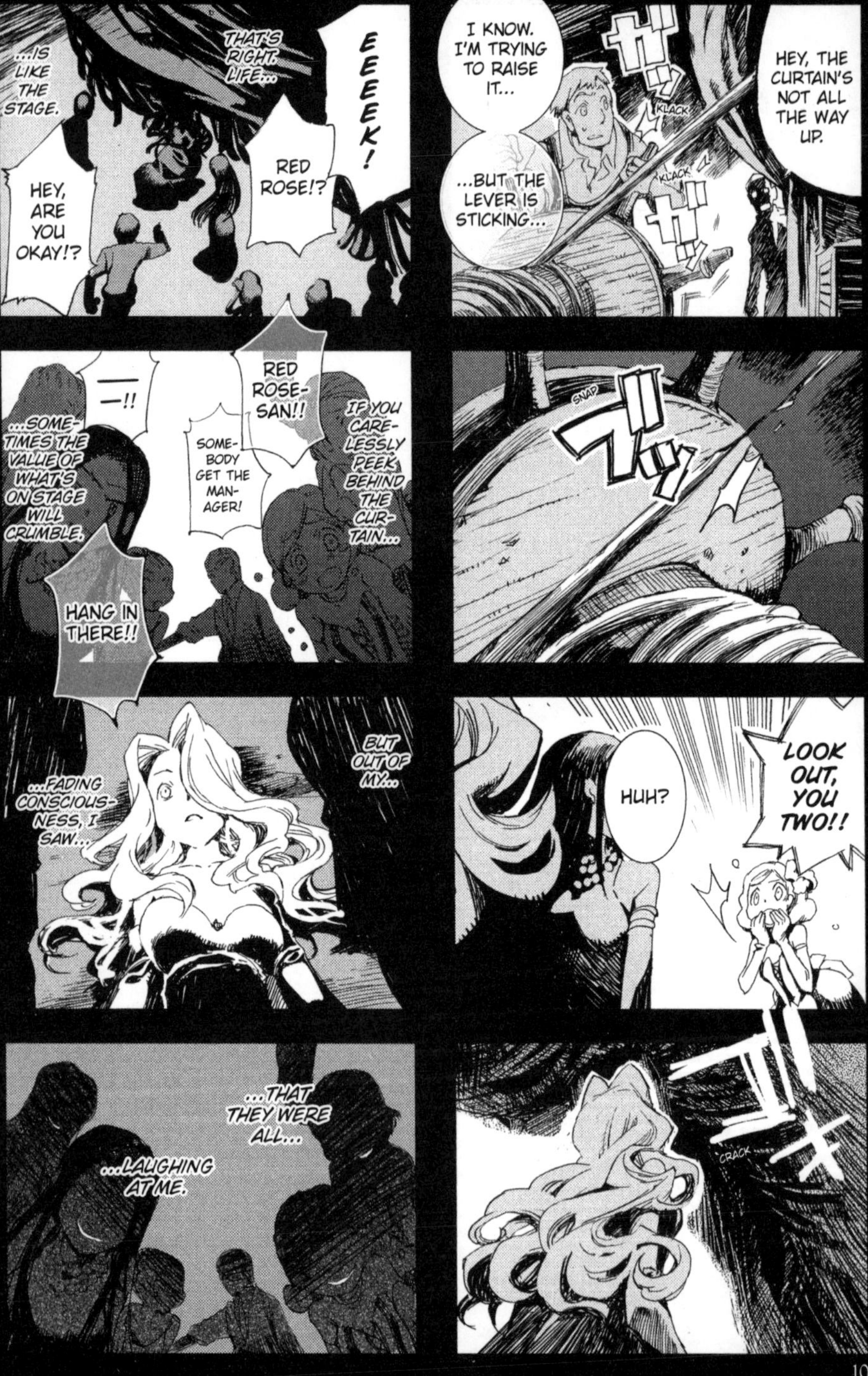
HEY, THE CURTAIN'S NOT ALL THE WAY UP.
I KNOW. I'M TRYING TO RAISE IT...
...BUT THE LEVER IS STICKING...
KLACK
KLACK
EEEEEK!
RED ROSE!?
THAT'S RIGHT. LIFE...
...IS LIKE THE STAGE.
HEY, ARE YOU OKAY!?
SNAP
IF YOU CARELESSLY PEEK BEHIND THE CURTAIN...
RED ROSE-SAN!!
SOMEBODY GET THE MANAGER!
——!!
...SOMETIMES THE VALUE OF WHAT'S ON STAGE WILL CRUMBLE.
HANG IN THERE!!
LOOK OUT, YOU TWO!!
HUH?
BUT OUT OF MY...
...FADING CONSCIOUSNESS, I SAW...
CRACK
...THAT THEY WERE ALL...
...LAUGHING AT ME.

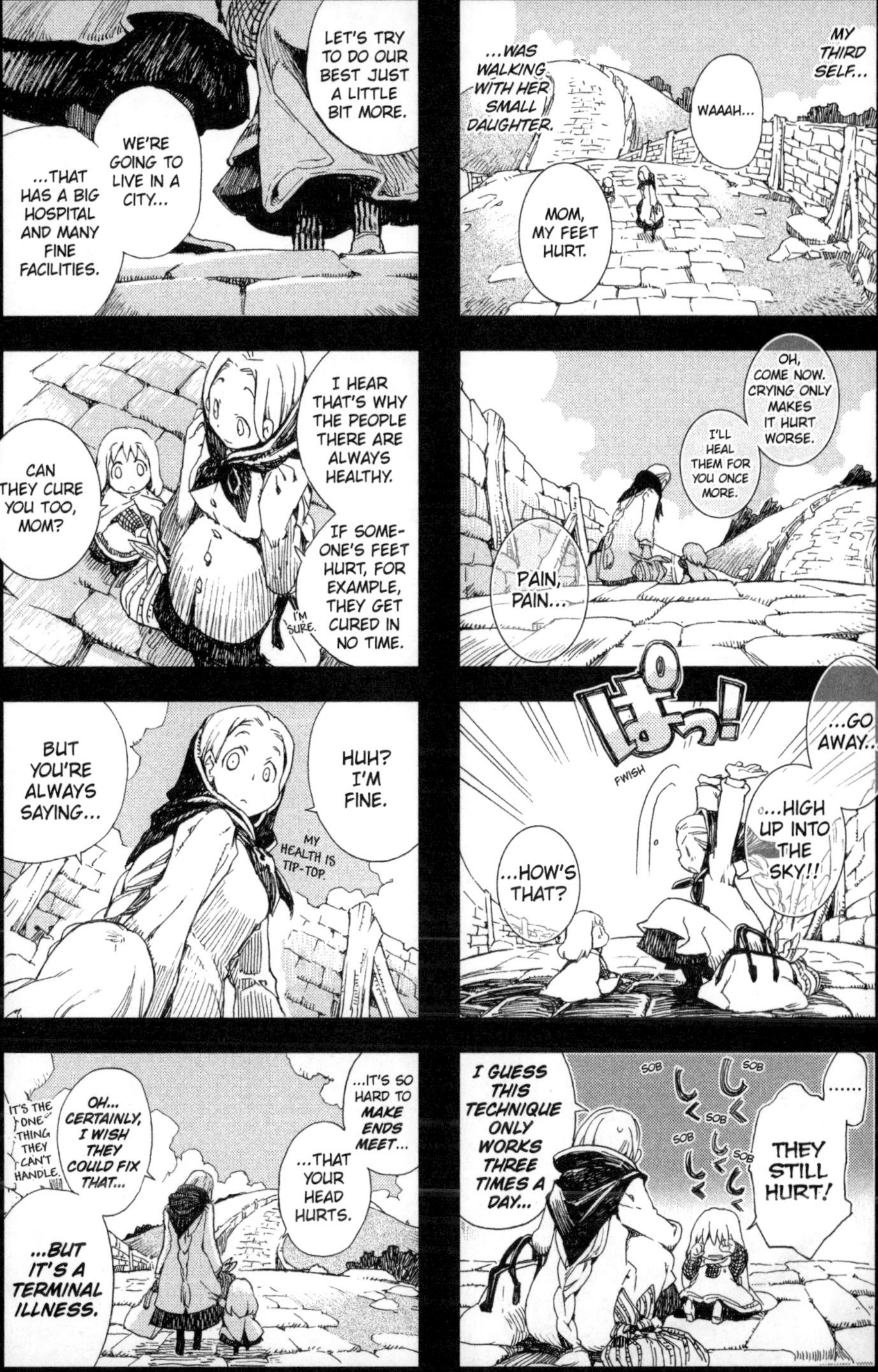

MY THIRD SELF...
...WAS WALKING WITH HER SMALL DAUGHTER.
WAAAH...
MOM, MY FEET HURT.
LET'S TRY TO DO OUR BEST JUST A LITTLE BIT MORE.
WE'RE GOING TO LIVE IN A CITY...
...THAT HAS A BIG HOSPITAL AND MANY FINE FACILITIES.
OH, COME NOW. CRYING ONLY MAKES IT HURT WORSE.
I'LL HEAL THEM FOR YOU ONCE MORE.
PAIN, PAIN...
I HEAR THAT'S WHY THE PEOPLE THERE ARE ALWAYS HEALTHY.
IF SOME-ONE'S FEET HURT, FOR EXAMPLE, THEY GET CURED IN NO TIME.
I'M SURE.
CAN THEY CURE YOU TOO, MOM?
...GO AWAY...
ぱっ!
FWISH
...HIGH UP INTO THE SKY!!
...HOW'S THAT?
HUH? I'M FINE.
MY HEALTH IS TIP-TOP.
BUT YOU'RE ALWAYS SAYING...
......
THEY STILL HURT!
SOB SOB SOB SOB
I GUESS THIS TECHNIQUE ONLY WORKS THREE TIMES A DAY...
...IT'S SO HARD TO MAKE ENDS MEET...
...THAT YOUR HEAD HURTS.
OH... CERTAINLY, I WISH THEY COULD FIX THAT...
IT'S THE ONE THING THEY CAN'T HANDLE.
...BUT IT'S A TERMINAL ILLNESS.

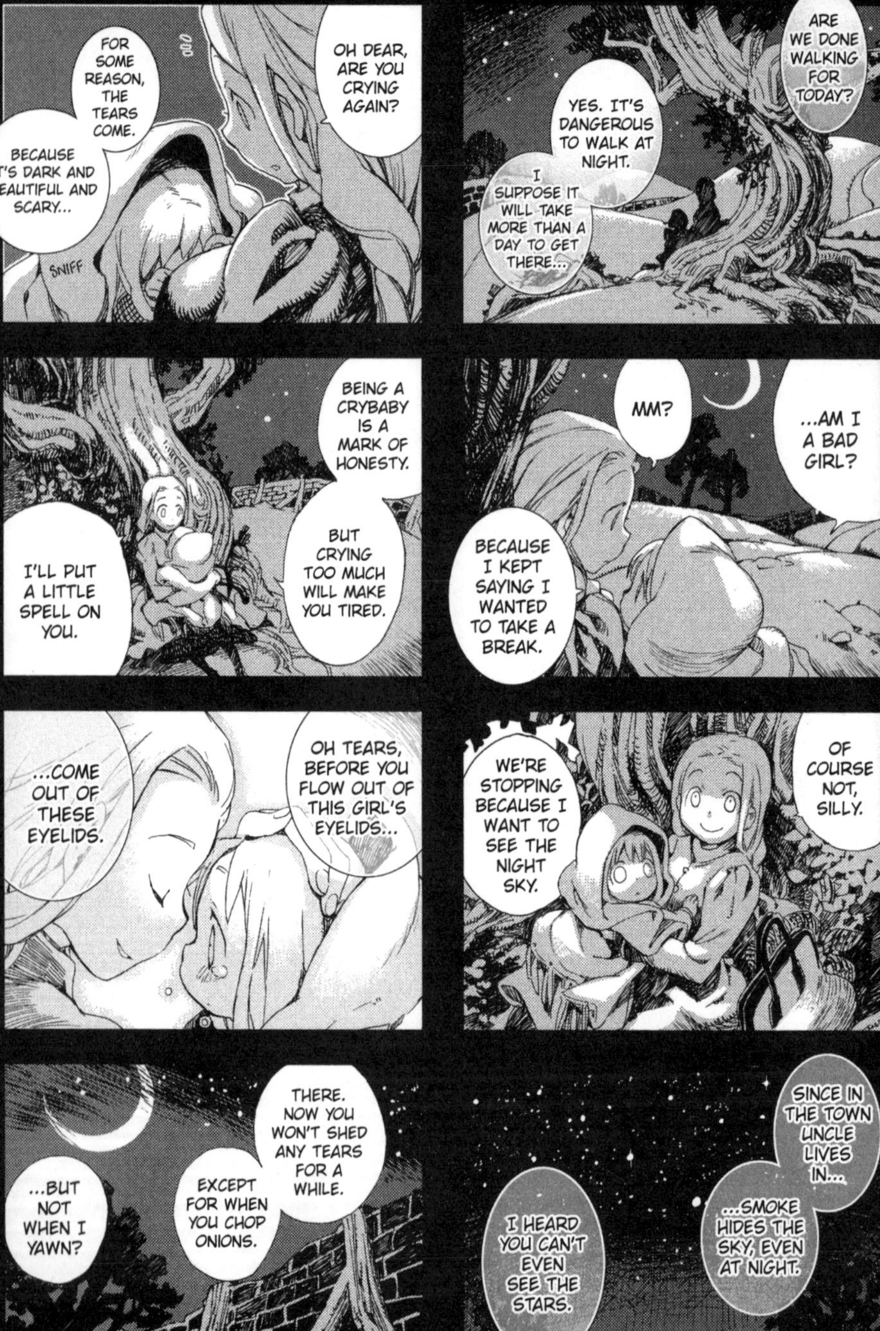
ARE WE DONE WALKING FOR TODAY?
YES. IT'S DANGEROUS TO WALK AT NIGHT.
I SUPPOSE IT WILL TAKE MORE THAN A DAY TO GET THERE...
OH DEAR, ARE YOU CRYING AGAIN?
FOR SOME REASON, THE TEARS COME.
BECAUSE IT'S DARK AND BEAUTIFUL AND SCARY...
SNIFF
...AM I A BAD GIRL?
MM?
BECAUSE I KEPT SAYING I WANTED TO TAKE A BREAK.
BEING A CRYBABY IS A MARK OF HONESTY.
BUT CRYING TOO MUCH WILL MAKE YOU TIRED.
I'LL PUT A LITTLE SPELL ON YOU.
OF COURSE NOT, SILLY.
WE'RE STOPPING BECAUSE I WANT TO SEE THE NIGHT SKY.
OH TEARS, BEFORE YOU FLOW OUT OF THIS GIRL'S EYELIDS...
...COME OUT OF THESE EYELIDS.
SINCE IN THE TOWN UNCLE LIVES IN...
...SMOKE HIDES THE SKY, EVEN AT NIGHT.
I HEARD YOU CAN'T EVEN SEE THE STARS.
THERE. NOW YOU WON'T SHED ANY TEARS FOR A WHILE.
EXCEPT FOR WHEN YOU CHOP ONIONS.
...BUT NOT WHEN I YAWN?

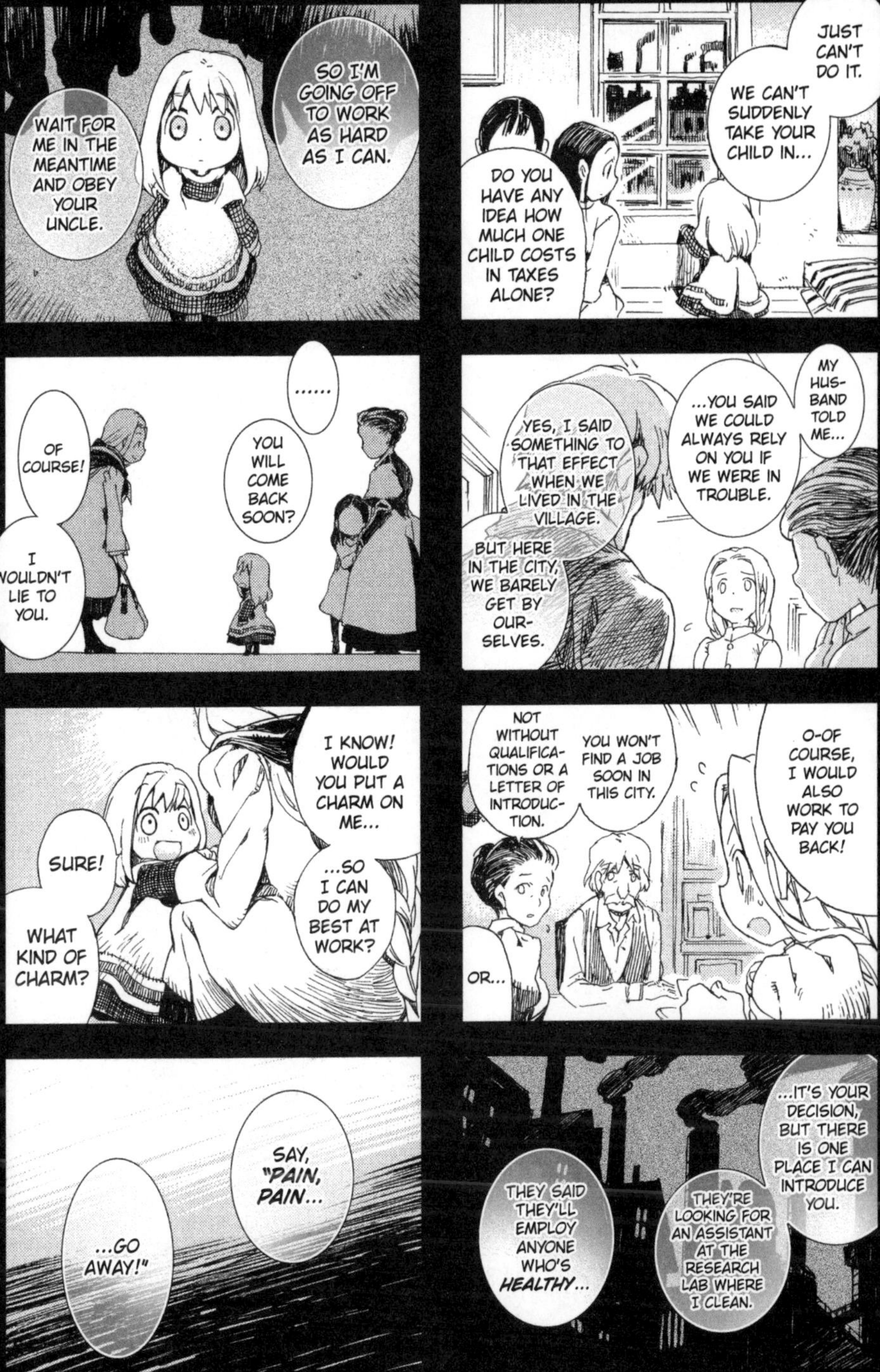
JUST CAN'T DO IT.
WE CAN'T SUDDENLY TAKE YOUR CHILD IN...
DO YOU HAVE ANY IDEA HOW MUCH ONE CHILD COSTS IN TAXES ALONE?
SO I'M GOING OFF TO WORK AS HARD AS I CAN.
WAIT FOR ME IN THE MEANTIME AND OBEY YOUR UNCLE.
MY HUS-BAND TOLD ME...
...YOU SAID WE COULD ALWAYS RELY ON YOU IF WE WERE IN TROUBLE.
YES, I SAID SOMETHING TO THAT EFFECT WHEN WE LIVED IN THE VILLAGE.
BUT HERE IN THE CITY, WE BARELY GET BY OUR-SELVES.
......
YOU WILL COME BACK SOON?
OF COURSE!
I WOULDN'T LIE TO YOU.
O-OF COURSE, I WOULD ALSO WORK TO PAY YOU BACK!
YOU WON'T FIND A JOB SOON IN THIS CITY.
NOT WITHOUT QUALIFICA-TIONS OR A LETTER OF INTRODUC-TION.
OR...
I KNOW! WOULD YOU PUT A CHARM ON ME...
...SO I CAN DO MY BEST AT WORK?
SURE!
WHAT KIND OF CHARM?
...IT'S YOUR DECISION, BUT THERE IS ONE PLACE I CAN INTRODUCE YOU.
THEY'RE LOOKING FOR AN ASSISTANT AT THE RESEARCH LAB WHERE I CLEAN.
THEY SAID THEY'LL EMPLOY ANYONE WHO'S *HEALTHY*...
SAY, *"PAIN, PAIN*...
...GO AWAY!"

SO THAT I MAY ONE DAY TAKE THE STAGE AGAIN...

I WANT TO LEAVE BEHIND MY BODY.

THE SECOND WOMAN SAID...

I'M PROUD OF IT.

GURGLE, GURGLE...

GURGLE, GURGLE...

SO THAT ONE DAY, MY HUSBAND AND DAUGHTER WILL RECOGNIZE ME...

I DON'T WANT TO FORGET MY FAMILY...

THE THIRD WOMAN SAID...

...SO I WOULD LIKE TO KEEP AT LEAST A LITTLE BIT OF MY HEART.

I HEAR A VOICE BEYOND THE STEAM.

AM I IN A CAULDRON?

...AND IF POSSIBLE, I WOULD LIKE TO APOLOGIZE TO HIM ONCE SOME- DAY...

I LEFT NO LOOSE ENDS BEHIND...

THE FIRST WOMAN SAID...

...BUT I WAS ALWAYS PROUD OF THIS HAIR...

I'M GOING TO REMAKE YOU INTO ONE NEW HUMAN.

YOU THREE ARE DEAD.

...SO MY VOICE.

...IS THERE SOMETHING THAT YOU WOULD LIKE TO LEAVE BEHIND?

BUT AS PROOF THAT YOU ONCE EXISTED SEPA- RATELY...

AND SO...

...THE WITCH'S SPELL WAS BROKEN.

THE PRINCE AND PRINCESS RETURNED TO NORMAL...

HUH?

...AND LIVED HAPPILY EVER AFTER.

HAPPY ENDING.

HAPPY ENDING?

WHAT IS "DIFFER-ENT"?

...I tHOUGHT you were telling a Different story.

THE THREE...

WHAT WAS it AGAIN?

THEN HOW ABOUT THIS STORY NEXT?

YOU'RE BEING WEIRD.

THE THREE LITTLE PIGS...

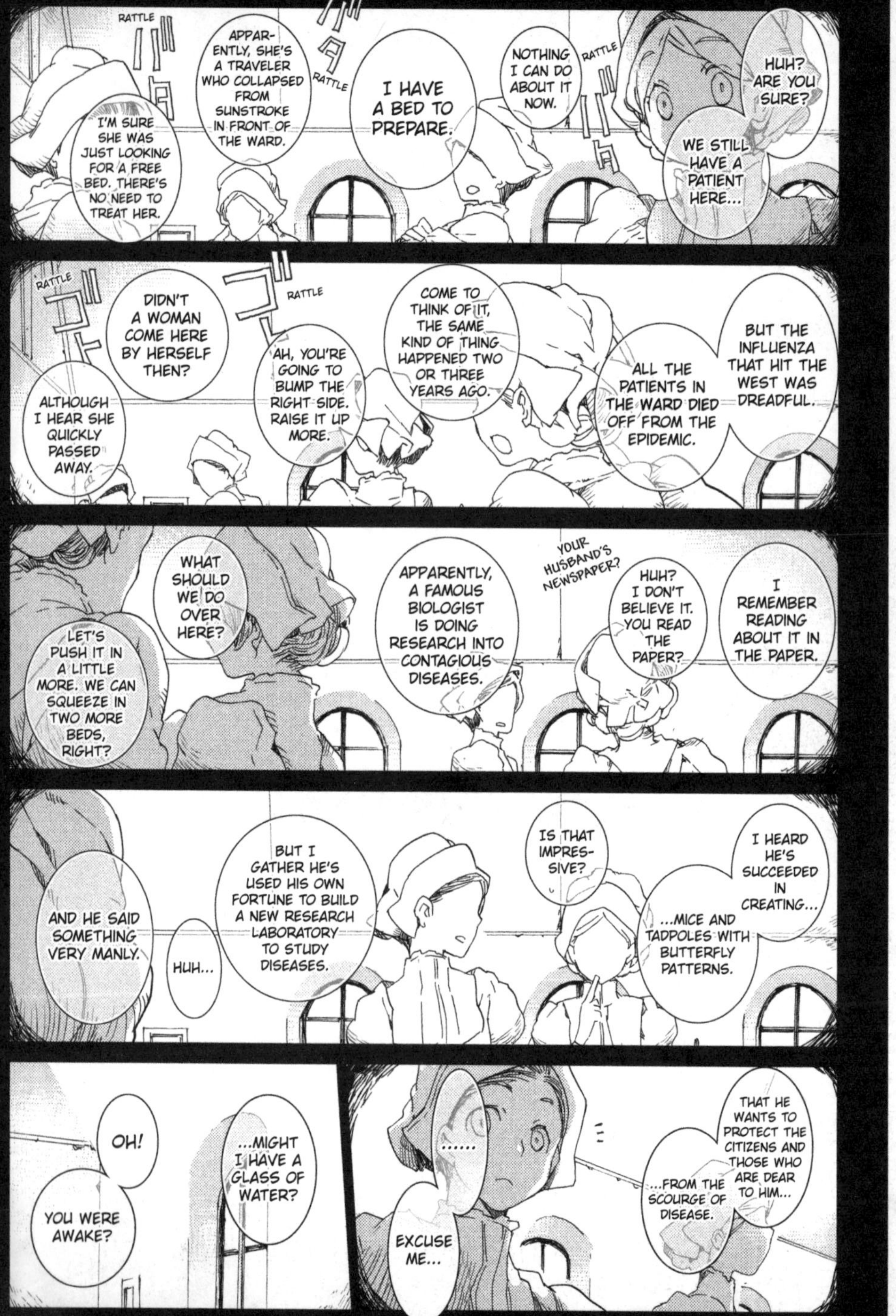
HUH? ARE YOU SURE?
WE STILL HAVE A PATIENT HERE...
RATTLE
NOTHING I CAN DO ABOUT IT NOW.
I HAVE A BED TO PREPARE.
RATTLE
APPARENTLY, SHE'S A TRAVELER WHO COLLAPSED FROM SUNSTROKE IN FRONT OF THE WARD.
RATTLE
I'M SURE SHE WAS JUST LOOKING FOR A FREE BED. THERE'S NO NEED TO TREAT HER.
BUT THE INFLUENZA THAT HIT THE WEST WAS DREADFUL.
ALL THE PATIENTS IN THE WARD DIED OFF FROM THE EPIDEMIC.
COME TO THINK OF IT, THE SAME KIND OF THING HAPPENED TWO OR THREE YEARS AGO.
RATTLE
AH, YOU'RE GOING TO BUMP THE RIGHT SIDE. RAISE IT UP MORE.
DIDN'T A WOMAN COME HERE BY HERSELF THEN?
RATTLE
ALTHOUGH I HEAR SHE QUICKLY PASSED AWAY.
I REMEMBER READING ABOUT IT IN THE PAPER.
HUH? I DON'T BELIEVE IT. YOU READ THE PAPER?
YOUR HUSBAND'S NEWSPAPER?
APPARENTLY, A FAMOUS BIOLOGIST IS DOING RESEARCH INTO CONTAGIOUS DISEASES.
WHAT SHOULD WE DO OVER HERE?
LET'S PUSH IT IN A LITTLE MORE. WE CAN SQUEEZE IN TWO MORE BEDS, RIGHT?
I HEARD HE'S SUCCEEDED IN CREATING...
...MICE AND TADPOLES WITH BUTTERFLY PATTERNS.
IS THAT IMPRESSIVE?
BUT I GATHER HE'S USED HIS OWN FORTUNE TO BUILD A NEW RESEARCH LABORATORY TO STUDY DISEASES.
HUH...
AND HE SAID SOMETHING VERY MANLY.
THAT HE WANTS TO PROTECT THE CITIZENS AND THOSE WHO ARE DEAR TO HIM...
...FROM THE SCOURGE OF DISEASE.
......
EXCUSE ME...
...MIGHT I HAVE A GLASS OF WATER?
OH!
YOU WERE AWAKE?

Shoulder-a-Coffin Kuro by Satoko Kiyuduki

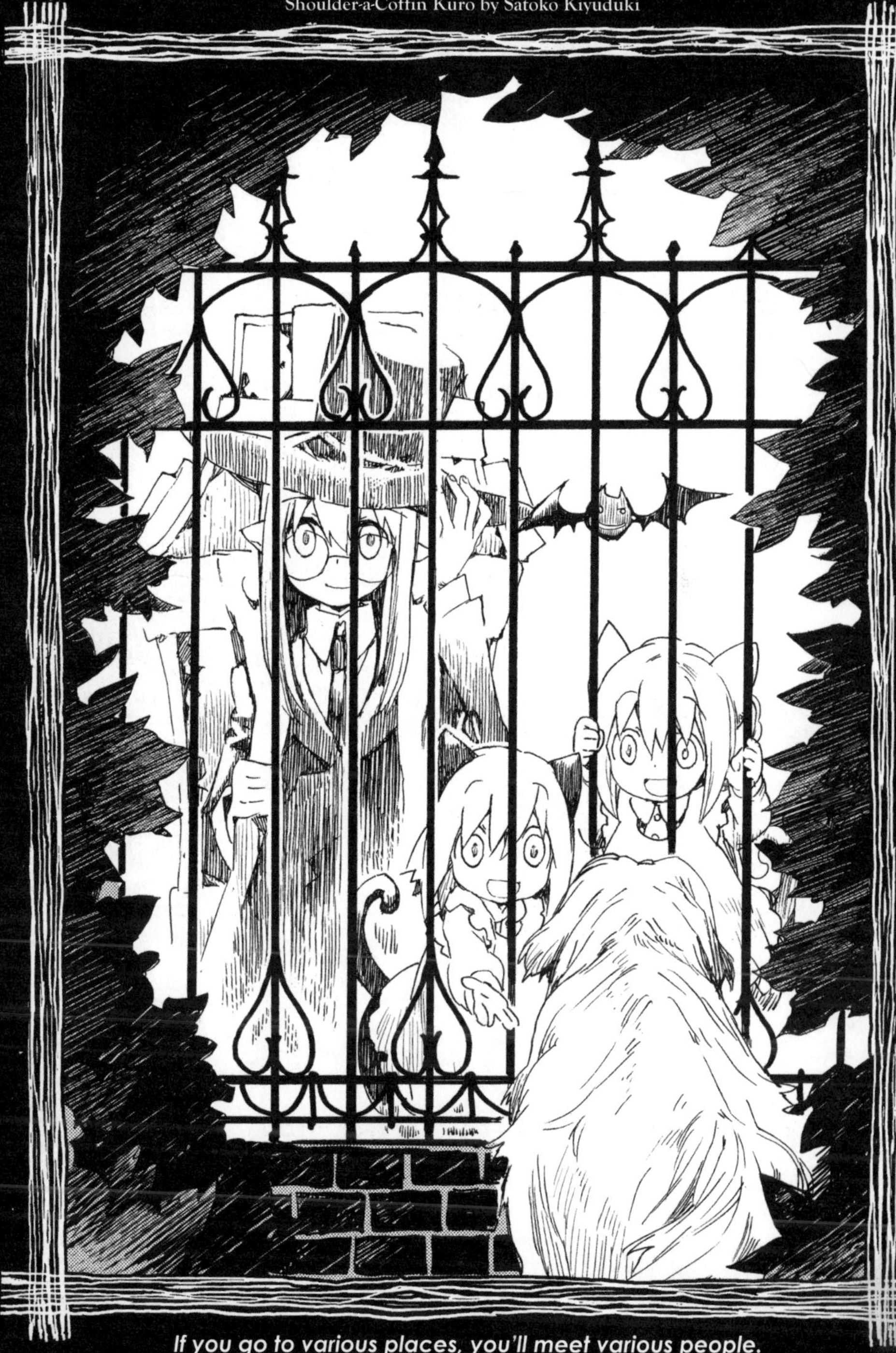

If you go to various places, you'll meet various people.
If you come across travelers like these, something may change,
or you may just feel that something has changed.

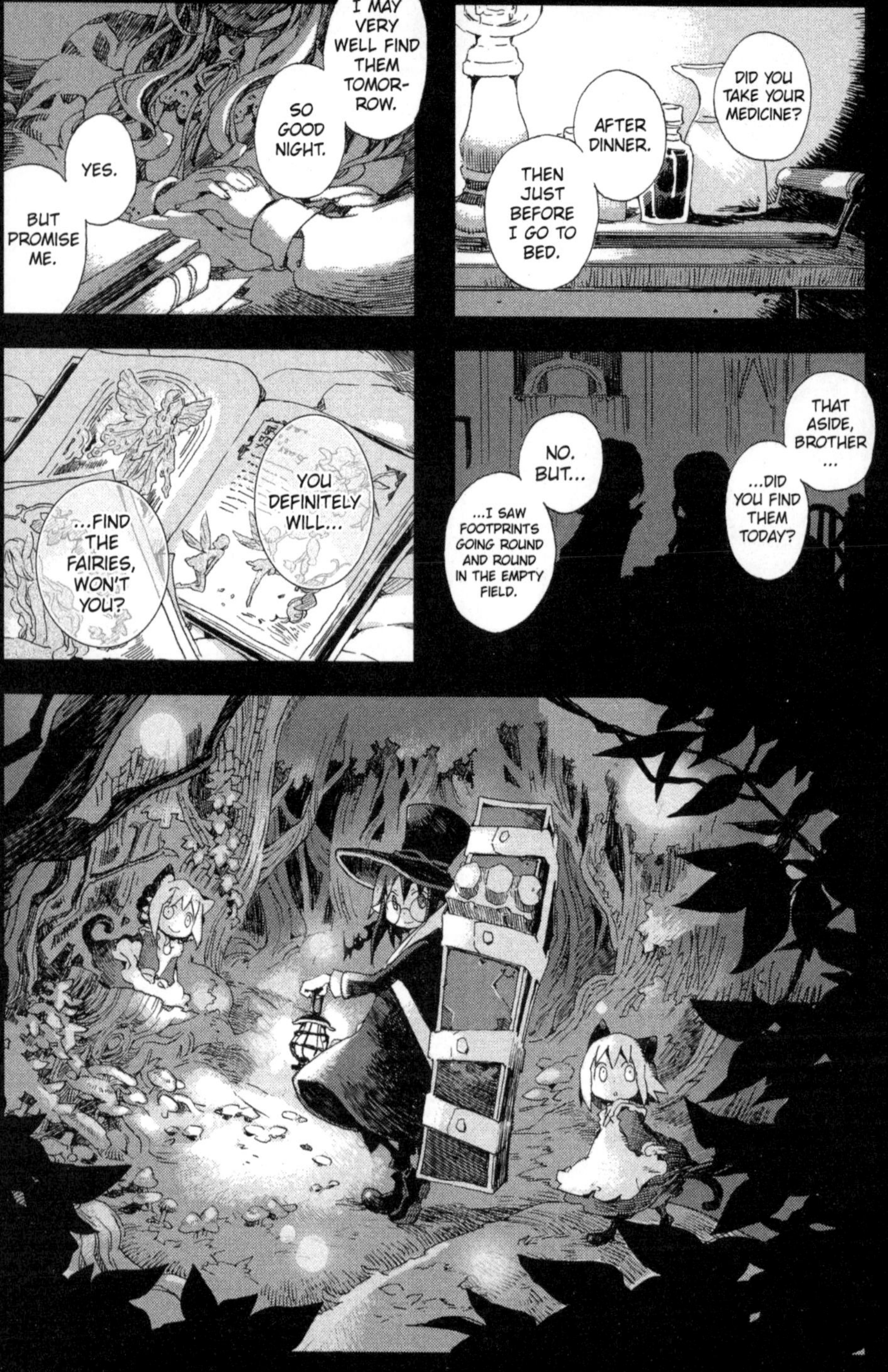
DID YOU TAKE YOUR MEDICINE?
AFTER DINNER.
THEN JUST BEFORE I GO TO BED.
I MAY VERY WELL FIND THEM TOMORROW.
SO GOOD NIGHT.
YES.
BUT PROMISE ME.
THAT ASIDE, BROTHER ...
...DID YOU FIND THEM TODAY?
NO. BUT...
...I SAW FOOTPRINTS GOING ROUND AND ROUND IN THE EMPTY FIELD.
YOU DEFINITELY WILL...
...FIND THE FAIRIES, WON'T YOU?

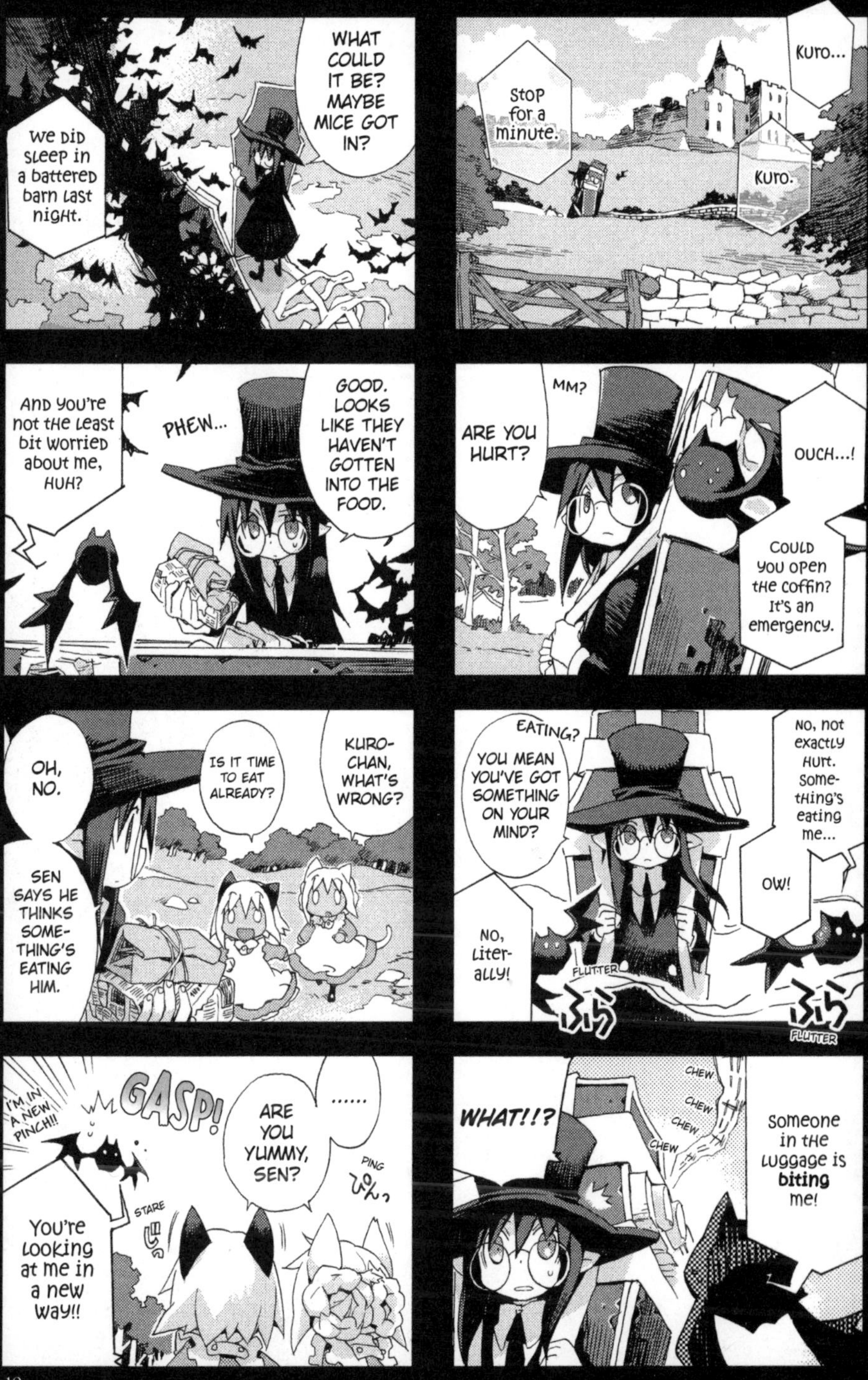

Kuro...
Kuro.
Stop for a minute.
MM?
OUCH...!
ARE YOU HURT?
COULD YOU OPEN THE COFFIN? IT'S AN EMERGENCY.
No, not exactly hurt. Some-thing's eating me...
OW!
EATING?
YOU MEAN YOU'VE GOT SOMETHING ON YOUR MIND?
NO, Liter-ally!
FLUTTER
ふら
ふら
FLUTTER
CHEW
CHEW
CHEW
CHEW
Someone in the luggage is **biting** me!
WHAT!!?
WHAT COULD IT BE? MAYBE MICE GOT IN?
We DID sleep in a battered barn last night.
GOOD. LOOKS LIKE THEY HAVEN'T GOTTEN INTO THE FOOD.
PHEW...
And you're not the least bit worried about me, HUH?
KURO-CHAN, WHAT'S WRONG?
IS IT TIME TO EAT ALREADY?
OH, NO.
SEN SAYS HE THINKS SOME-THING'S EATING HIM.
......
ARE YOU YUMMY, SEN?
PING
ぴん
GASP!
I'M IN A NEW PINCH!!
STARE
じー
You're looking at me in a new way!!

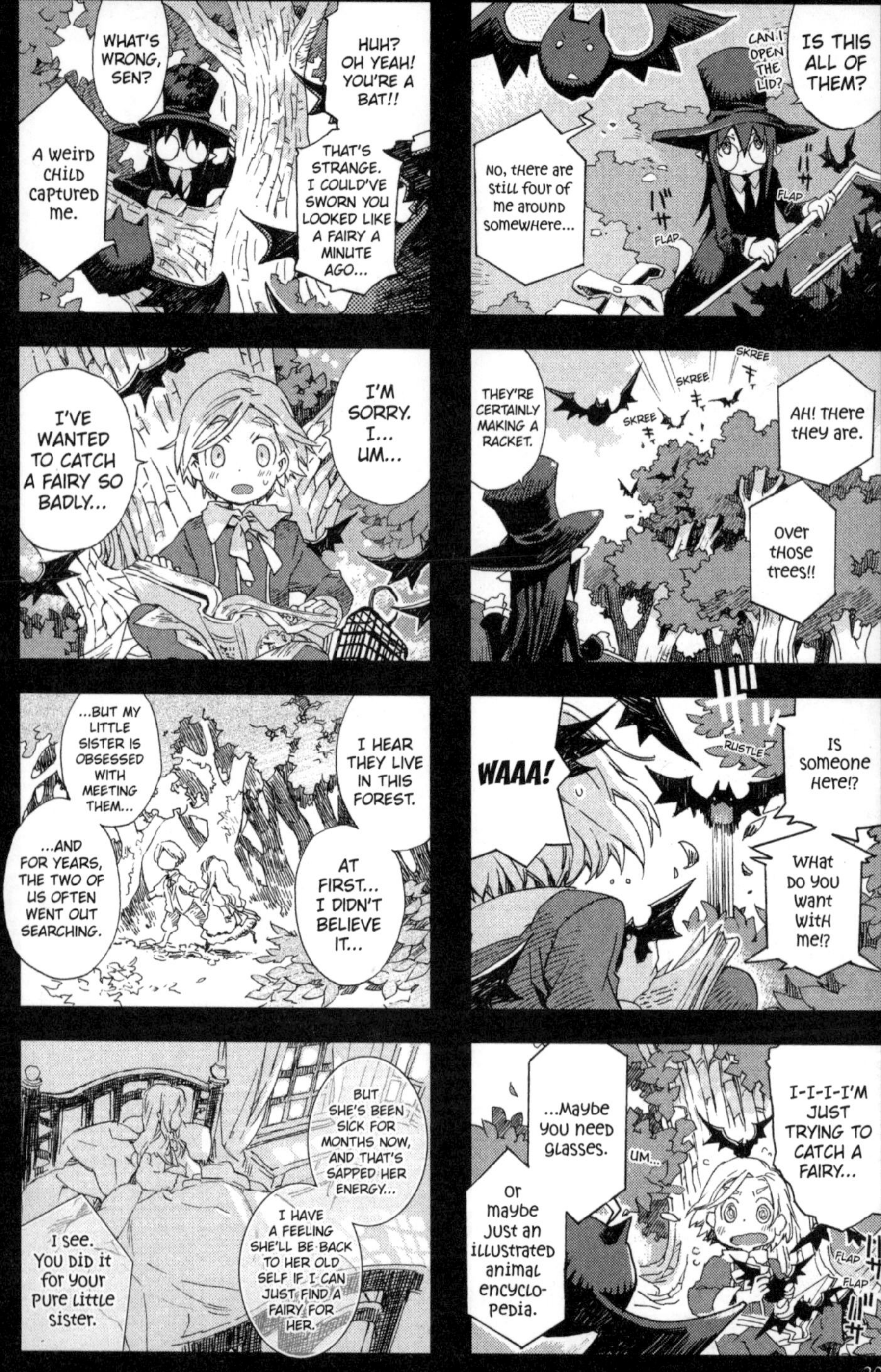
IS THIS ALL OF THEM?
CAN I OPEN THE LID?
FLAP
No, there are still four of me around somewhere...
FLAP
HUH? OH YEAH! YOU'RE A BAT!!
WHAT'S WRONG, SEN?
THAT'S STRANGE. I COULD'VE SWORN YOU LOOKED LIKE A FAIRY A MINUTE AGO...
A weird child captured me.
SKREE
SKREE
AH! There they are.
SKREE
THEY'RE CERTAINLY MAKING A RACKET.
Over those trees!!
I'M SORRY. I... UM...
I'VE WANTED TO CATCH A FAIRY SO BADLY...
IS someone Here!?
RUSTLE
WAAA!
WHat do you want with me!?
I HEAR THEY LIVE IN THIS FOREST.
AT FIRST... I DIDN'T BELIEVE IT...
...BUT MY LITTLE SISTER IS OBSESSED WITH MEETING THEM...
...AND FOR YEARS, THE TWO OF US OFTEN WENT OUT SEARCHING.
I-I-I-I'M JUST TRYING TO CATCH A FAIRY...
UM...
...Maybe you need glasses.
Or maybe just an illustrated animal encyclopedia.
FLAP
FLAP
BUT SHE'S BEEN SICK FOR MONTHS NOW, AND THAT'S SAPPED HER ENERGY...
I HAVE A FEELING SHE'LL BE BACK TO HER OLD SELF IF I CAN JUST FIND A FAIRY FOR HER.
I see. You did it for your pure little sister.

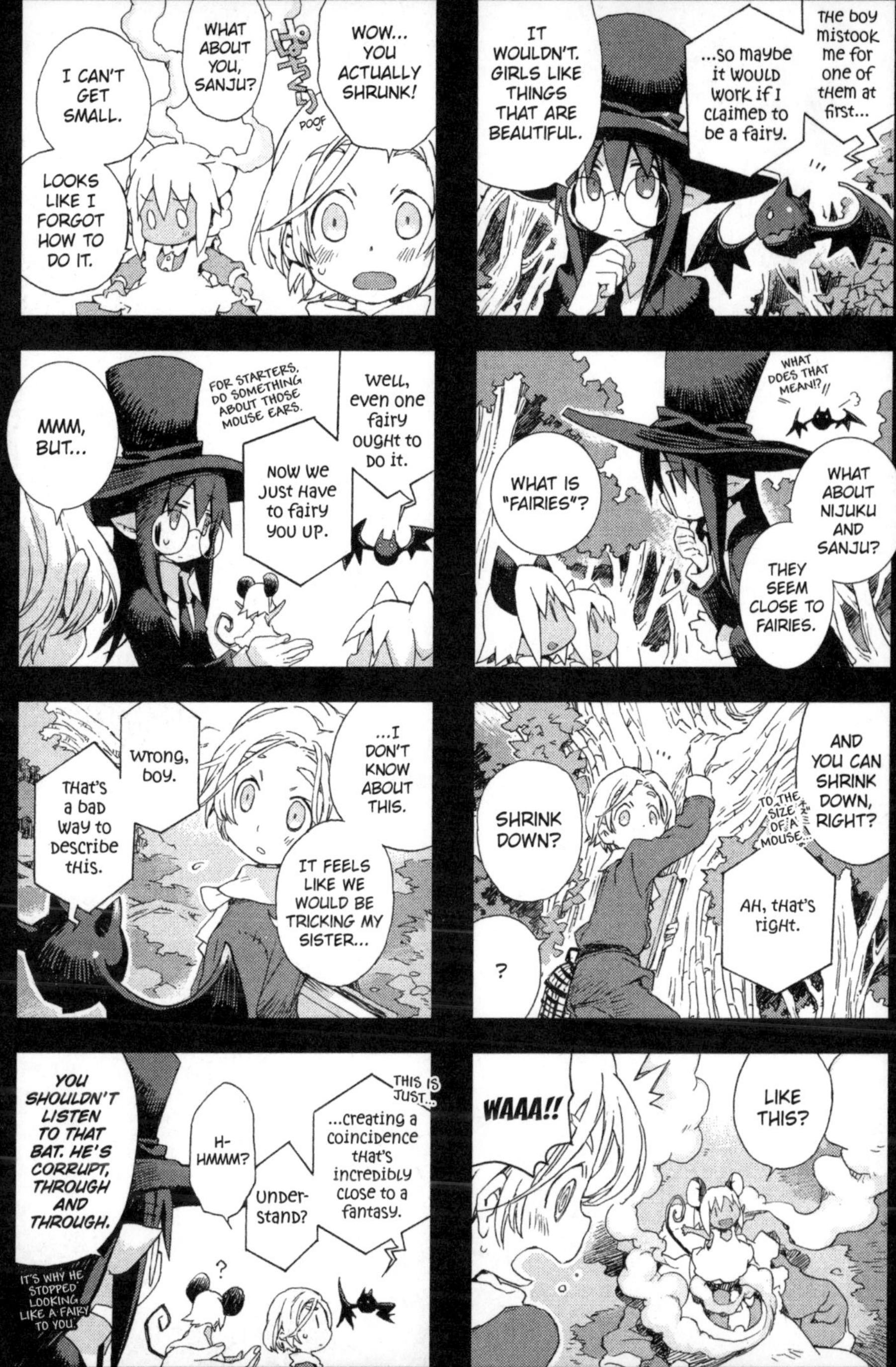
THE boy mistook me for one of tHem at first...
...so maybe it would work if I claimed to be a fairy.
IT WOULDN'T. GIRLS LIKE THINGS THAT ARE BEAUTIFUL.
WOW... YOU ACTUALLY SHRUNK!
POOF
WHAT ABOUT YOU, SANJU?
I CAN'T GET SMALL.
LOOKS LIKE I FORGOT HOW TO DO IT.
WHAT DOES THAT MEAN!?
WHAT ABOUT NIJUKU AND SANJU?
THEY SEEM CLOSE TO FAIRIES.
WHAT IS "FAIRIES"?
Well, even one fairy ought to do it.
FOR STARTERS, DO SOMETHING ABOUT THOSE MOUSE EARS.
Now we just Have to fairy you up.
MMM, BUT...
AND YOU CAN SHRINK DOWN, RIGHT?
TO THE SIZE OF A MOUSE...
AH, tHat's right.
SHRINK DOWN?
...
?
...I DON'T KNOW ABOUT THIS.
IT FEELS LIKE WE WOULD BE TRICKING MY SISTER...
wrong, boy.
THat's a bad way to describe tHis.
LIKE THIS?
WAAA!!
THIS IS JUST...
...creating a coincidence tHat's incredibly close to a fantasy.
H-HMMM?
Under-stand?
?
YOU SHOULDN'T LISTEN TO THAT BAT. HE'S CORRUPT, THROUGH AND THROUGH.
IT'S WHY HE STOPPED LOOKING LIKE A FAIRY TO YOU.

THIS IS... A FAIRY?

YEP. IT'S THE FIRST TIME YOU'VE SEEN ONE, RIGHT?

ZZZ...

GLISY, I'M BACK!

HOW DO YOU FEEL?

ITS FEATHERS ARE COMING OFF...

...IT'S A LITTLE DIFFERENT THAN WHAT I HAD IMAGINED.

W-WELL, THAT'S TO BE EXPECTED...

PERK

BROTHER! WELCOME HOME. I'VE BEEN WAITING FOR YOU!

I SORTED OUT MY MEDICINE AND TOOK IT BY MYSELF TODAY!

UM, WAIT, I DIDN'T...

...CAPTURE THIS FAIRY MYSELF.

UH...

THUMP

BUT I'M SO HAPPY TO FINALLY SEE ONE!

I'LL RAISE IT WITH CARE FOR THE REST OF MY LIFE!

YAY! COULD IT BE...?

I WAS JUST PRAYING TO GOD FOR IT!

I'M GLAD TO SEE YOU'RE FEELING BETTER!

ESPECIALLY SINCE THERE'S SOMETHING I HAVE TO SHOW YOU!

...REALLY?

SHE LET ME BORROW ONE FROM HER COLLECTION FOR JUST ONE DAY!

IT WAS DR. KURO, A FAIRY COLLECTOR WHO JUST HAPPENED TO BE PASSING BY!!

we weren't sure if it's okay for slightly sleazy people like us to go in.

I SAW A BLUE BIRD!

AH!

OH... THE AIR IN THERE IS JUST SO PURE...

HUH? WHAT'S WRONG, KURO-SAN?

GASP!

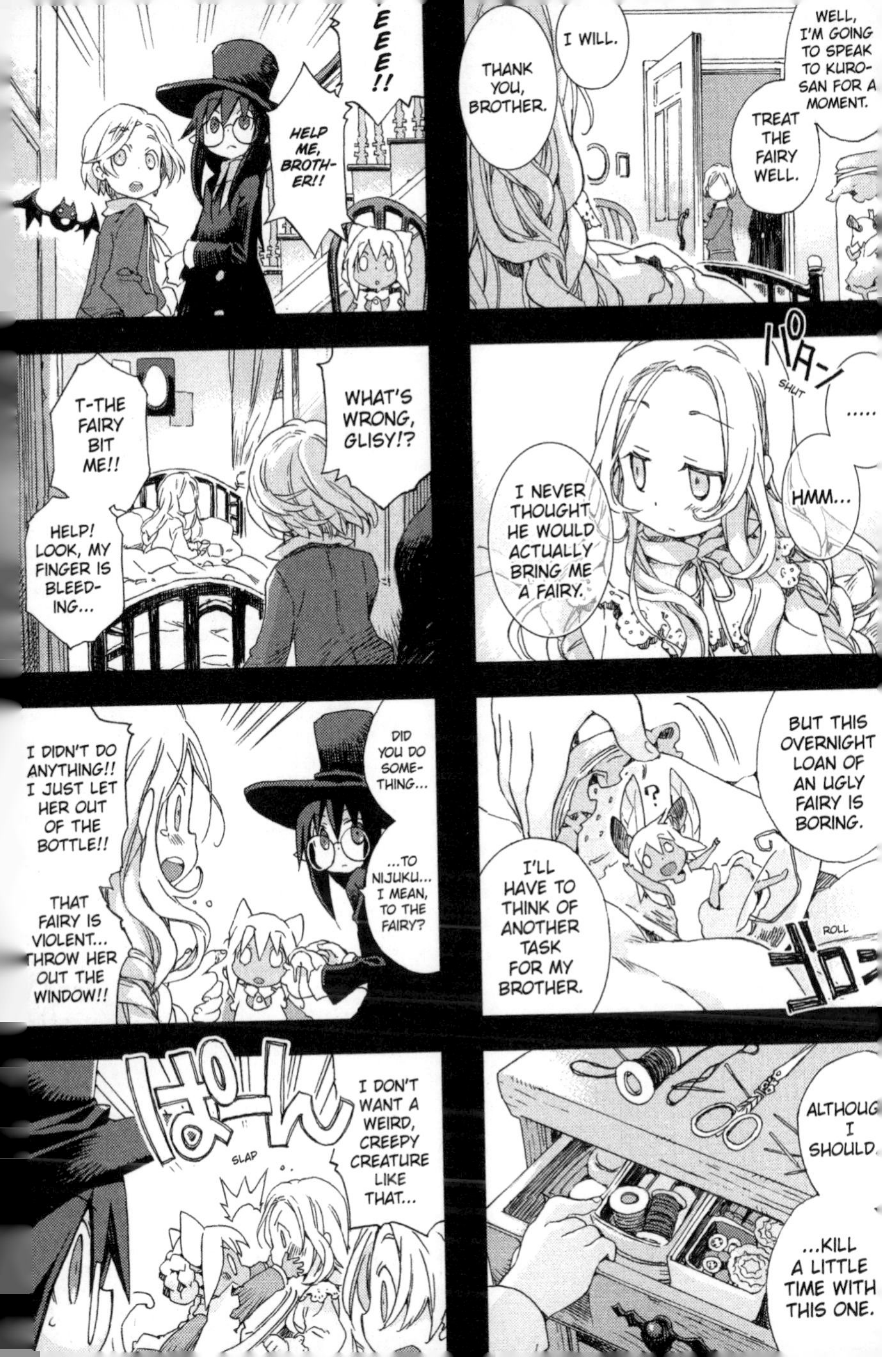
WELL, I'M GOING TO SPEAK TO KURO-SAN FOR A MOMENT.
TREAT THE FAIRY WELL.
I WILL.
THANK YOU, BROTHER.
EEE!!
HELP ME, BROTHER!!
パターン
SHUT
.....
HMM...
I NEVER THOUGHT HE WOULD ACTUALLY BRING ME A FAIRY.
WHAT'S WRONG, GLISY!?
T-THE FAIRY BIT ME!!
HELP! LOOK, MY FINGER IS BLEEDING...
BUT THIS OVERNIGHT LOAN OF AN UGLY FAIRY IS BORING.
I'LL HAVE TO THINK OF ANOTHER TASK FOR MY BROTHER.
ROLL
DID YOU DO SOMETHING...
...TO NIJUKU... I MEAN, TO THE FAIRY?
I DIDN'T DO ANYTHING!! I JUST LET HER OUT OF THE BOTTLE!!
THAT FAIRY IS VIOLENT... THROW HER OUT THE WINDOW!!
ALTHOUG I SHOULD.
...KILL A LITTLE TIME WITH THIS ONE.
I DON'T WANT A WEIRD, CREEPY CREATURE LIKE THAT...
SLAP

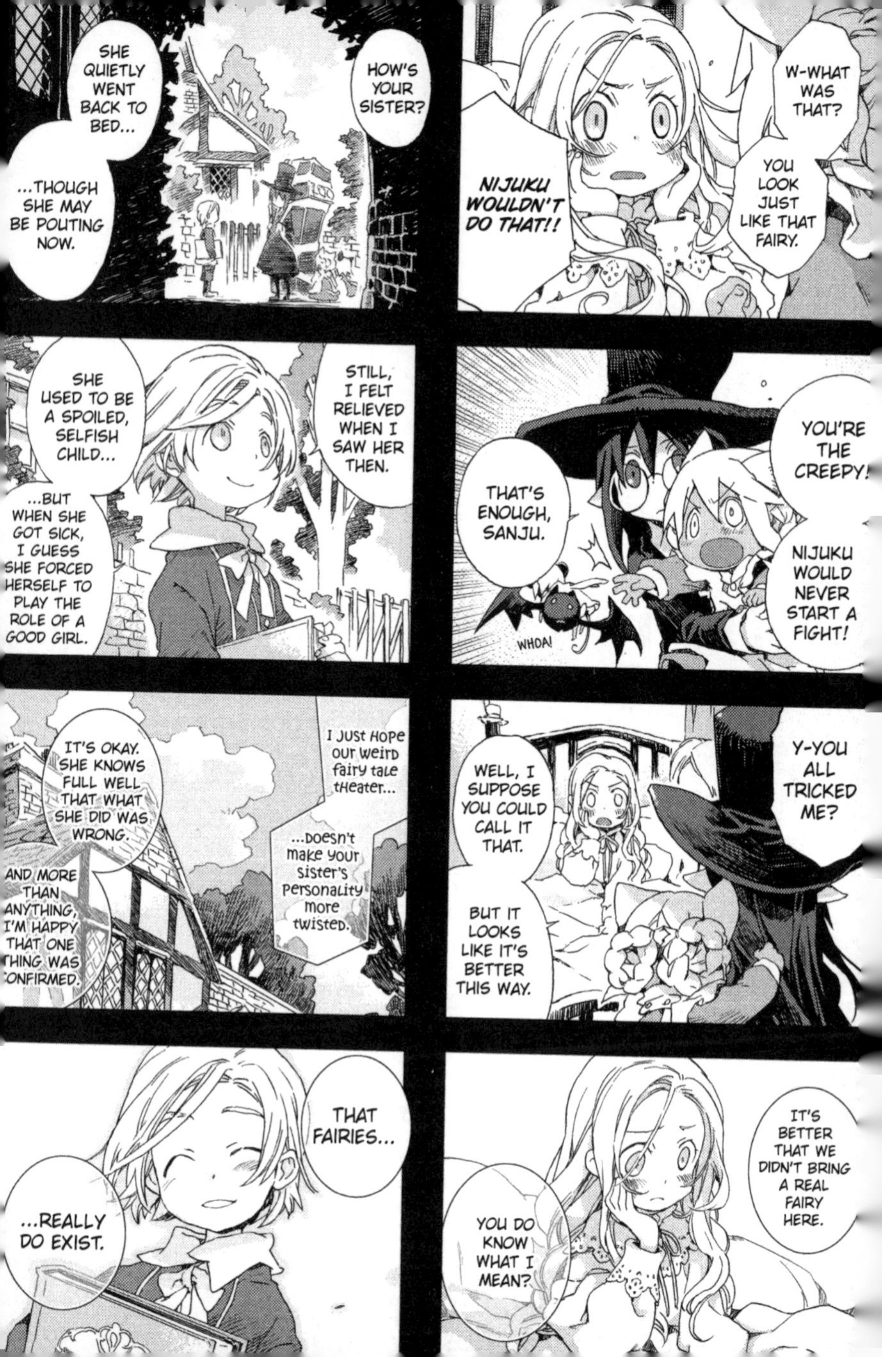
W-WHAT WAS THAT?
YOU LOOK JUST LIKE THAT FAIRY.
NIJUKU WOULDN'T DO THAT!!
YOU'RE THE CREEPY!
NIJUKU WOULD NEVER START A FIGHT!
THAT'S ENOUGH, SANJU.
WHOA!
Y-YOU ALL TRICKED ME?
WELL, I SUPPOSE YOU COULD CALL IT THAT.
BUT IT LOOKS LIKE IT'S BETTER THIS WAY.
IT'S BETTER THAT WE DIDN'T BRING A REAL FAIRY HERE.
YOU DO KNOW WHAT I MEAN?
HOW'S YOUR SISTER?
SHE QUIETLY WENT BACK TO BED...
...THOUGH SHE MAY BE POUTING NOW.
STILL, I FELT RELIEVED WHEN I SAW HER THEN.
SHE USED TO BE A SPOILED, SELFISH CHILD...
...BUT WHEN SHE GOT SICK, I GUESS SHE FORCED HERSELF TO PLAY THE ROLE OF A GOOD GIRL.
I JUST HOPE OUR WEIRD FAIRY TALE THEATER...
...DOESN'T MAKE YOUR SISTER'S PERSONALITY MORE TWISTED.
IT'S OKAY. SHE KNOWS FULL WELL THAT WHAT SHE DID WAS WRONG.
AND MORE THAN ANYTHING, I'M HAPPY THAT ONE THING WAS CONFIRMED.
THAT FAIRIES...
...REALLY DO EXIST.

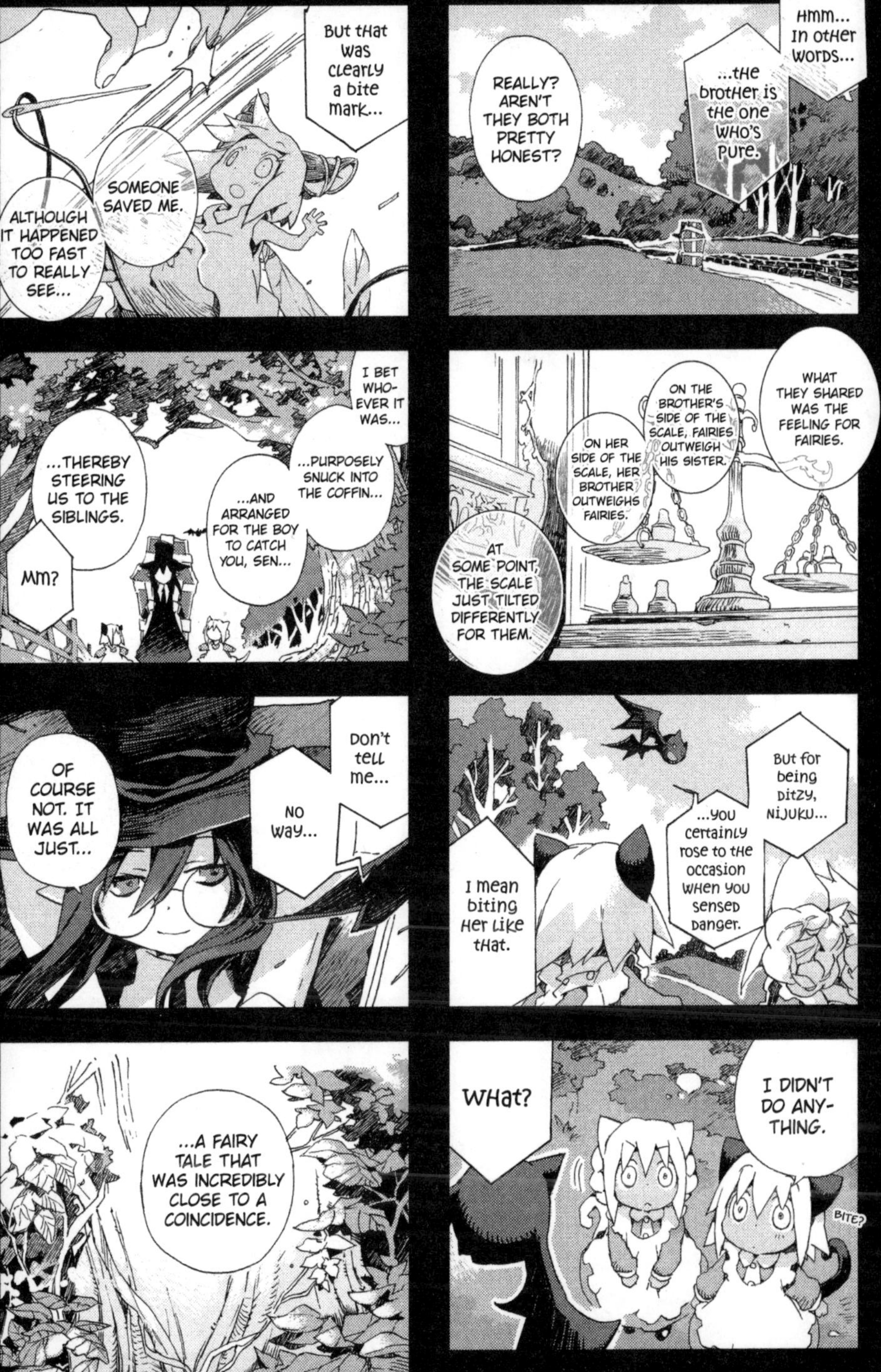
Hmm... In other words...
...the brother is the one who's pure.
REALLY? AREN'T THEY BOTH PRETTY HONEST?
But that was clearly a bite mark...
SOMEONE SAVED ME.
ALTHOUGH IT HAPPENED TOO FAST TO REALLY SEE...
WHAT THEY SHARED WAS THE FEELING FOR FAIRIES.
ON THE BROTHER'S SIDE OF THE SCALE, FAIRIES OUTWEIGH HIS SISTER.
ON HER SIDE OF THE SCALE, HER BROTHER OUTWEIGHS FAIRIES.
AT SOME POINT, THE SCALE JUST TILTED DIFFERENTLY FOR THEM.
I BET WHO-EVER IT WAS...
...PURPOSELY SNUCK INTO THE COFFIN...
...AND ARRANGED FOR THE BOY TO CATCH YOU, SEN...
...THEREBY STEERING US TO THE SIBLINGS.
MM?
But for being ditzy, Nijuku...
...you certainly rose to the occasion when you sensed danger.
I mean biting her like that.
Don't tell me...
NO way...
OF COURSE NOT. IT WAS ALL JUST...
I DIDN'T DO ANY-THING.
BITE?
WHat?
...A FAIRY TALE THAT WAS INCREDIBLY CLOSE TO A COINCIDENCE.

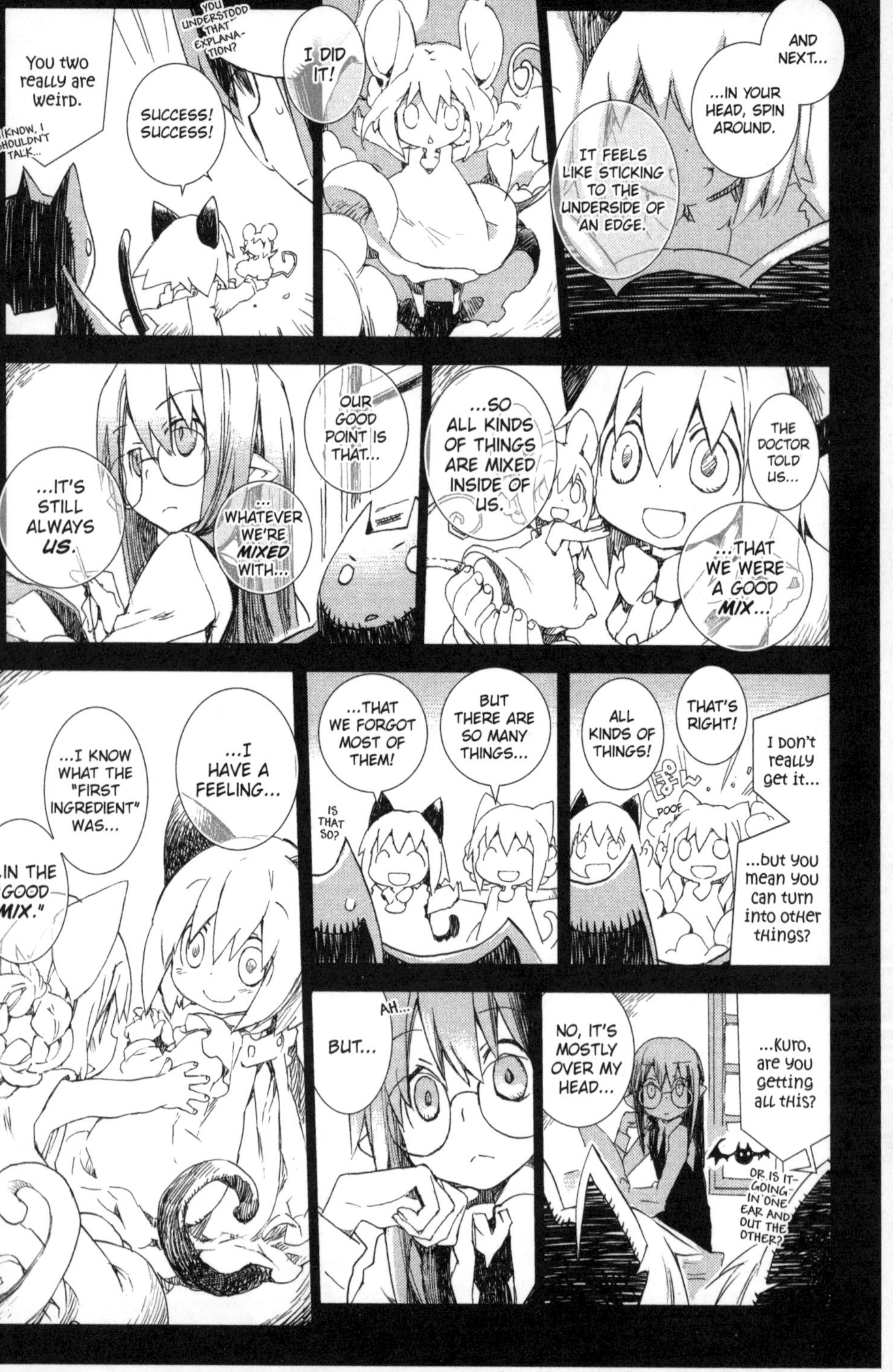
AND NEXT...
...IN YOUR HEAD, SPIN AROUND.
IT FEELS LIKE STICKING TO THE UNDERSIDE OF AN EDGE.
I DID IT!
YOU UNDERSTOOD THAT EXPLANATION?
SUCCESS! SUCCESS!
You two really are weird.
I KNOW, I SHOULDN'T TALK...
THE DOCTOR TOLD US...
...THAT WE WERE A GOOD **MIX**...
...SO ALL KINDS OF THINGS ARE MIXED INSIDE OF US.
OUR GOOD POINT IS THAT...
...WHATEVER WE'RE **MIXED** WITH...
...IT'S STILL ALWAYS **US**.
THAT'S RIGHT!
I Don't really get it...
ALL KINDS OF THINGS!
POOF
...but you mean you can turn into other things?
BUT THERE ARE SO MANY THINGS...
...THAT WE FORGOT MOST OF THEM!
IS THAT SO?
...Kuro, are you getting all this?
NO, IT'S MOSTLY OVER MY HEAD...
OR IS IT GOING IN ONE EAR AND OUT THE OTHER?
AH...
BUT...
...I HAVE A FEELING...
...I KNOW WHAT THE "FIRST INGREDIENT" WAS...
...IN THE "GOOD **MIX**."

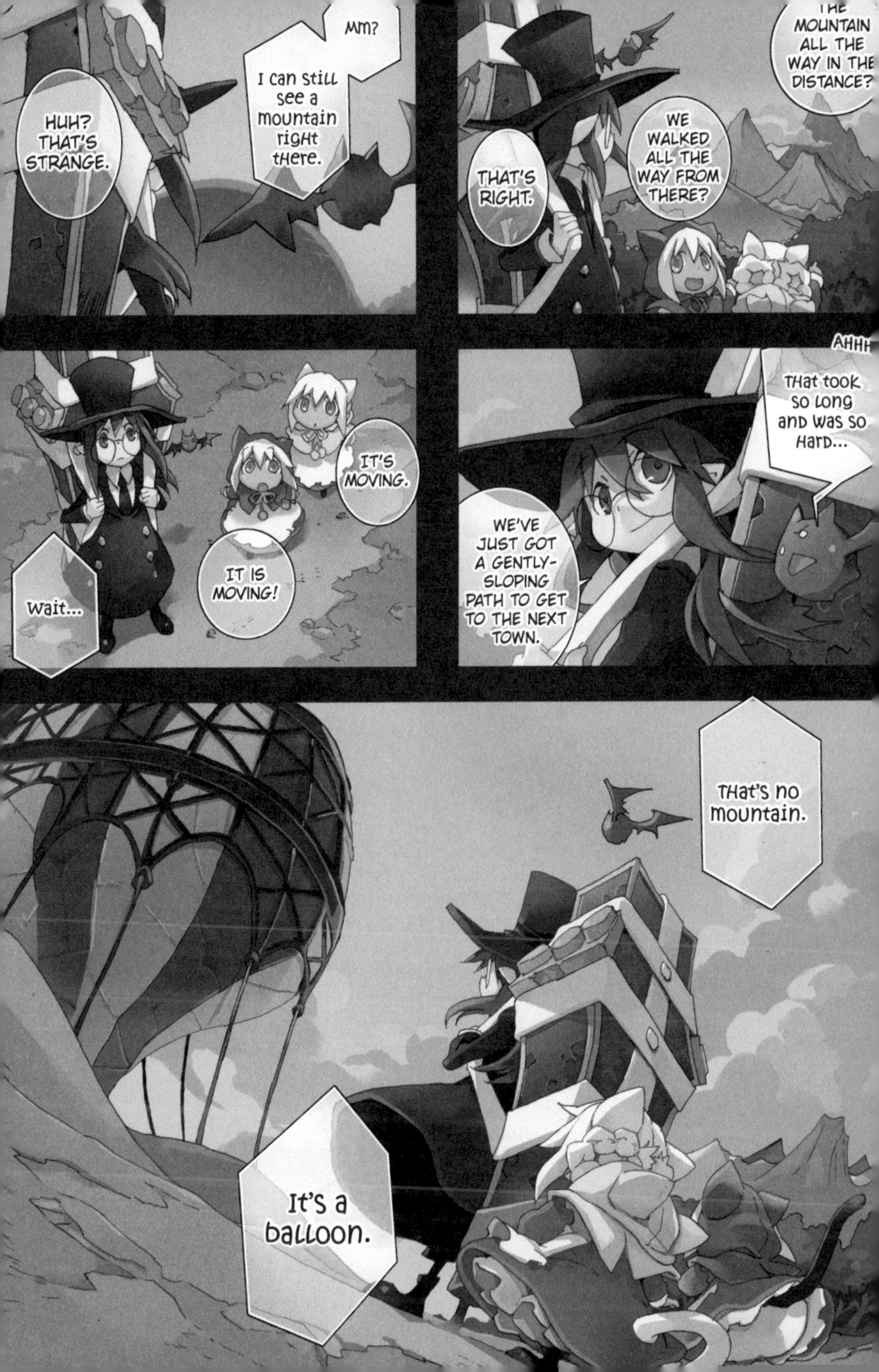
THE MOUNTAIN ALL THE WAY IN THE DISTANCE?
WE WALKED ALL THE WAY FROM THERE?
THAT'S RIGHT.
MM?
I can still see a mountain right there.
HUH? THAT'S STRANGE.
AHHH
That took so long and was so hard...
WE'VE JUST GOT A GENTLY-SLOPING PATH TO GET TO THE NEXT TOWN.
IT'S MOVING.
IT IS MOVING!
Wait...
That's no mountain.
It's a balloon.

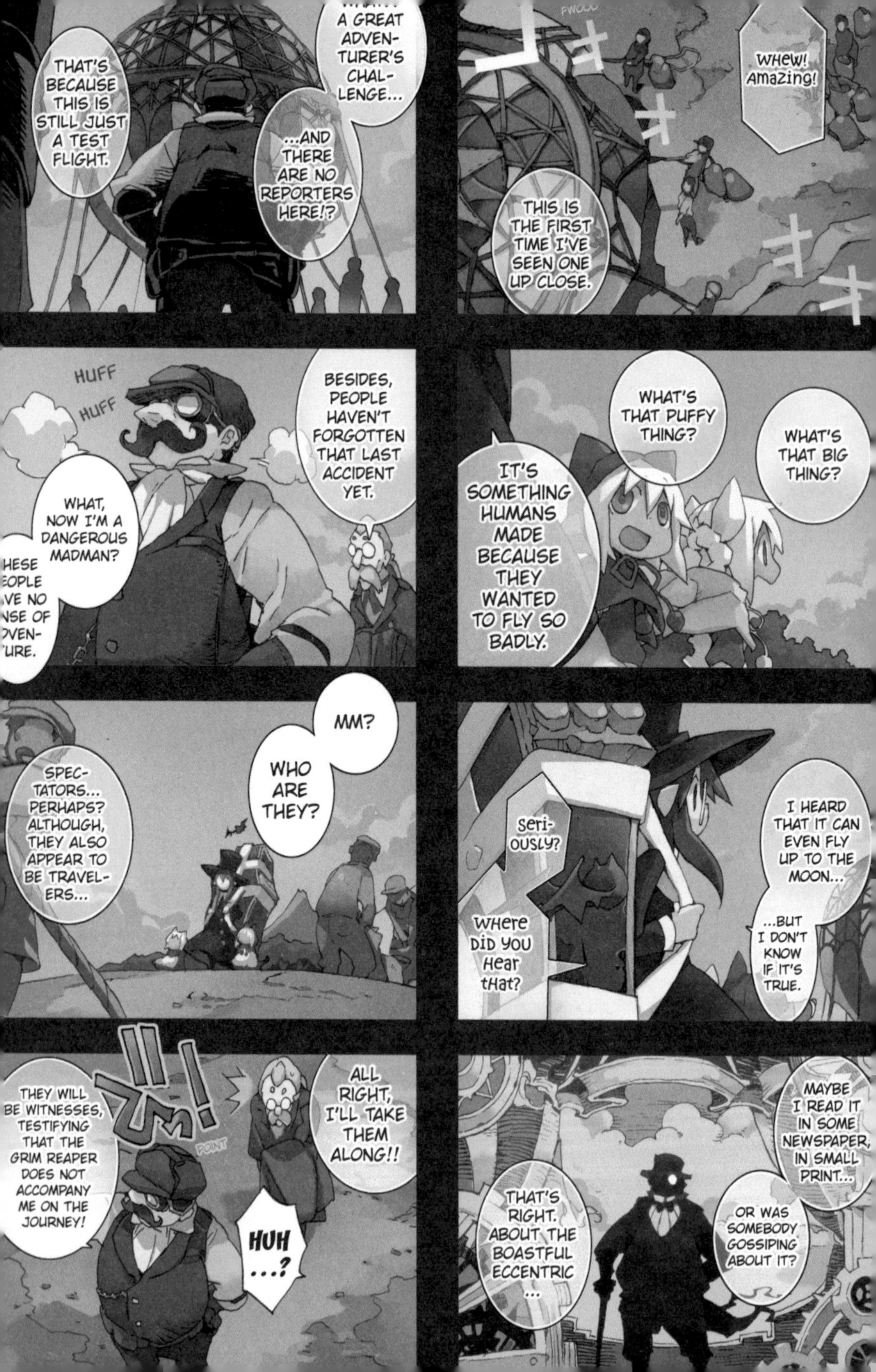

FWOOO
WHEW! AMAZING!
THIS IS THE FIRST TIME I'VE SEEN ONE UP CLOSE.
A GREAT ADVENTURER'S CHALLENGE...
...AND THERE ARE NO REPORTERS HERE!?
THAT'S BECAUSE THIS IS STILL JUST A TEST FLIGHT.
WHAT'S THAT BIG THING?
WHAT'S THAT PUFFY THING?
IT'S SOMETHING HUMANS MADE BECAUSE THEY WANTED TO FLY SO BADLY.
BESIDES, PEOPLE HAVEN'T FORGOTTEN THAT LAST ACCIDENT YET.
HUFF
HUFF
WHAT, NOW I'M A DANGEROUS MADMAN?
HESE EOPLE VE NO NSE OF DVEN-TURE.
I HEARD THAT IT CAN EVEN FLY UP TO THE MOON...
SERIOUSLY?
...BUT I DON'T KNOW IF IT'S TRUE.
WHERE DID YOU HEAR THAT?
MM?
WHO ARE THEY?
SPECTATORS... PERHAPS? ALTHOUGH, THEY ALSO APPEAR TO BE TRAVELERS...
MAYBE I READ IT IN SOME NEWSPAPER, IN SMALL PRINT...
OR WAS SOMEBODY GOSSIPING ABOUT IT?
THAT'S RIGHT. ABOUT THE BOASTFUL ECCENTRIC...
ALL RIGHT, I'LL TAKE THEM ALONG!!
THEY WILL BE WITNESSES, TESTIFYING THAT THE GRIM REAPER DOES NOT ACCOMPANY ME ON THE JOURNEY!
POINT
HUH...?

BE CARE-FUL!

SEE YOU LATER!

BYE-BYE!

HUH?

YOU WANT US TO RIDE IN THE BALLOON?

WHAT, again?

WHAT DO YOU THINK? AN EXQUISITE VIEW, IS IT NOT?

Kuro, I'm hanging on to you tight.

THE SCENERY BECOMES SMALL BEFORE YOU KNOW IT...

BY WHAT?

POINT

I'M INTRIGUED BY THAT!

He probably means the coffin.

LOOK, KURO!

THERE.

THE mountains we crossed.

I think we've been ensnared by a weirdo.

GLOOMY YOUTH WHO WALKS WHILE BEARING A COFFIN...

...I SHALL SHOW YOU HOW WONDERFUL LIFE CAN BE!

...we've retraced our steps in a matter of minutes.

THE MOUNTAINS THAT TOOK US A WEEK TO GET THROUGH BECAUSE I DIDN'T WANT TO TRAVEL BY SHIP...

YES. IT SEEMS YOU'RE STRUCK WITH WONDER AT THE CONVENIENCE OF CIVILIZATION.

UH-HUH...

THEY'RE SAFE WITH ME.

STILL, IT WOULDN'T DO TO TAKE ALONG THE TWO CHILDREN...

...SO THE CHILDREN CAN RIDE ALONG.

I'LL DRIVE AFTER THE BALLOON DURING THE FLIGHT...

HELLO THERE, COUNT RITTOCK!

EVEN AFTER YOU LOST AN EYE AND AN ARM, I HEARD YOU WERE COMING BACK UP TO COURT DEATH, SO I CAME TO PAY MY RESPECTS.

LONG TIME NO SEE, MRS. SIVRAC!

BE AT EASE. THIS IS JUST AN EXPERIMENT.

TO SEE WHETHER I CAN GET TO THE HEIGHT I'M AIMING FOR.

HOW FAR ARE WE FLYING?

I DON'T WANT YOU TO TAKE US TO THE ENDS OF THE EARTH.

SHE IS MY BAD PENNY, THE CAT TO MY DOG, THE ONE WHO ALWAYS HORNS IN ON MY CHALLENGES.

BUT THIS TIME, SHE SHALL NOT INTERFERE.

TUG

IS THAT LADY AN ADVENTURER TOO?

I'D RATHER RIDE IN HER BALLOON...

CERTAINLY, IT'S NOT LIKE YOU WOULD RUN ACROSS SOMEONE ALL THE WAY UP HERE...

STILL, IT IS NICE TO HAVE COMPANY FOR ONCE.

THESE FLIGHTS ARE ALWAYS SO LONELY THAT I END UP TALKING TO MYSELF.

FSSSHT

WHAT, MIGRATORY BIRDS?

NO, THAT'S...

SOMETHING'S APPROACHING.

OUR DESTINATION LIES HIGHER.

FOLLOW ALONG IF YOU CAN, AND I'LL DEAL WITH YOU AGAIN.

COUGH COUGH

W-WAIT!!

A FELLOW BALLOONIST!

...ANOTHER BALLOON!

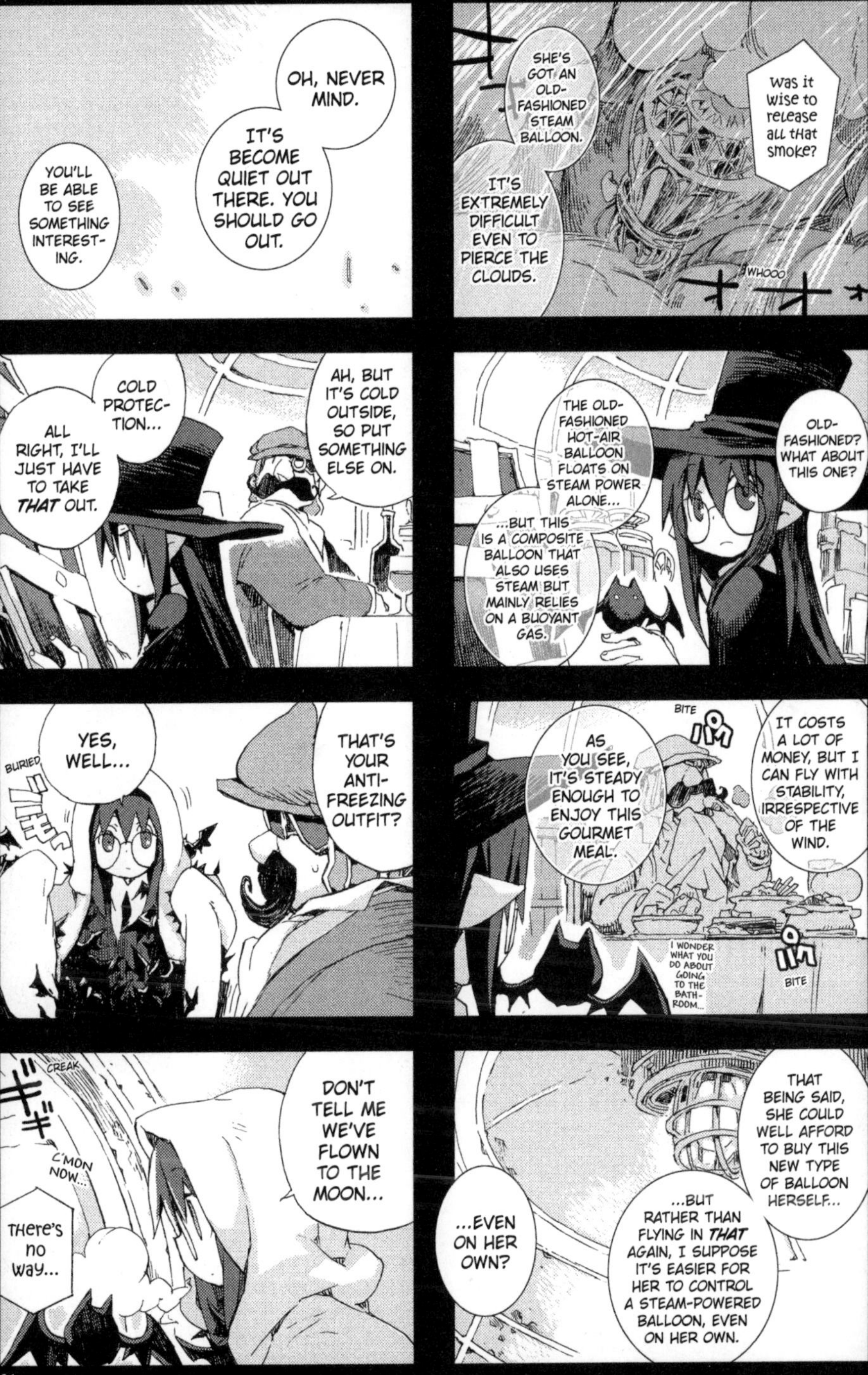
Was it wise to release all that smoke?
SHE'S GOT AN OLD-FASHIONED STEAM BALLOON.
IT'S EXTREMELY DIFFICULT EVEN TO PIERCE THE CLOUDS.
WHOOO
OH, NEVER MIND.
IT'S BECOME QUIET OUT THERE. YOU SHOULD GO OUT.
YOU'LL BE ABLE TO SEE SOMETHING INTEREST-ING.
OLD-FASHIONED? WHAT ABOUT THIS ONE?
THE OLD-FASHIONED HOT-AIR BALLOON FLOATS ON STEAM POWER ALONE...
...BUT THIS IS A COMPOSITE BALLOON THAT ALSO USES STEAM BUT MAINLY RELIES ON A BUOYANT GAS.
AH, BUT IT'S COLD OUTSIDE, SO PUT SOMETHING ELSE ON.
COLD PROTEC-TION...
ALL RIGHT, I'LL JUST HAVE TO TAKE *THAT* OUT.
IT COSTS A LOT OF MONEY, BUT I CAN FLY WITH STABILITY, IRRESPECTIVE OF THE WIND.
BITE
AS YOU SEE, IT'S STEADY ENOUGH TO ENJOY THIS GOURMET MEAL.
I WONDER WHAT YOU DO ABOUT GOING TO THE BATH-ROOM...
BITE
THAT'S YOUR ANTI-FREEZING OUTFIT?
YES, WELL...
BURIED
THAT BEING SAID, SHE COULD WELL AFFORD TO BUY THIS NEW TYPE OF BALLOON HERSELF...
...BUT RATHER THAN FLYING IN *THAT* AGAIN, I SUPPOSE IT'S EASIER FOR HER TO CONTROL A STEAM-POWERED BALLOON, EVEN ON HER OWN.
...EVEN ON HER OWN?
DON'T TELL ME WE'VE FLOWN TO THE MOON...
CREAK
C'MON NOW...
There's no way...

....

BEAUTI-
FUL,
ISN'T IT?

OF COURSE
YOUR SENSES
DON'T WORK
OUT HERE.

THIS
WORLD
REJECTS
HUMANS.

A SEA OF
CLOUDS.

BUT
BEFORE THE
VASTNESS
OF THIS
WORLD...

...I CAN
SENSE HOW
PRECIOUS
MY OWN
LIFE IS.

NO
SOUND,
NO WIND,
NO
SENSE OF
DISTANCE
...

IT'S
LIKE I
DON'T
KNOW
WHICH
SENSES
TO USE...

WHAT IS IT?
IT FEELS
STRANGE...

I'M SURE JEAN WOULD HAVE BEEN SURPRISED TOO.

VERY IMPRESSIVE, SOPHIE!

POOP

CHUCKLE

OH! SHE MANAGED TO BYPASS THOSE CLOUDS.

MRS. SIVRAC'S BALLOON.

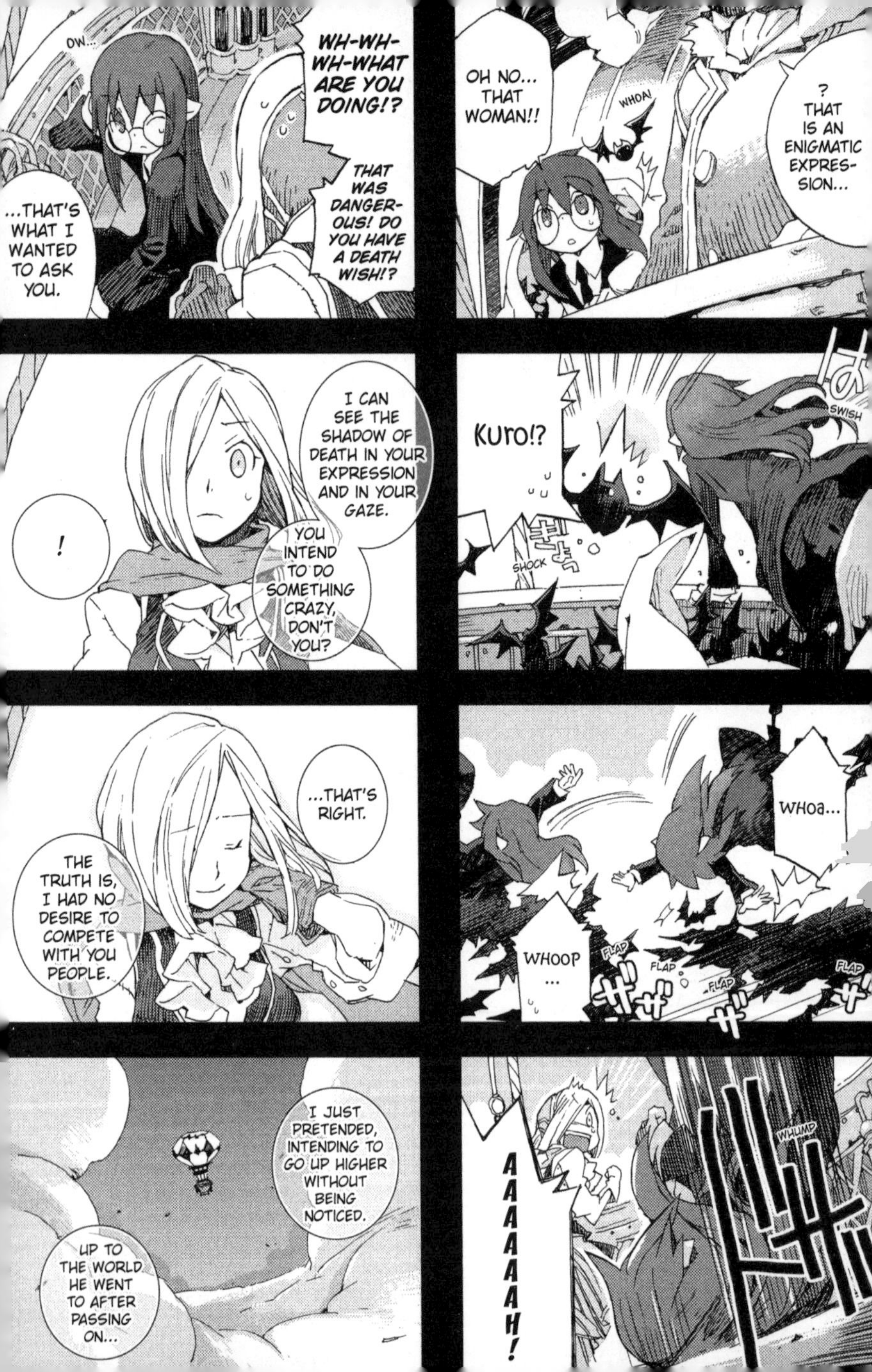

? THAT IS AN ENIGMATIC EXPRES-SION...
WHOA!
OH NO... THAT WOMAN!!
WH-WH-WH-WHAT ARE YOU DOING!?
THAT WAS DANGER-OUS! DO YOU HAVE A DEATH WISH!?
OW...
...THAT'S WHAT I WANTED TO ASK YOU.
SWISH
Kuro!?
SHOCK
I CAN SEE THE SHADOW OF DEATH IN YOUR EXPRESSION AND IN YOUR GAZE.
YOU INTEND TO DO SOMETHING CRAZY, DON'T YOU?
!
Whoa...
WHOOP ...
FLAP
FLAP
FLAP
FLAP
...THAT'S RIGHT.
THE TRUTH IS, I HAD NO DESIRE TO COMPETE WITH YOU PEOPLE.
WHUMP
AAAAAAAAH!
I JUST PRETENDED, INTENDING TO GO UP HIGHER WITHOUT BEING NOTICED.
UP TO THE WORLD HE WENT TO AFTER PASSING ON...

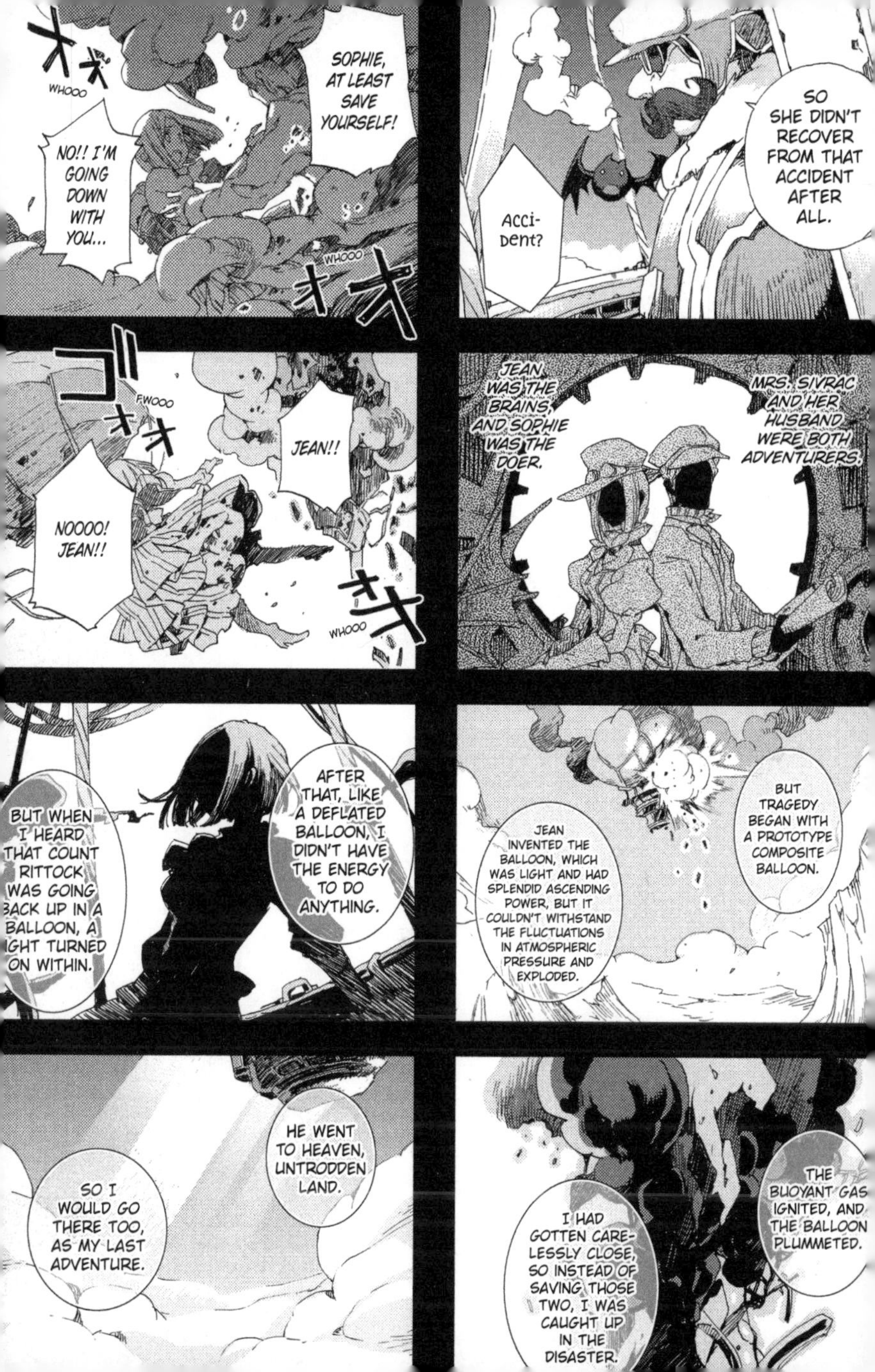
SO SHE DIDN'T RECOVER FROM THAT ACCIDENT AFTER ALL.
Acci-dent?
WHOOO
SOPHIE, AT LEAST SAVE YOURSELF!
NO!! I'M GOING DOWN WITH YOU...
WHOOO
MRS. SIVRAC AND HER HUSBAND WERE BOTH ADVENTURERS.
JEAN WAS THE BRAINS, AND SOPHIE WAS THE DOER.
FWOOO
JEAN!!
NOOOO! JEAN!!
WHOOO
BUT TRAGEDY BEGAN WITH A PROTOTYPE COMPOSITE BALLOON.
JEAN INVENTED THE BALLOON, WHICH WAS LIGHT AND HAD SPLENDID ASCENDING POWER, BUT IT COULDN'T WITHSTAND THE FLUCTUATIONS IN ATMOSPHERIC PRESSURE AND EXPLODED.
AFTER THAT, LIKE A DEFLATED BALLOON, I DIDN'T HAVE THE ENERGY TO DO ANYTHING.
BUT WHEN I HEARD THAT COUNT RITTOCK WAS GOING ACK UP IN A BALLOON, A IGHT TURNED ON WITHIN.
THE BUOYANT GAS IGNITED, AND THE BALLOON PLUMMETED.
I HAD GOTTEN CARE-LESSLY CLOSE, SO INSTEAD OF SAVING THOSE TWO, I WAS CAUGHT UP IN THE DISASTER.
HE WENT TO HEAVEN, UNTRODDEN LAND.
SO I WOULD GO THERE TOO, AS MY LAST ADVENTURE.

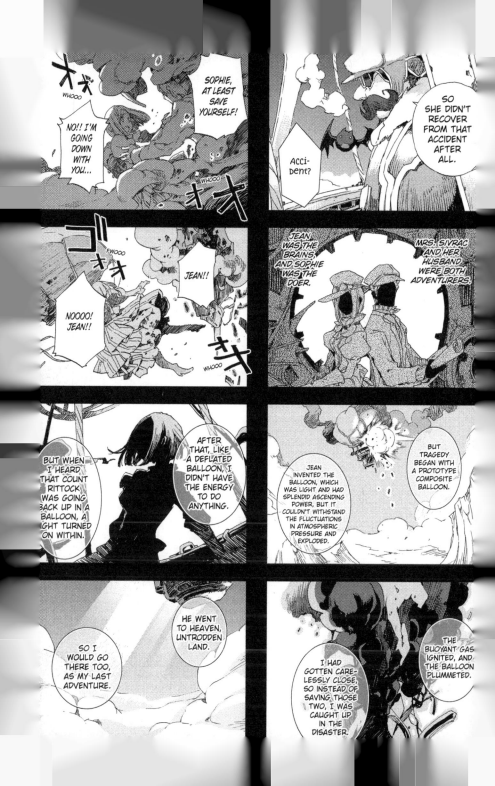

WAIT... IT CAN'T BE!!

WA-HA-HA-HA! YOU REALLY DID IT NOW, MRS. SIVRAC!

AH!! I'M ALMOST OUT OF FUEL!!!

...I CONFIRMED IT AFTER COMING HERE.

THAT HE'S BEYOND THIS SCENERY...

UGH...!

GULP

...I'M SURE YOU FOOLISHLY BURNED THROUGH YOUR STEAM.

WITHOUT THINKING BEFORE-HAND...

IN ORDER TO CLEAR THAT THICK CLOUD COVER...

FOOO

THAT'S WHY I'M GOING TO KEEP ASCENDING IN THIS BALLOON.

NOW RETURN TO THAT BALLOON BEFORE IT'S TOO LATE FOR YOU TO GO BACK...

...MM?

DON'T YOU UNDER-STAND, SOPHIE?

CLATTER

THAT'S RIDICU-LOUS

CLATTER

I'M NOT GIVING UP YET!!

YOU! IF YOU'RE A TRAVELER, CALL ONE OR TWO RISING BALLOONS OVER!!

NO, THAT'S NOT IT...

THAT NASTY MAN.

HE'S GONE UP HIGHER THAN ME AGAIN!

HE'S SAYING IT'S TOO SOON FOR YOU TO COME.

JEAN IS GIVING YOU A MESSAGE.

WHAT!?

I BELIEVE WE'RE LOSING ALTITUDE...

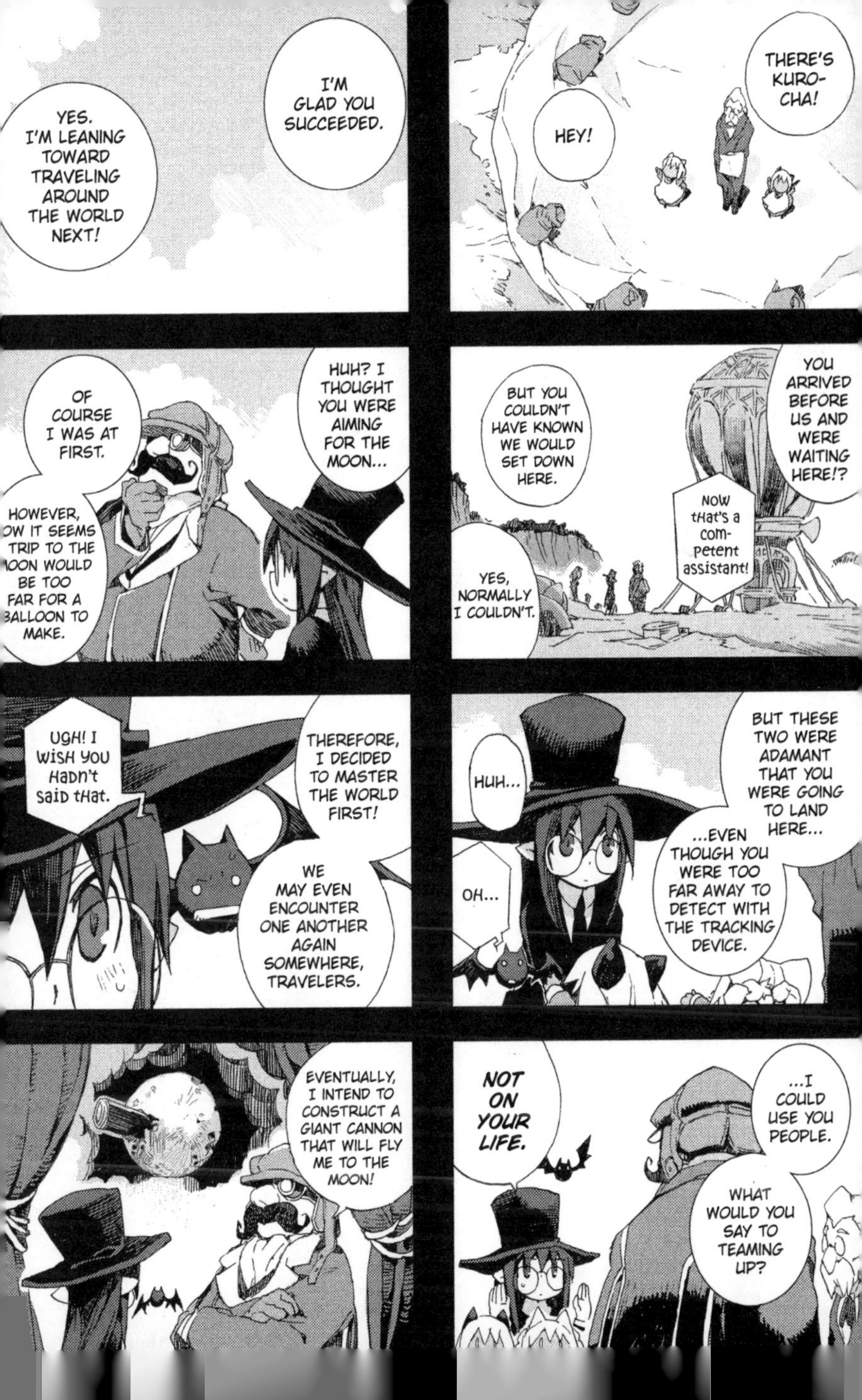
THERE'S KURO-CHA!
HEY!
I'M GLAD YOU SUCCEEDED.
YES. I'M LEANING TOWARD TRAVELING AROUND THE WORLD NEXT!
YOU ARRIVED BEFORE US AND WERE WAITING HERE!?
BUT YOU COULDN'T HAVE KNOWN WE WOULD SET DOWN HERE.
NOW THAT'S A COM-PETENT ASSISTANT!
YES, NORMALLY I COULDN'T.
HUH? I THOUGHT YOU WERE AIMING FOR THE MOON...
OF COURSE I WAS AT FIRST.
HOWEVER, OW IT SEEMS TRIP TO THE OON WOULD BE TOO FAR FOR A BALLOON TO MAKE.
BUT THESE TWO WERE ADAMANT THAT YOU WERE GOING TO LAND HERE...
HUH...
...EVEN THOUGH YOU WERE TOO FAR AWAY TO DETECT WITH THE TRACKING DEVICE.
OH...
THEREFORE, I DECIDED TO MASTER THE WORLD FIRST!
UGH! I WISH YOU HADN'T SAID THAT.
WE MAY EVEN ENCOUNTER ONE ANOTHER AGAIN SOMEWHERE, TRAVELERS.
...I COULD USE YOU PEOPLE.
WHAT WOULD YOU SAY TO TEAMING UP?
NOT ON YOUR LIFE.
EVENTUALLY, I INTEND TO CONSTRUCT A GIANT CANNON THAT WILL FLY ME TO THE MOON!

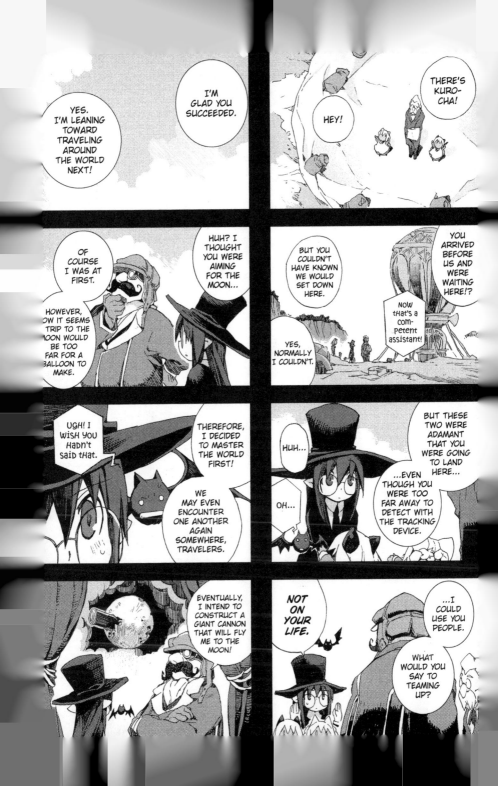

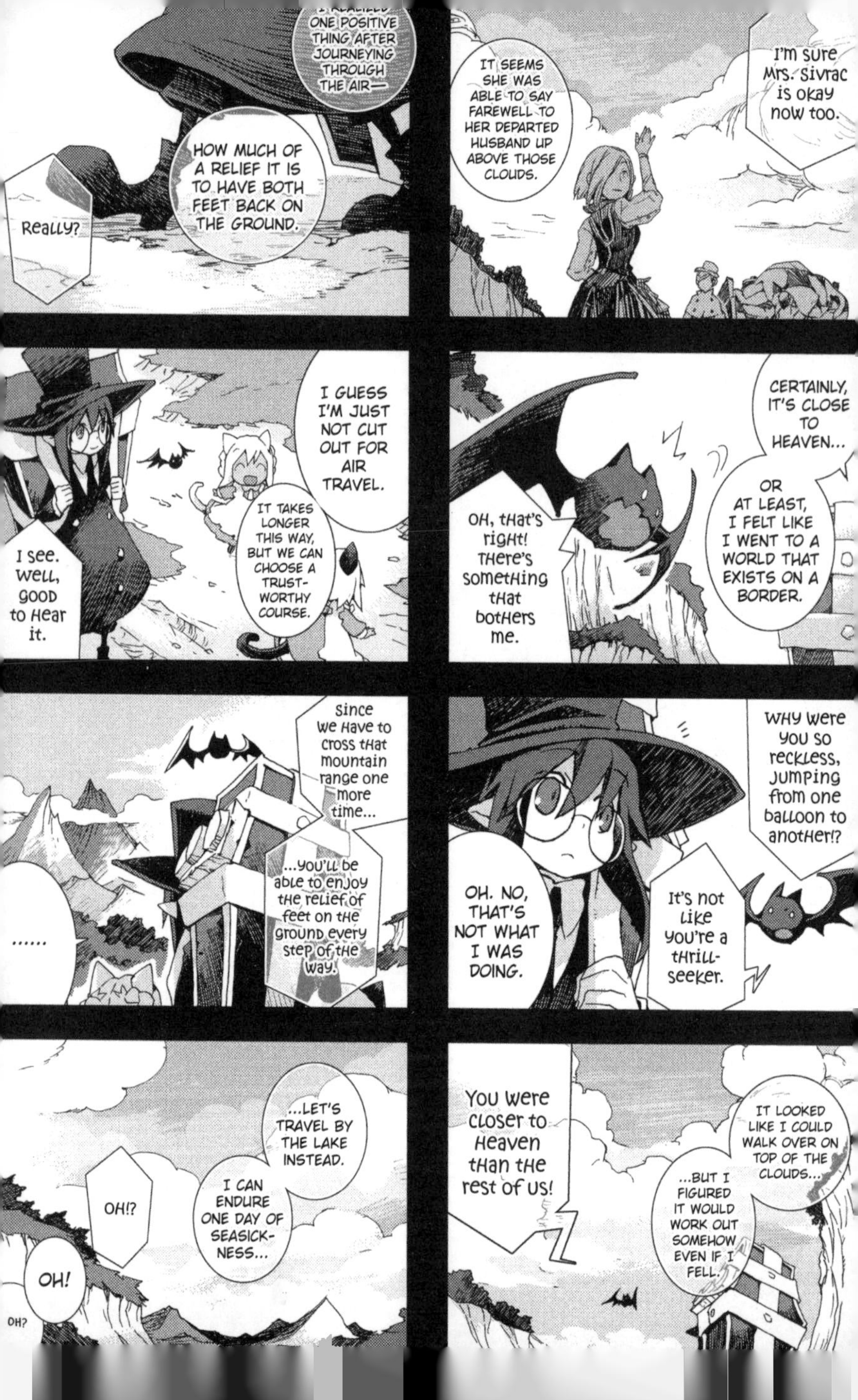
I'm sure Mrs. Sivrac is okay now too.
IT SEEMS SHE WAS ABLE TO SAY FAREWELL TO HER DEPARTED HUSBAND UP ABOVE THOSE CLOUDS.
ONE POSITIVE THING AFTER JOURNEYING THROUGH THE AIR—
HOW MUCH OF A RELIEF IT IS TO HAVE BOTH FEET BACK ON THE GROUND.
Really?
CERTAINLY, IT'S CLOSE TO HEAVEN...
OR AT LEAST, I FELT LIKE I WENT TO A WORLD THAT EXISTS ON A BORDER.
OH, that's right! There's something that bothers me.
I GUESS I'M JUST NOT CUT OUT FOR AIR TRAVEL.
IT TAKES LONGER THIS WAY, BUT WE CAN CHOOSE A TRUST-WORTHY COURSE.
I see. Well, good to hear it.
Why were you so reckless, jumping from one balloon to another!?
It's not like you're a thrill-seeker.
OH. NO, THAT'S NOT WHAT I WAS DOING.
Since we have to cross that mountain range one more time...
...you'll be able to enjoy the relief of feet on the ground every step of the way.
......
IT LOOKED LIKE I COULD WALK OVER ON TOP OF THE CLOUDS...
...BUT I FIGURED IT WOULD WORK OUT SOMEHOW EVEN IF I FELL.
You were closer to Heaven than the rest of us!
...LET'S TRAVEL BY THE LAKE INSTEAD.
I CAN ENDURE ONE DAY OF SEASICK-NESS...
OH!?
OH!
OH?

WE WERE PUTTING OUR LATE MASTER'S ATELIER IN ORDER WHEN IT HAPPENED...

AH!!

RATTLE

A BLACK HAT AND BLACK SUIT...

IS THAT THE MASTER'S ...!?

ANY-THING BRO-KEN?

IT DIDN'T SOUND THAT BAD...

AAAH... THEY REALLY TOOK A TUMBLE.

I'M SORRY! I'M SORRY!

THE STORY THE MASTER TOLD US ABOUT A PARTICULAR "ENCOUNTER"...

WE, HER DISCIPLES, QUICKLY CONNECTED THEM TO "THAT STORY."

...WHICH SEEMED TO HAVE BEEN STORED AWAY IN THAT DRAWER FOR AGES.

THERE WERE MANY UNFINISHED CANVASES...

HUH!? YOU THINK A WITCH LIVES HERE?

ARE YOU SHE?

I WAS TOLD I'D BE ABLE TO MEET HER IF I KNOCKED ON THE DOOR OF A HOUSE DEEP IN THIS PINE FOREST.

HMM...

I DON'T KNOW WHO TOLD YOU THAT OR HOW MUCH TROUBLE YOU HAD GETTING HERE...

...BUT UNFORTUNATELY, THE ONLY PERSON THAT LIVES HERE IS A HERMIT.

...THAT'S THE FEELING I'M GETTING.

AHHH, NO GOOD. I GIVE UP!

SCRABBLE

I'M SICK OF WOOD MANNEQUINS.

I DIDN'T THINK YOU WOULD BELIEVE ME RIGHT AWAY.

YES, WELL...

TAKE A LOAD OFF FOR A WHILE.

...WAIT, NOBODY'S TURNING YOU AWAY.

I'M SORRY TO HAVE BOTHERED YOU.

I WISH SOMEONE WOULD COME HERE TO DIE.

OR SOMEONE WHO'S ALREADY CURSED...

KNOCK

SIGH...

KNOCK

AND WHO ARE YOU, THEN?

...YOU'RE NOT THE WITCH I'M ACQUAINTED WITH, SO...

ACQUAINTED WITH...

KNOCK

KNOCK

KNOCK

EXCUSE ME.

I'M A TRAVELER...

MM?

40

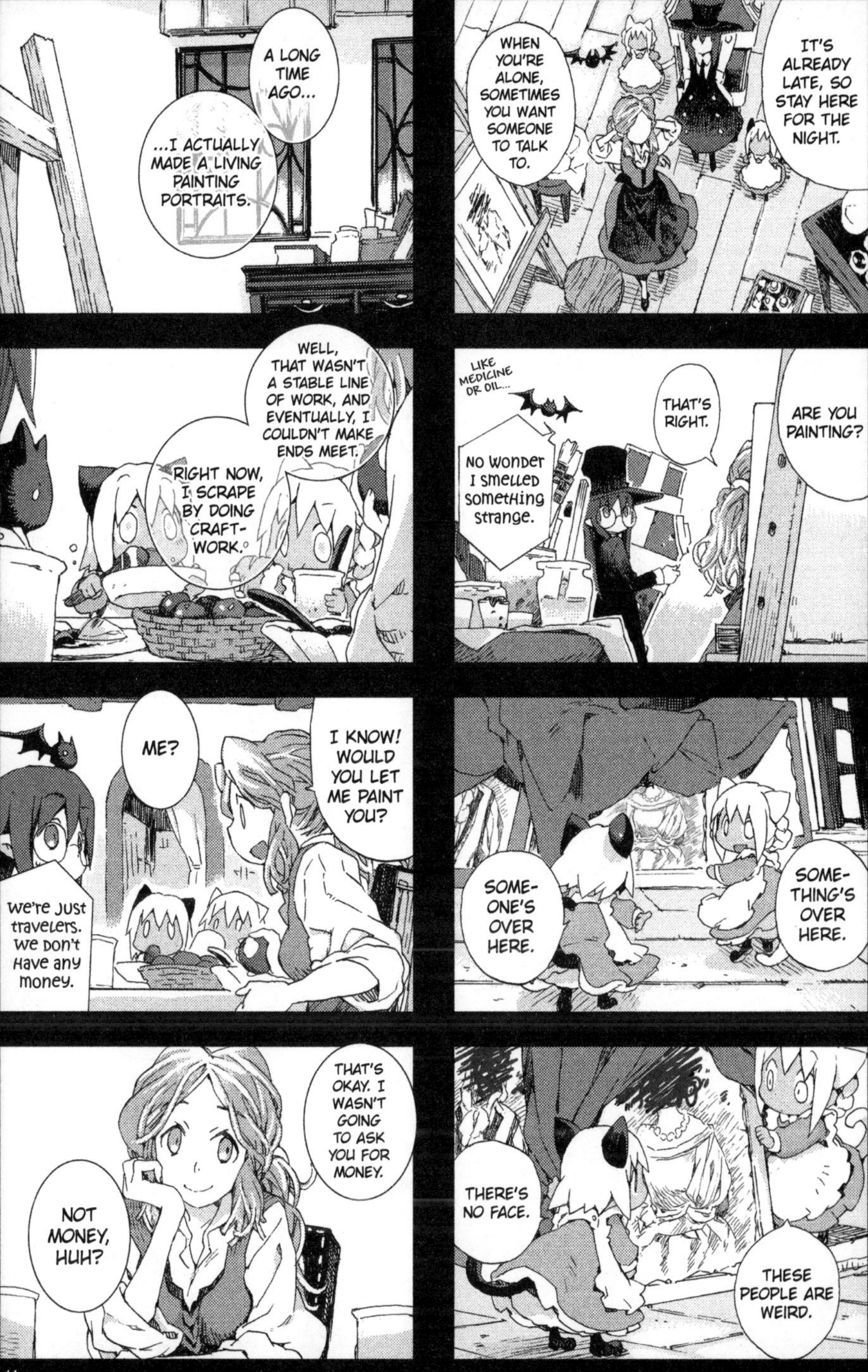
IT'S ALREADY LATE, SO STAY HERE FOR THE NIGHT.
WHEN YOU'RE ALONE, SOMETIMES YOU WANT SOMEONE TO TALK TO.
A LONG TIME AGO...
...I ACTUALLY MADE A LIVING PAINTING PORTRAITS.
ARE YOU PAINTING?
THAT'S RIGHT.
LIKE MEDICINE OR OIL...
No wonder I smelled something strange.
WELL, THAT WASN'T A STABLE LINE OF WORK, AND EVENTUALLY, I COULDN'T MAKE ENDS MEET.
RIGHT NOW, I SCRAPE BY DOING CRAFT-WORK.
SOME-THING'S OVER HERE.
SOME-ONE'S OVER HERE.
I KNOW! WOULD YOU LET ME PAINT YOU?
ME?
We're just travelers. We don't have any money.
THERE'S NO FACE.
THESE PEOPLE ARE WEIRD.
THAT'S OKAY. I WASN'T GOING TO ASK YOU FOR MONEY.
NOT MONEY, HUH?

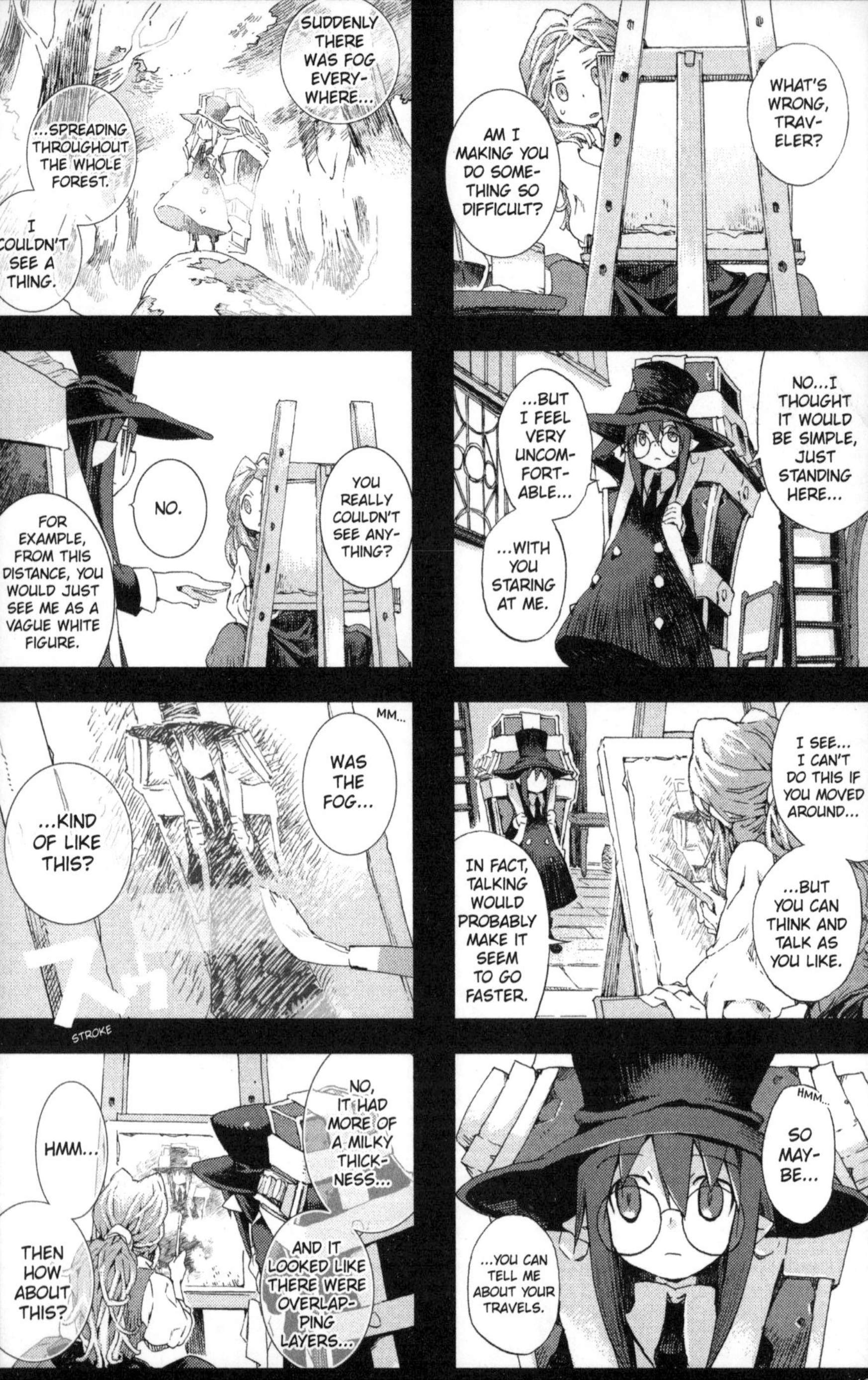
WHAT'S WRONG, TRAVELER?
AM I MAKING YOU DO SOMETHING SO DIFFICULT?
SUDDENLY THERE WAS FOG EVERYWHERE...
...SPREADING THROUGHOUT THE WHOLE FOREST.
I COULDN'T SEE A THING.
NO...I THOUGHT IT WOULD BE SIMPLE, JUST STANDING HERE...
...BUT I FEEL VERY UNCOMFORTABLE...
...WITH YOU STARING AT ME.
YOU REALLY COULDN'T SEE ANYTHING?
NO.
FOR EXAMPLE, FROM THIS DISTANCE, YOU WOULD JUST SEE ME AS A VAGUE WHITE FIGURE.
I SEE... I CAN'T DO THIS IF YOU MOVED AROUND...
...BUT YOU CAN THINK AND TALK AS YOU LIKE.
IN FACT, TALKING WOULD PROBABLY MAKE IT SEEM TO GO FASTER.
MM...
WAS THE FOG...
...KIND OF LIKE THIS?
STROKE
HMM...
SO MAYBE...
...YOU CAN TELL ME ABOUT YOUR TRAVELS.
NO, IT HAD MORE OF A MILKY THICKNESS...
AND IT LOOKED LIKE THERE WERE OVERLAPPING LAYERS...
HMM...
THEN HOW ABOUT THIS?

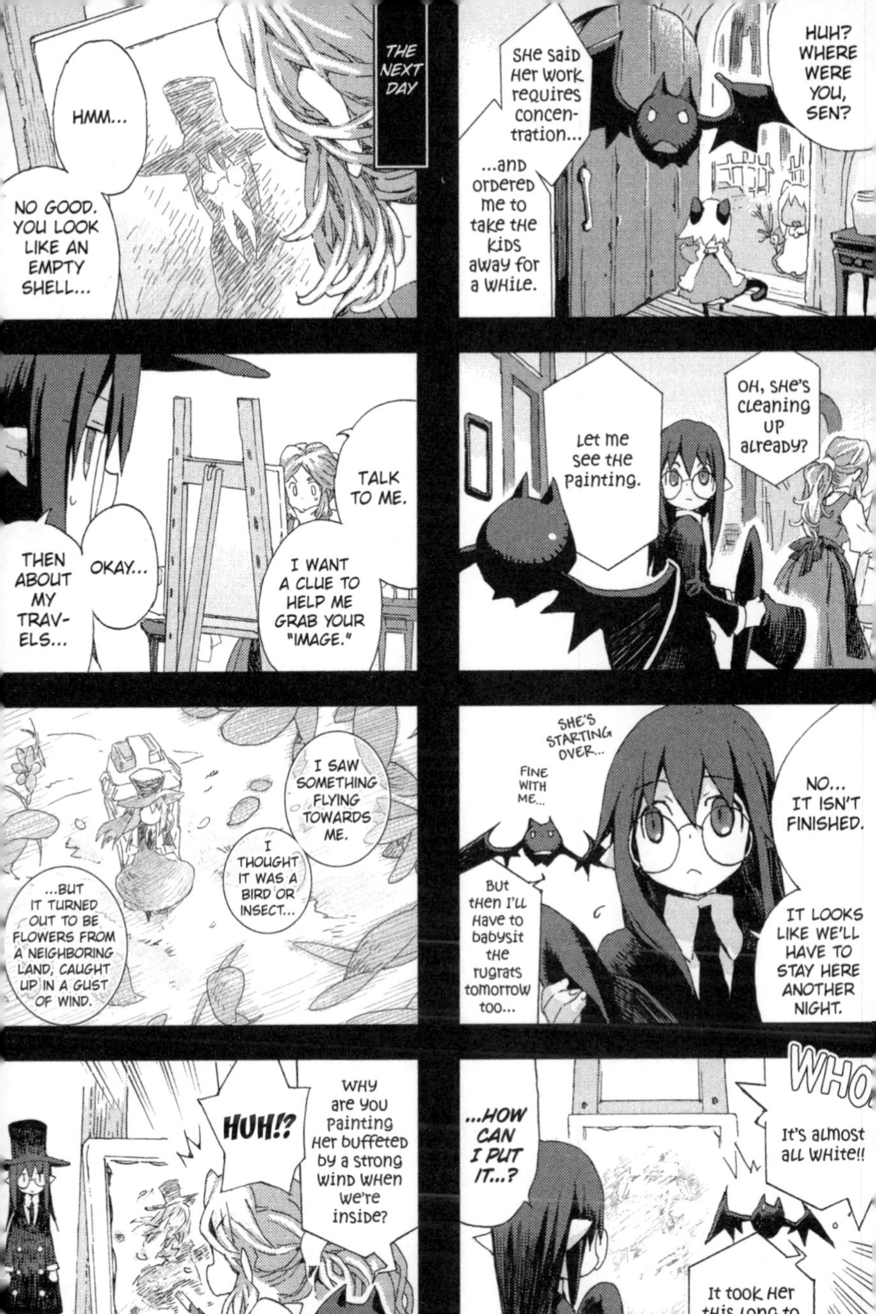
HUH? WHERE WERE YOU, SEN?
SHE SAID HER WORK REQUIRES CONCEN-TRATION...
...AND ORDERED ME TO TAKE THE KIDS AWAY FOR A WHILE.
THE NEXT DAY
HMM...
NO GOOD. YOU LOOK LIKE AN EMPTY SHELL...
OH, SHE'S CLEANING UP ALREADY?
LET ME SEE THE PAINTING.
TALK TO ME.
I WANT A CLUE TO HELP ME GRAB YOUR "IMAGE."
OKAY...
THEN ABOUT MY TRAV-ELS...
NO... IT ISN'T FINISHED.
SHE'S STARTING OVER...
FINE WITH ME...
IT LOOKS LIKE WE'LL HAVE TO STAY HERE ANOTHER NIGHT.
BUT THEN I'LL HAVE TO BABYSIT THE RUGRATS TOMORROW TOO...
I SAW SOMETHING FLYING TOWARDS ME.
I THOUGHT IT WAS A BIRD OR INSECT...
...BUT IT TURNED OUT TO BE FLOWERS FROM A NEIGHBORING LAND, CAUGHT UP IN A GUST OF WIND.
WHO
IT'S ALMOST ALL WHITE!!
IT TOOK HER THIS LONG TO PAINT THAT!?
...HOW CAN I PUT IT...?
WHY ARE YOU PAINTING HER BUFFETED BY A STRONG WIND WHEN WE'RE INSIDE?
HUH!?

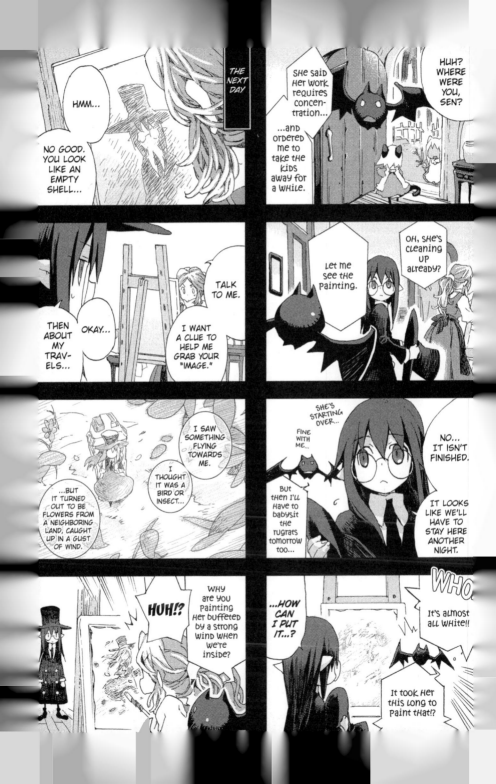

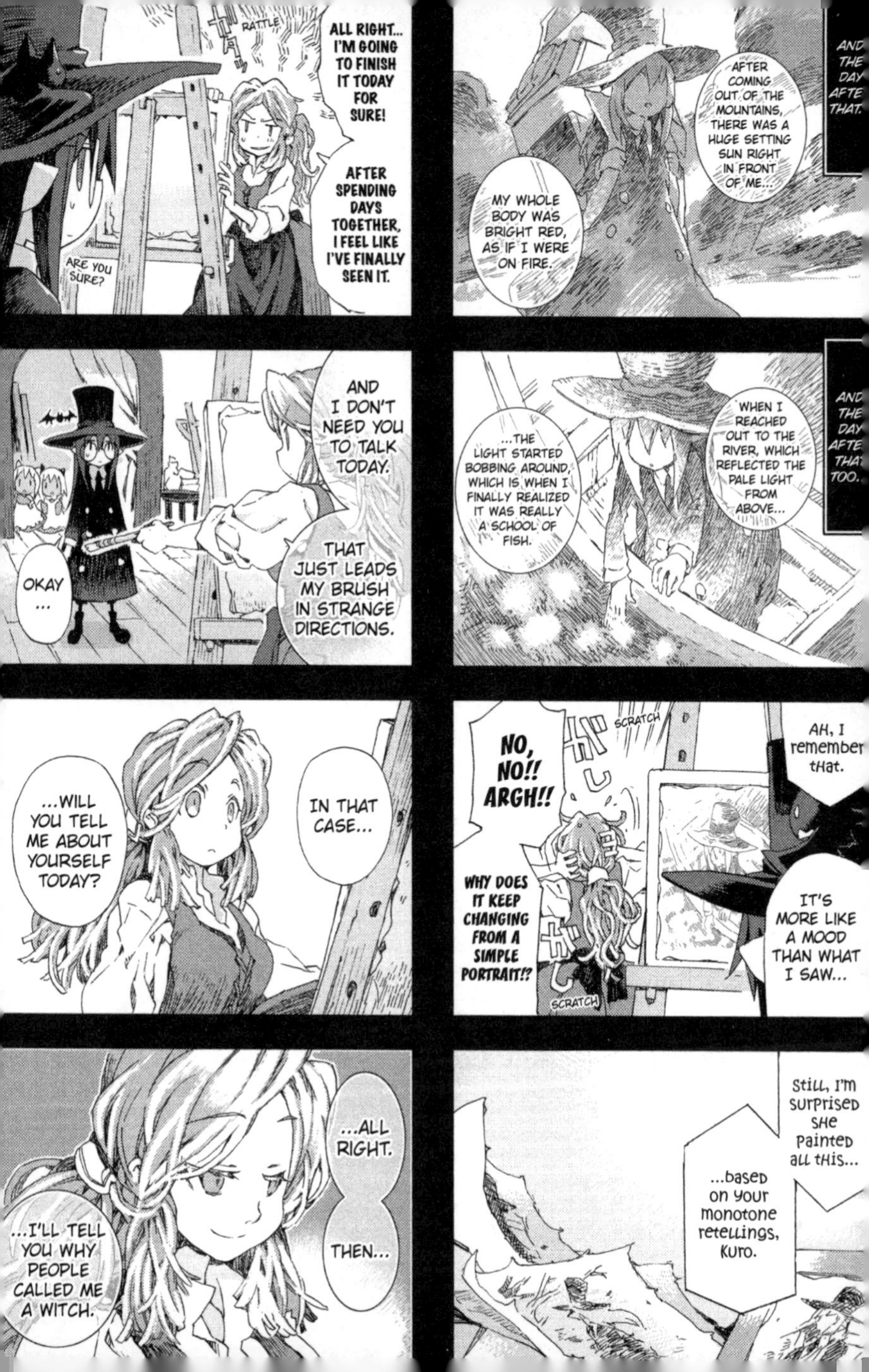
AND THE DAY AFTE THAT.
AFTER COMING OUT OF THE MOUNTAINS, THERE WAS A HUGE SETTING SUN RIGHT IN FRONT OF ME...
MY WHOLE BODY WAS BRIGHT RED, AS IF I WERE ON FIRE.
AND THE DAY AFTE THAT TOO...
WHEN I REACHED OUT TO THE RIVER, WHICH REFLECTED THE PALE LIGHT FROM ABOVE...
...THE LIGHT STARTED BOBBING AROUND, WHICH IS WHEN I FINALLY REALIZED IT WAS REALLY A SCHOOL OF FISH.
AH, I remembe that.
IT'S MORE LIKE A MOOD THAN WHAT I SAW...
SCRATCH
NO, NO!! ARGH!!
WHY DOES IT KEEP CHANGING FROM A SIMPLE PORTRAIT!?
SCRATCH
Still, I'm surprised she painted all this...
...based on your monotone retellings, Kuro.
ALL RIGHT... I'M GOING TO FINISH IT TODAY FOR SURE!
RATTLE
AFTER SPENDING DAYS TOGETHER, I FEEL LIKE I'VE FINALLY SEEN IT.
ARE YOU SURE?
AND I DON'T NEED YOU TO TALK TODAY.
THAT JUST LEADS MY BRUSH IN STRANGE DIRECTIONS.
OKAY...
IN THAT CASE...
...WILL YOU TELL ME ABOUT YOURSELF TODAY?
...ALL RIGHT.
THEN...
...I'LL TELL YOU WHY PEOPLE CALLED ME A WITCH.

?

YES, I AM, BUT...

ARE YOU THE ONE WHO PAINTED...

...THE DUKE'S POR- TRAIT?

BUT FEMALE PAINTERS LACK SKILL AND TEND TO ARRANGE COLORS LIKE A PEACOCK.

IS THAT THE PAINTER EVEN THE GUILD TALKS ABOUT?

SHE'S STILL A YOUNG WOMAN.

EXCUSE ME, BUT WHAT ARE YOU DOING!?

RATTLE

WE ARE TAKING THIS PAINTING.

IT'S NOT ABOUT WHETHER THEY ARE GOOD OR NOT.

IT'S WHETHER THEY PAINT WITH CONVICTION.

TOO MANY PAINTERS THESE DAYS...

...DRAW *THINGS THAT SHOULDN'T BE DRAWN.*

THAT WON'T BE NECES- SARY.

AT LEAST LET ME OBTAIN THE DUKE'S PERMIS- SION...

BUT I'M NOT FINISHED WITH IT!

TH- THANK YOU.

I'M GLAD I COMMIS- SIONED YOU FOR THE WORK.

YES, YOU PAINTED HIM WITH A VERY GENTLE EXPRES- SION.

AND AS SUCH, THIS PAINTING WILL BE BURNED AS A WARNING TO THE PEOPLE.

THE DUKE IS GOING TO BE EXECUTED FOR THE CRIME OF PLOTTING TREASON AGAINST THE NATION.

R- RIGHT!

NOW JUST DEEPEN HIS MUSTACHE A LITTLE TO BRING OUT A SENSE OF GRAVITY.

AND MAKE THE GOLD EMBROIDERY ON HIS SLEEVES AND COLLAR STAND OUT MORE.

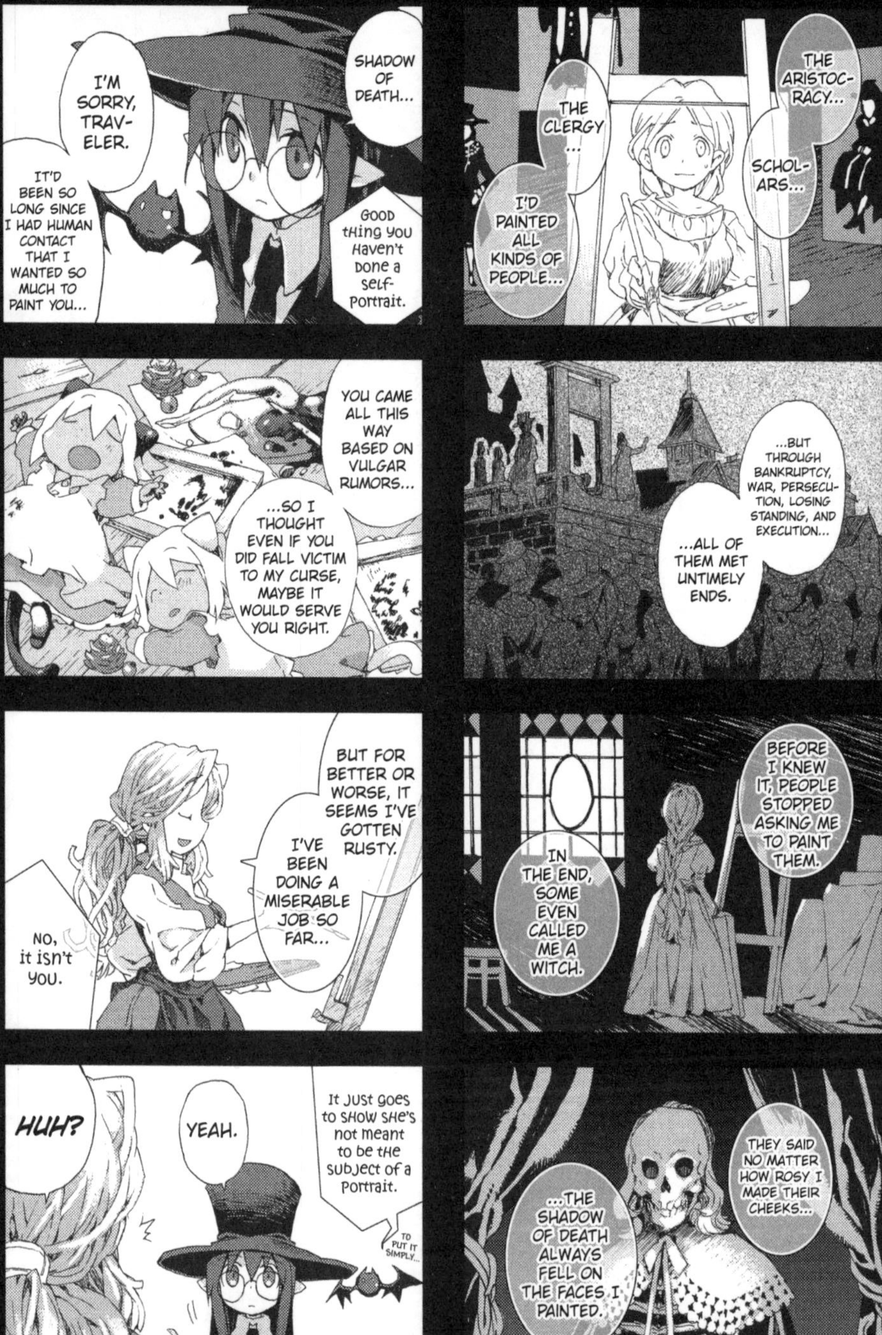
THE ARISTOCRACY...
SCHOLARS...
THE CLERGY...
I'D PAINTED ALL KINDS OF PEOPLE...
SHADOW OF DEATH...
I'M SORRY, TRAVELER.
Good thing you haven't done a self-portrait.
IT'D BEEN SO LONG SINCE I HAD HUMAN CONTACT THAT I WANTED SO MUCH TO PAINT YOU...
...BUT THROUGH BANKRUPTCY, WAR, PERSECUTION, LOSING STANDING, AND EXECUTION...
...ALL OF THEM MET UNTIMELY ENDS.
YOU CAME ALL THIS WAY BASED ON VULGAR RUMORS...
...SO I THOUGHT EVEN IF YOU DID FALL VICTIM TO MY CURSE, MAYBE IT WOULD SERVE YOU RIGHT.
BEFORE I KNEW IT, PEOPLE STOPPED ASKING ME TO PAINT THEM.
IN THE END, SOME EVEN CALLED ME A WITCH.
BUT FOR BETTER OR WORSE, IT SEEMS I'VE GOTTEN RUSTY.
I'VE BEEN DOING A MISERABLE JOB SO FAR...
No, it isn't you.
THEY SAID NO MATTER HOW ROSY I MADE THEIR CHEEKS...
...THE SHADOW OF DEATH ALWAYS FELL ON THE FACES I PAINTED.
It just goes to show she's not meant to be the subject of a portrait.
TO PUT IT SIMPLY...
YEAH.
HUH?

AFTER SIX DAYS...

...I WAS FINALLY...

...ABOUT TO ARRIVE AT THE SAME CONCLUSION MYSELF.

WHILE PAINTING ME, YOU KEPT SAYING...

...THAT YOU COULDN'T SEE MY "INNER SELF."

YOU DON'T NEED TO BE SO DOWN ON YOUR-SELF...

HUH?

Let's see.

ALL RIGHT, FINISHED.

WILL YOU LOOK TO SEE IF IT HAS THE SHADOW OF DEATH?

THEIR intentions for getting their portrait painted too.

THEN THAT makes me think you often did...

...see the true, inner selves of your clients.

IT'S KURO-CHA!

AH! KURO-CHAN!

I WAS FINALLY ABLE TO SEE YOU, TRAVELER.

AND IF THEY miss their footing at the peak, they'll fall or go into decline.

You just happened to meet a lot of them.

PEOPLE who spend a lot of money to leave a portrait behind...

...must think their current life is near its peak.

THAT'S YOUR PORTRAIT, TRAVELER.

SUR-ROUNDED BY WIND AND SCENERY...

THAT'S WHY YOU COULDN'T PAINT IT.

...A PORTRAIT LIKE THAT.

BUT I DON'T NEED...

...STARTING HER PURSUIT OF PAINTING FROM SCRATCH.

AND SO, THE MASTER TRAVELED AROUND THE WORLD...

WELL, WE'VE STAYED HERE TOO LONG ANYWAY.

ALTHOUGH SHE SEEMED TO BE IN A HURRY...

WHAT THE HELL?

SHE KICKS US OUT OF HER HOUSE AT DAWN...?

...AND NURTURED MANY DISCIPLES.

THEN SHE LED THE WAY TO A NEW AGE OF PAINTING...

I'M GOING TO TRAVEL TOO! FROM TODAY, WE'RE FELLOW TRAVELERS!!

MM?

AH!!

THAT'S WHEN SHE PAINTED WHAT WOULD LATER BE CALLED HER "BLACK TRAVELER" SERIES.

IN HER TWILIGHT YEARS, THE MASTER WOULD HOLE UP IN HER ATELIER AND QUIETLY PAINT.

YOU FASCINATED ME...

...WITH YOUR TALES THAT WENT BEYOND THE CANVAS.

OR PERHAPS IT WAS THE MASTER HERSELF, PAINTING "SELF-PORTRAITS."

WAS THE MOTIF TAKEN FROM THE TRAVELER IN HER PAST?

...THE KIND OF WORLD THAT YOU SAW.

I WANT TO TRY PAINTING...

Shoulder-a-Coffin Kuro by Satoko Kiyuduki

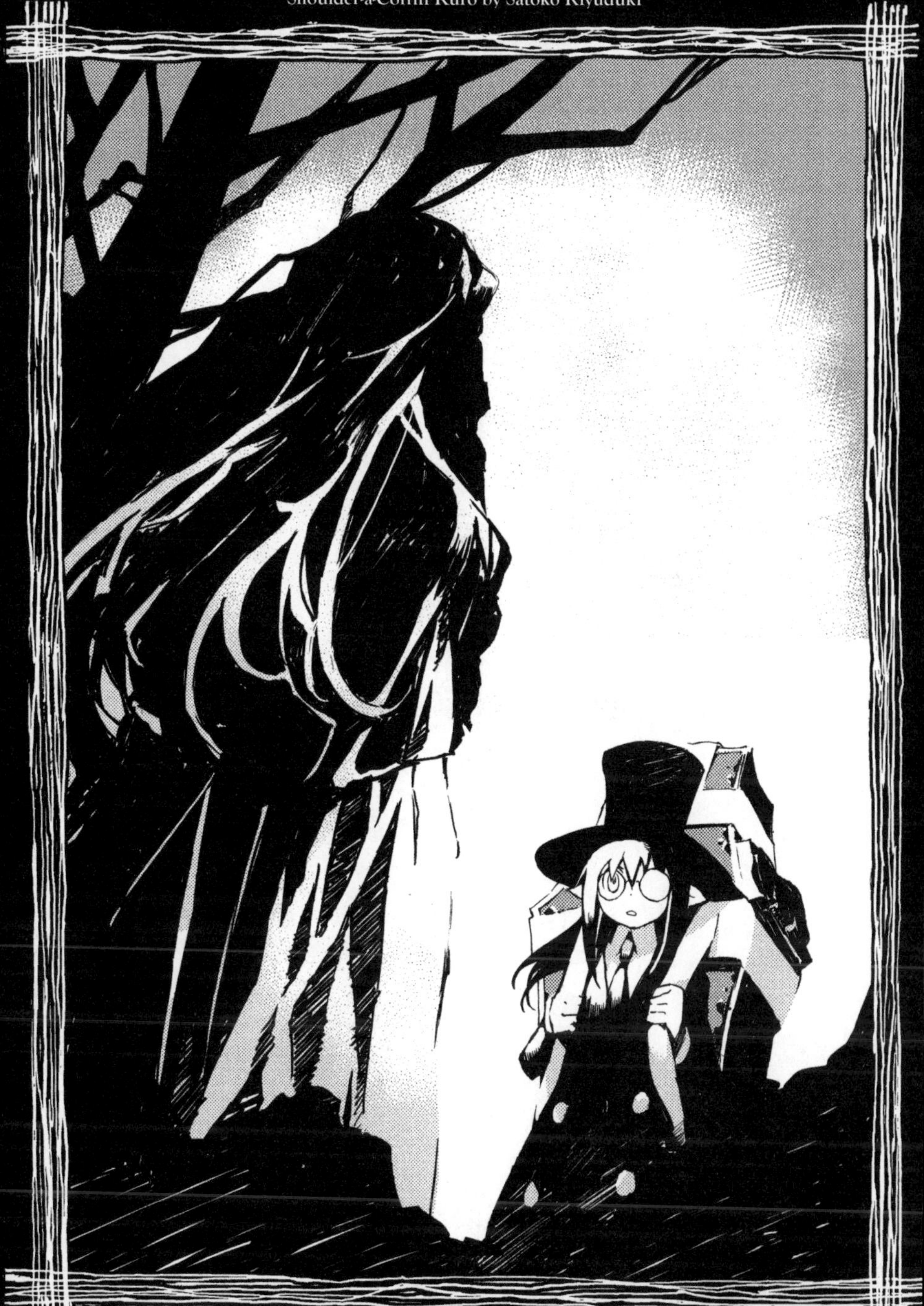

The traveler has a hard time talking about what happened here.
That's because it's difficult to convey to other people
what occurs in a dream.

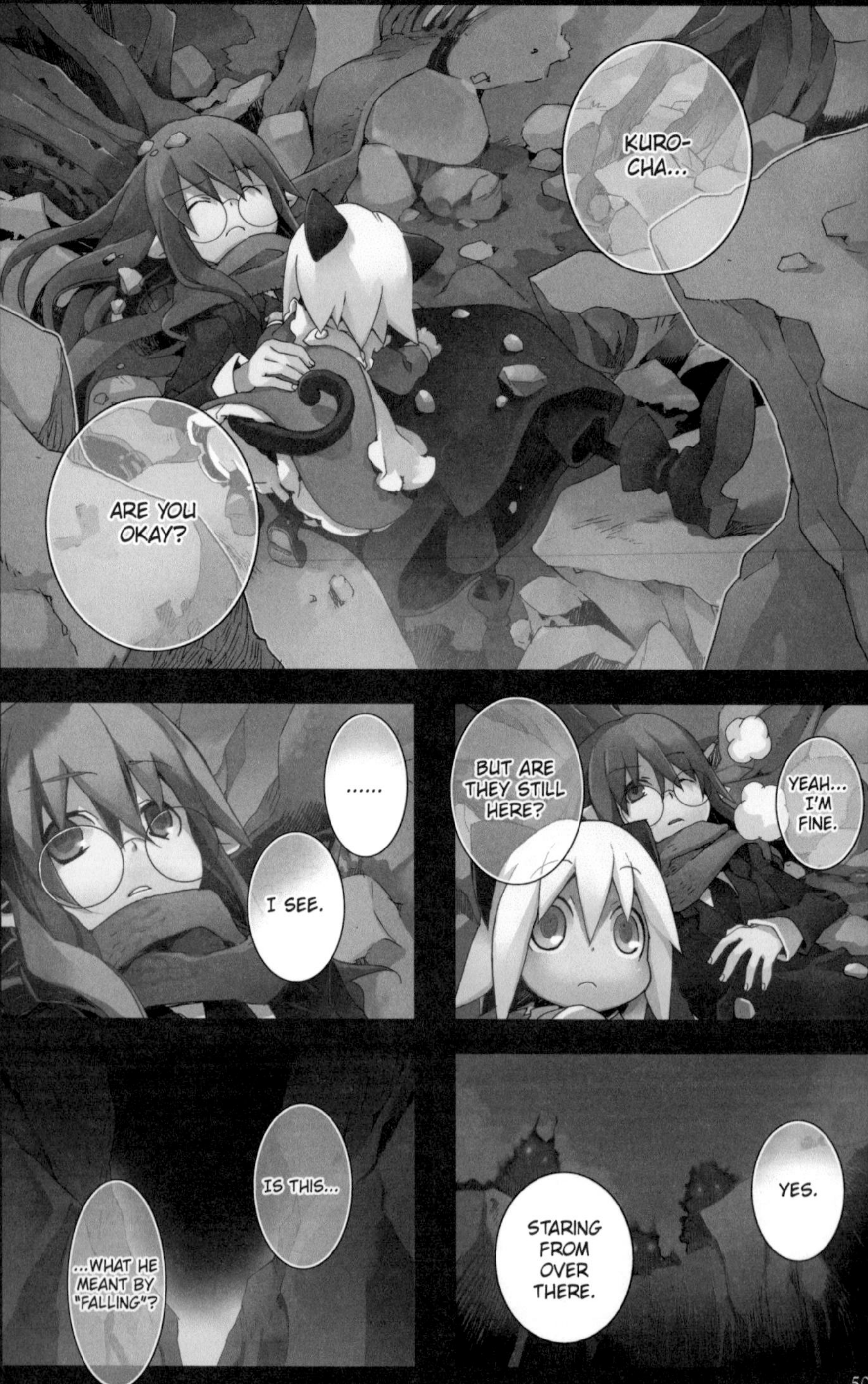
KURO-CHA...
ARE YOU OKAY?
YEAH... I'M FINE.
BUT ARE THEY STILL HERE?
......
I SEE.
YES.
STARING FROM OVER THERE.
IS THIS...
...WHAT HE MEANT BY "FALLING"?

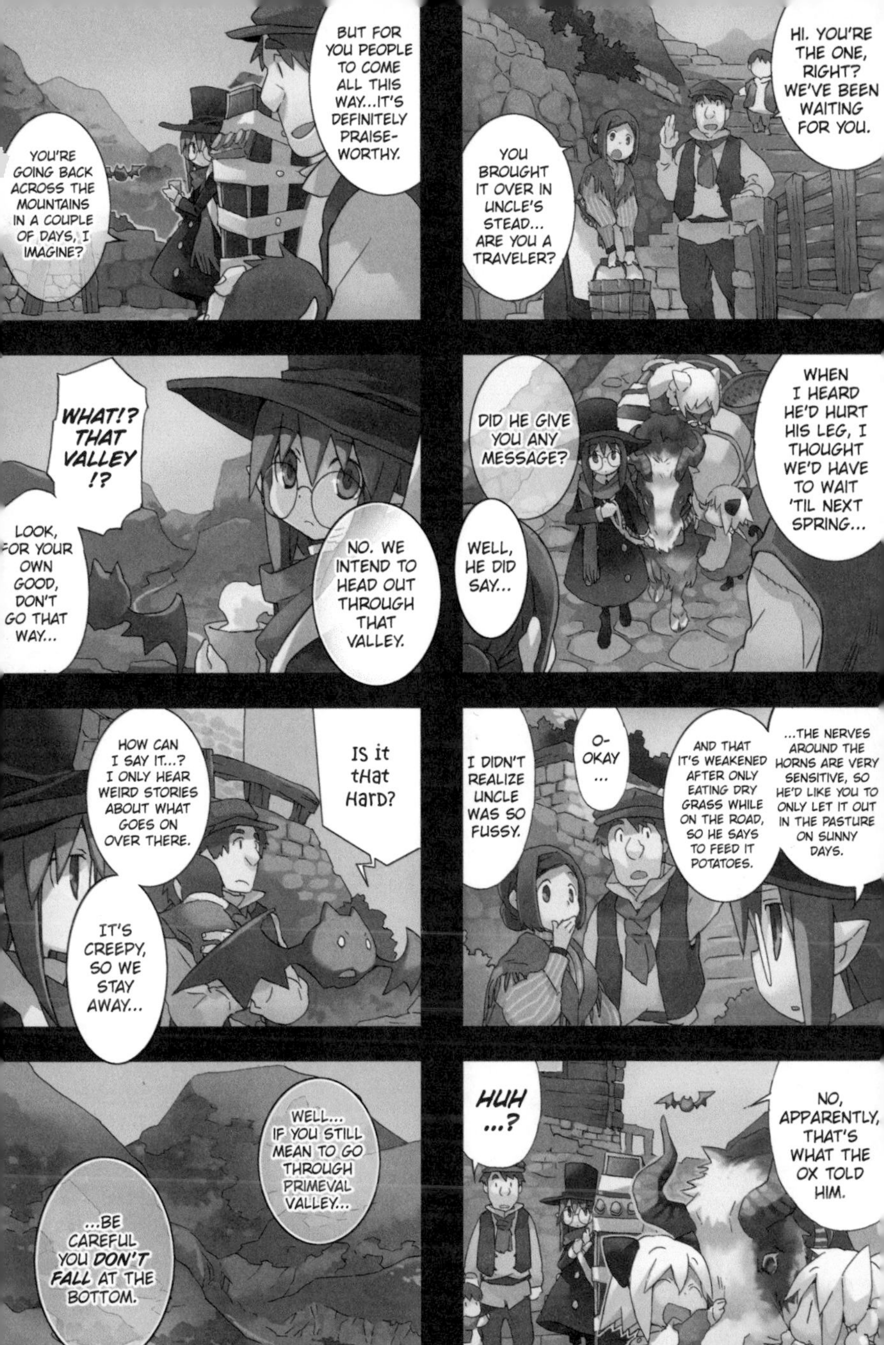
HI. YOU'RE THE ONE, RIGHT? WE'VE BEEN WAITING FOR YOU.
YOU BROUGHT IT OVER IN UNCLE'S STEAD... ARE YOU A TRAVELER?
WHEN I HEARD HE'D HURT HIS LEG, I THOUGHT WE'D HAVE TO WAIT 'TIL NEXT SPRING...
DID HE GIVE YOU ANY MESSAGE?
WELL, HE DID SAY...
...THE NERVES AROUND THE HORNS ARE VERY SENSITIVE, SO HE'D LIKE YOU TO ONLY LET IT OUT IN THE PASTURE ON SUNNY DAYS.
AND THAT IT'S WEAKENED AFTER ONLY EATING DRY GRASS WHILE ON THE ROAD, SO HE SAYS TO FEED IT POTATOES.
O-OKAY...
I DIDN'T REALIZE UNCLE WAS SO FUSSY.
NO, APPARENTLY, THAT'S WHAT THE OX TOLD HIM.
HUH...?
BUT FOR YOU PEOPLE TO COME ALL THIS WAY...IT'S DEFINITELY PRAISE-WORTHY.
YOU'RE GOING BACK ACROSS THE MOUNTAINS IN A COUPLE OF DAYS, I IMAGINE?
NO. WE INTEND TO HEAD OUT THROUGH THAT VALLEY.
WHAT!? THAT VALLEY!?
LOOK, FOR YOUR OWN GOOD, DON'T GO THAT WAY...
Is it tHat Hard?
HOW CAN I SAY IT...? I ONLY HEAR WEIRD STORIES ABOUT WHAT GOES ON OVER THERE.
IT'S CREEPY, SO WE STAY AWAY...
WELL... IF YOU STILL MEAN TO GO THROUGH PRIMEVAL VALLEY...
...BE CAREFUL YOU DON'T FALL AT THE BOTTOM.

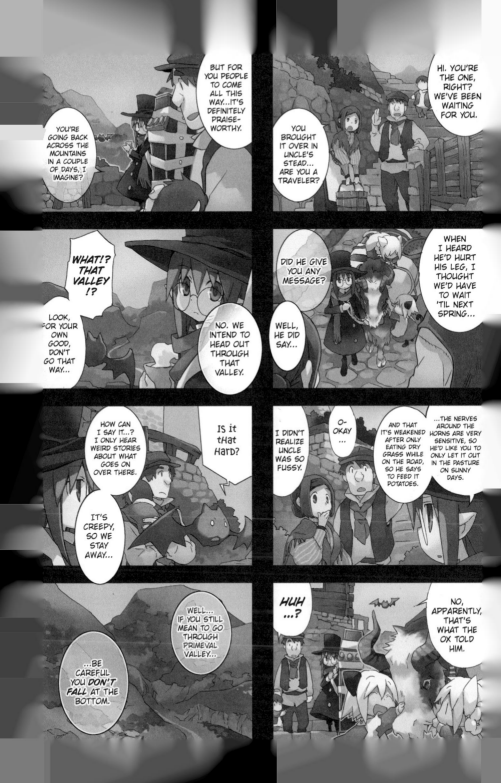

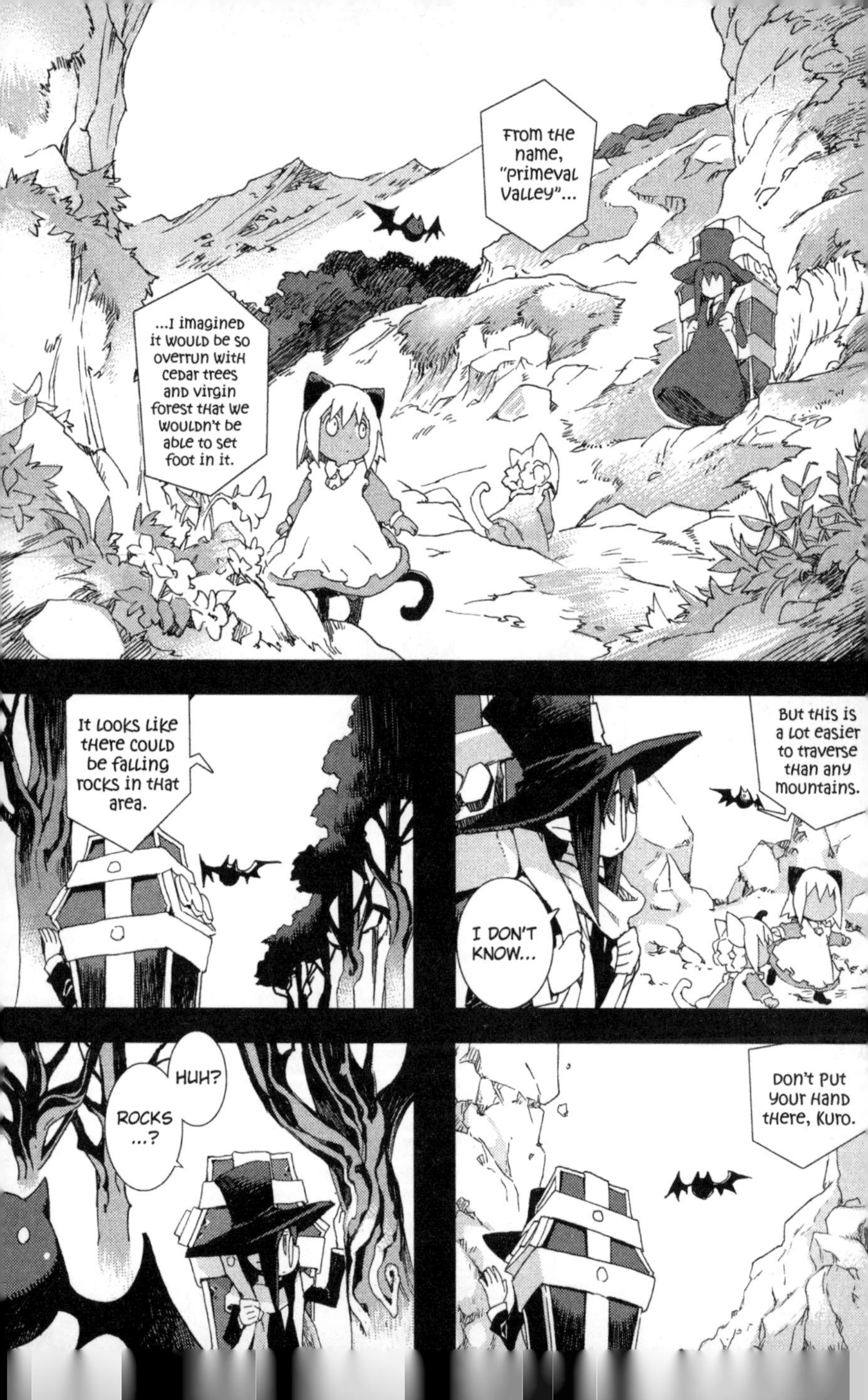
From the name, "primeval valley"...
...I imagined it would be so overrun with cedar trees and virgin forest that we wouldn't be able to set foot in it.
But this is a lot easier to traverse than any mountains.
I DON'T KNOW...
It looks like there could be falling rocks in that area.
Don't put your hand there, Kuro.
HUH?
ROCKS ...?

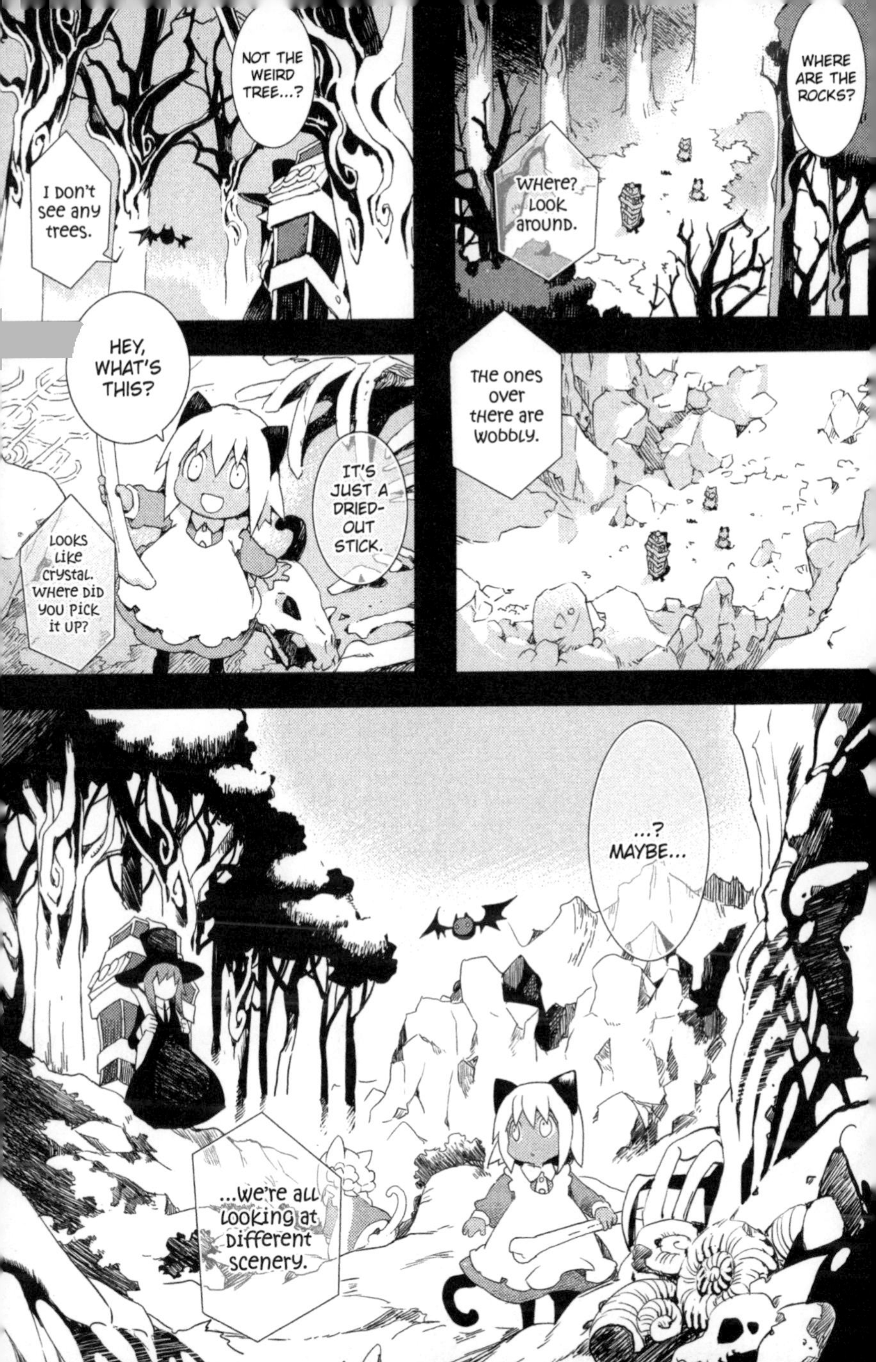
WHERE ARE THE ROCKS?
Where? Look around.
NOT THE WEIRD TREE...?
I don't see any trees.
The ones over there are wobbly.
HEY, WHAT'S THIS?
IT'S JUST A DRIED-OUT STICK.
Looks like crystal. Where did you pick it up?
...? MAYBE...
...we're all looking at different scenery.

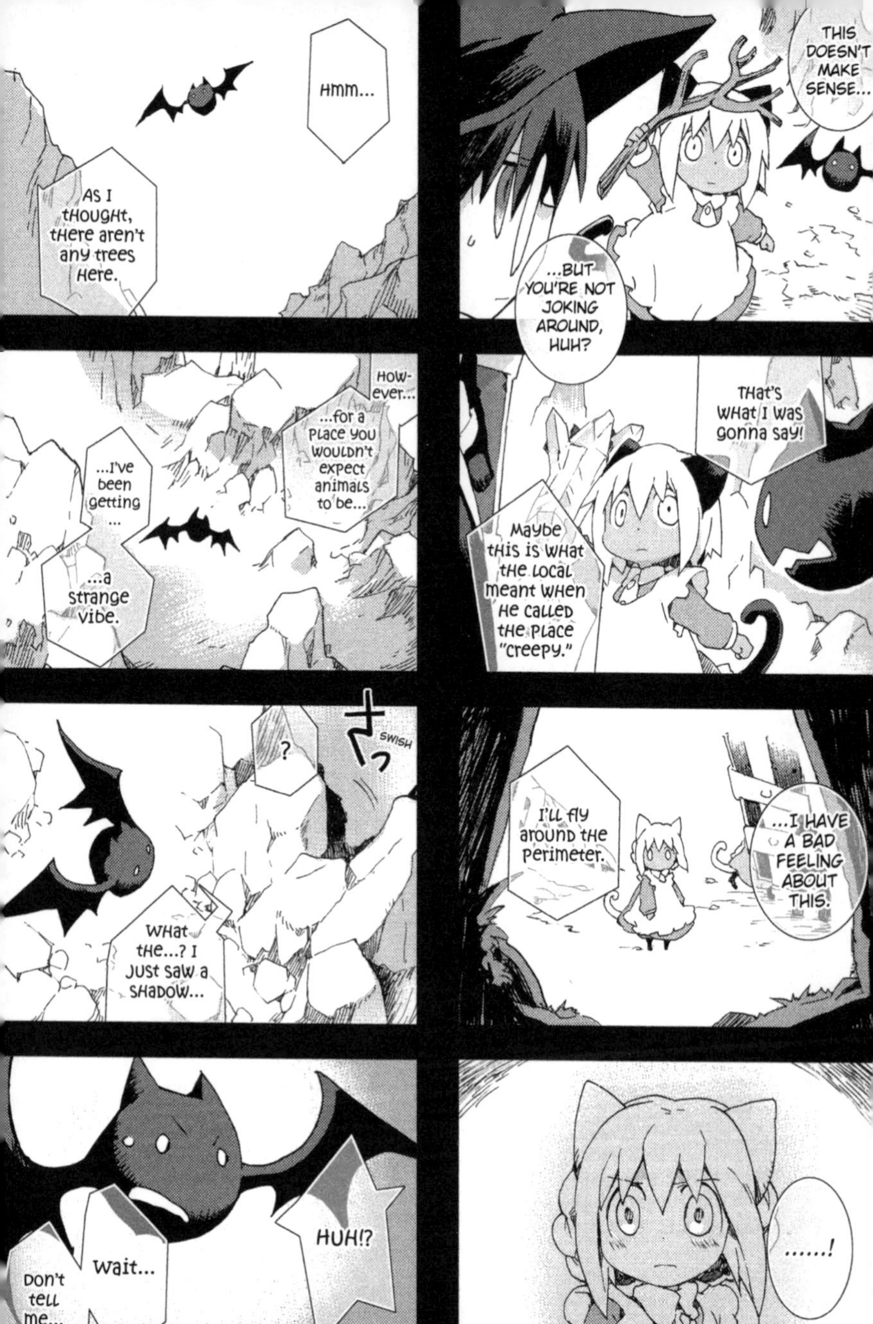
THIS DOESN'T MAKE SENSE...
...BUT YOU'RE NOT JOKING AROUND, HUH?
Hmm...
As I thought, there aren't any trees here.
That's what I was gonna say!
Maybe this is what the local meant when he called the place "creepy."
How-ever...
...for a place you wouldn't expect animals to be...
...I've been getting...
...a strange vibe.
...I HAVE A BAD FEELING ABOUT THIS.
I'll fly around the perimeter.
SWISH
?
What the...? I just saw a shadow...
......!
HUH!?
Wait...
Don't tell me...

I kind of picked up on their presence.

Maybe they've been here since we entered the valley.

...? WHO ARE THOSE GUYS?

WHEN DID THEY SHOW UP?

WHAT DOES IT LOOK LIKE TO YOU, SANJU?

TO ME, THIS LOOKS LIKE...

...SOMETHING FROM THE MIDDLE OF THE STONE AGE.

NAH.

At Least... I DON'T THINK SO.

MAYBE THEY'RE LOCALS?

OR BANDITS?

SANJU?

SWISH

...WE SHOULD HAVE LEFT WITHOUT ANY FURTHER ADO...

RIGHT...

?

A-anyway, WE SHOULD REALLY GET OUT OF HERE.

Remember the THIRTY-SIX Strata-gems.

LOOKING BACK...

I DON'T LIKE IT HERE.

HEY, LET'S LEAVE THIS PLACE.

...HIKING IN DEEPER.

If it is a dream...

Ha-Ha! True!

THIS IS LIKE A DREAM DURING A RESTLESS SLEEP.

...INSTEAD OF PER-VERSELY...

I DON'T LIKE THOSE PEOPLE EITHER.

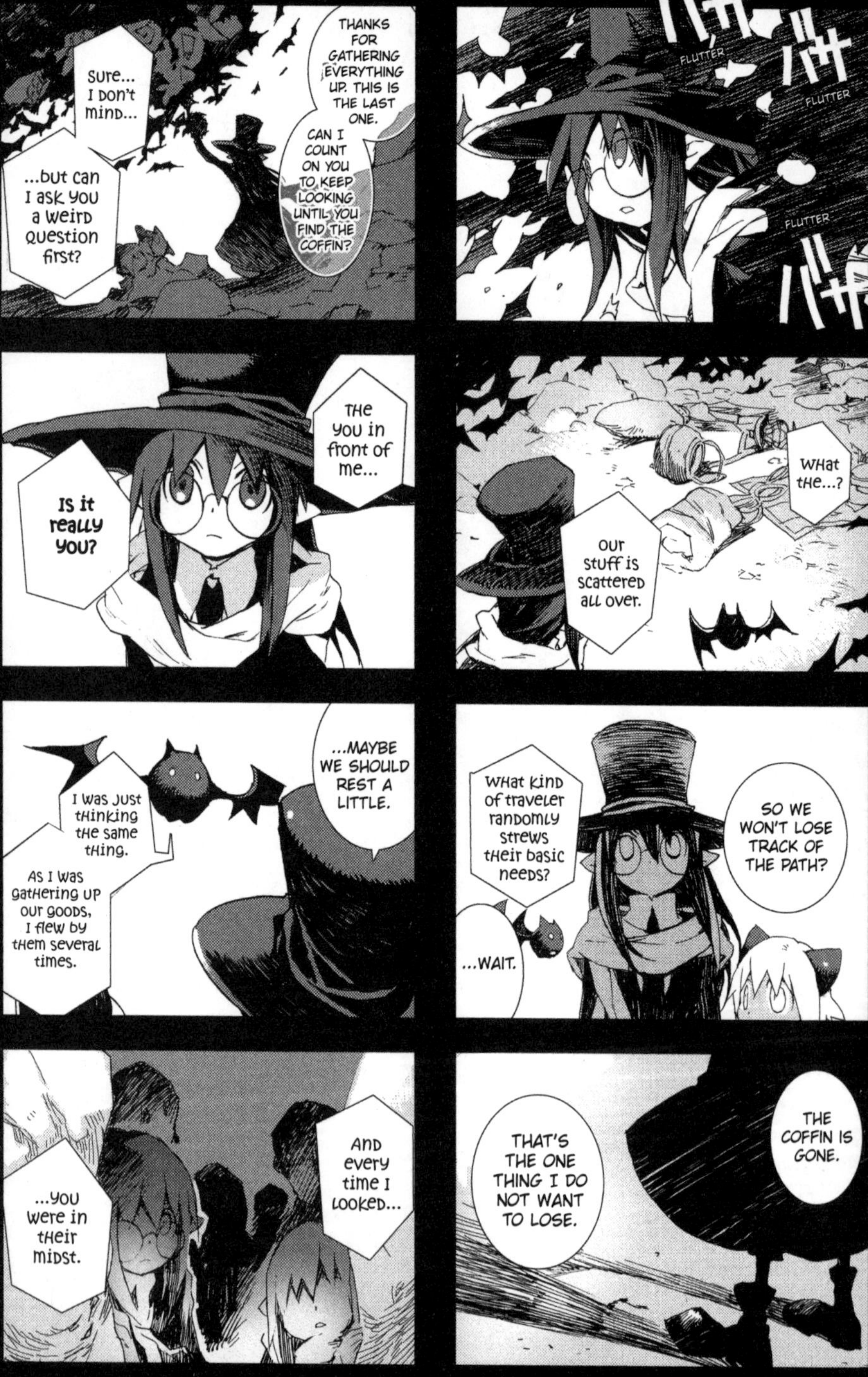

バサ
FLUTTER
バサ
FLUTTER
FLUTTER
バサ
THANKS FOR GATHERING EVERYTHING UP. THIS IS THE LAST ONE.
CAN I COUNT ON YOU TO KEEP LOOKING UNTIL YOU FIND THE COFFIN?
Sure... I don't mind...
...but can I ask you a weird question first?
What the...?
Our stuff is scattered all over.
The you in front of me...
Is it really you?
SO WE WON'T LOSE TRACK OF THE PATH?
What kind of traveler randomly strews their basic needs?
...WAIT.
...MAYBE WE SHOULD REST A LITTLE.
I was just thinking the same thing.
As I was gathering up our goods, I flew by them several times.
THE COFFIN IS GONE.
THAT'S THE ONE THING I DO NOT WANT TO LOSE.
And every time I looked...
...you were in their midst.

ARE YOU OKAY, KURO-CHA?

YOU LOOK DOWN.

......

...THE SAME THING TOO, SANJU?

DID YOU SEE...

I DO NOT.

BOTH OF THEM ARE YOU, KURO-CHA...

...BUT I DIDN'T WANT YOU TO GET ANGRY AT SANJU.

ARE YOU ALL RIGHT, NIJUKU?

Until now, I thought maybe I was just seeing things...

To be honest, it shook me up a little too.

Sorry, Kuro.

AH!

I HAVE NO IDEA WHAT'S GOING ON...

......

IS THAT YOUR LOST PROPERTY?

I'll take Sanju with me...

...so let's rendezvous after we clear the valley.

For the time being, let's split up.

THAT'S...

RATTLE

...OKAY.

GOT IT...

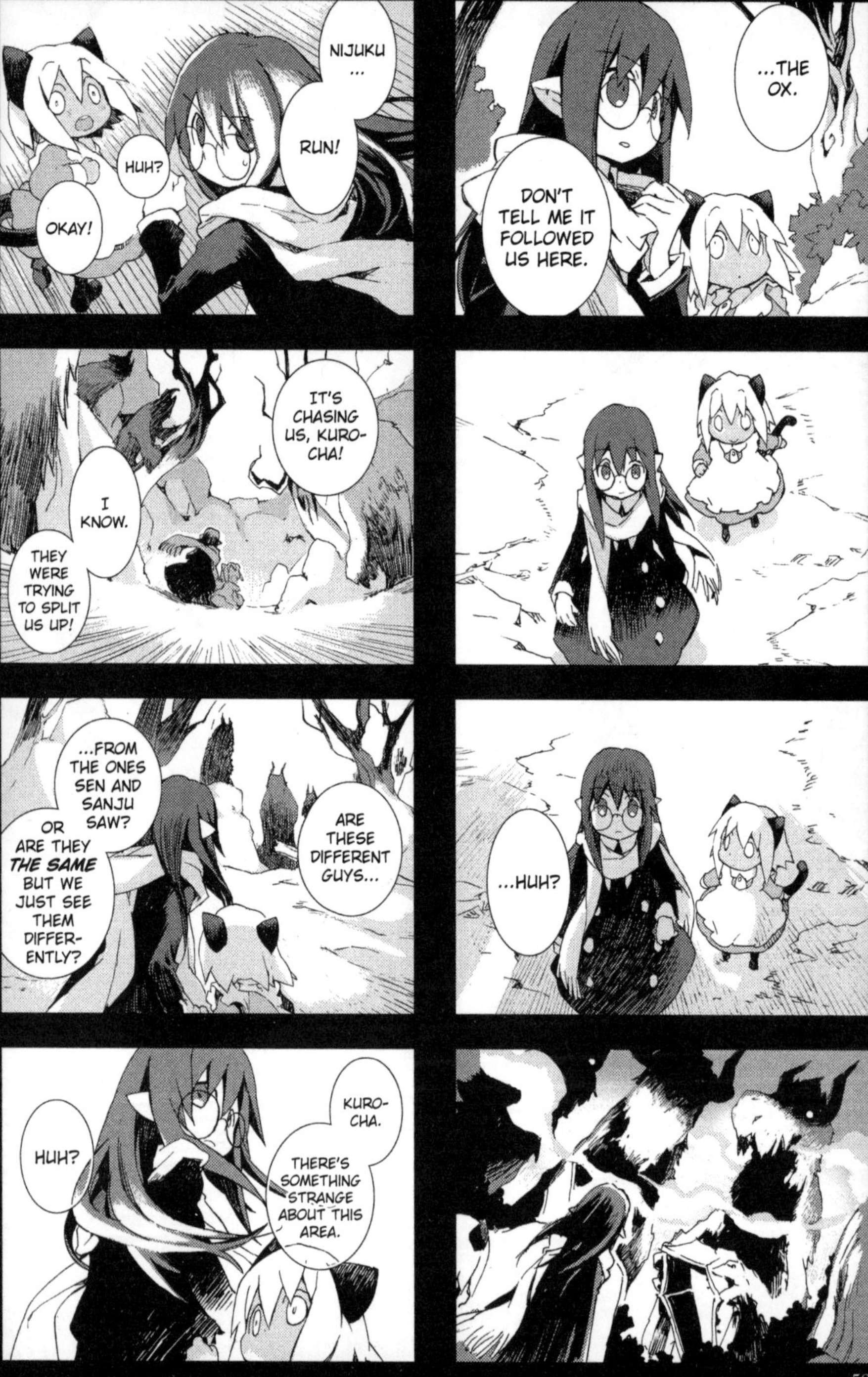
...THE OX.
DON'T TELL ME IT FOLLOWED US HERE.
NIJUKU ...
RUN!
HUH?
OKAY!
IT'S CHASING US, KURO-CHA!
I KNOW.
THEY WERE TRYING TO SPLIT US UP!
...HUH?
ARE THESE DIFFERENT GUYS...
...FROM THE ONES SEN AND SANJU SAW?
OR ARE THEY *THE SAME* BUT WE JUST SEE THEM DIFFERENTLY?
KURO-CHA.
THERE'S SOMETHING STRANGE ABOUT THIS AREA.
HUH?

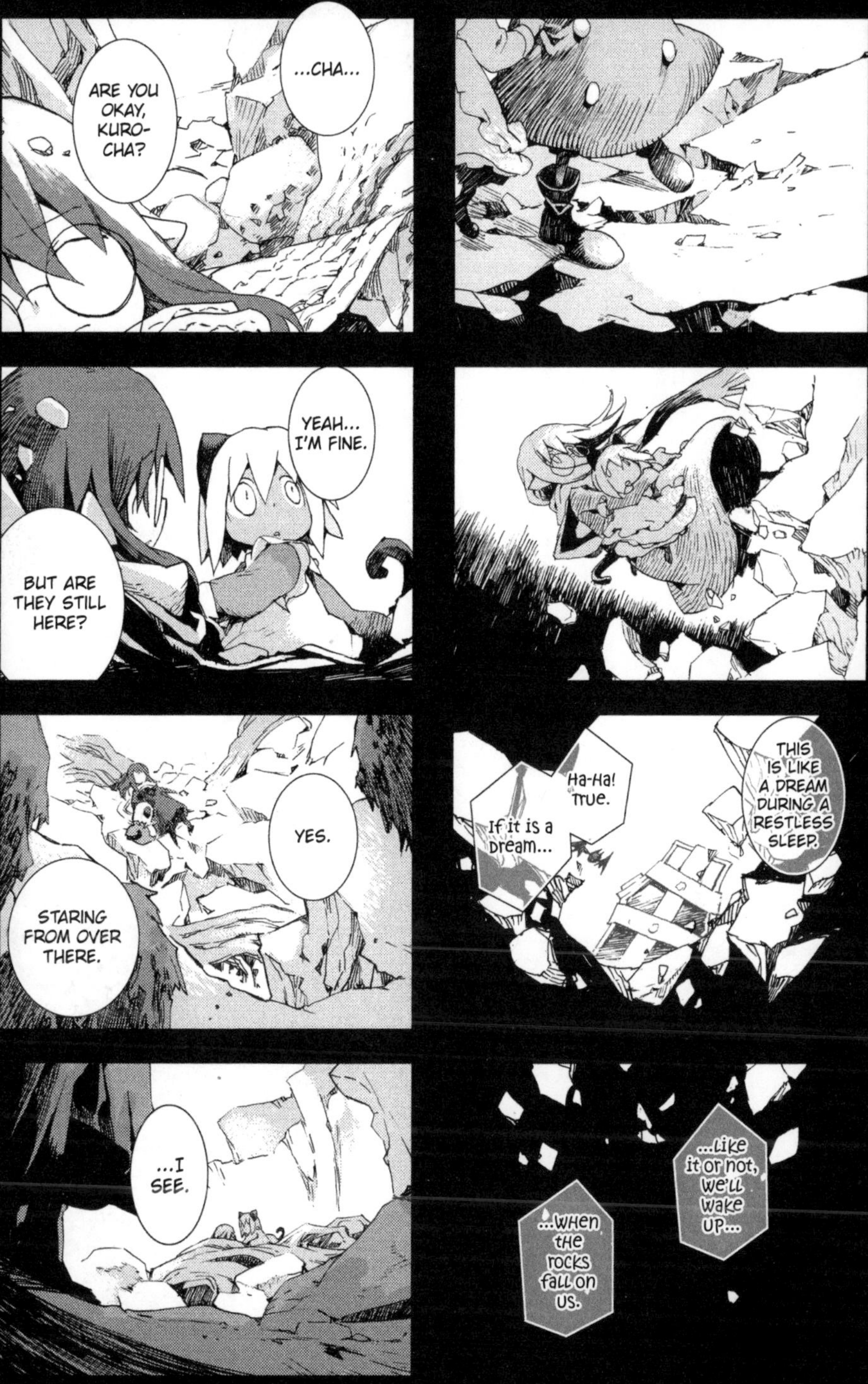
...CHA...
ARE YOU OKAY, KURO-CHA?
YEAH... I'M FINE.
BUT ARE THEY STILL HERE?
THIS IS LIKE A DREAM DURING A RESTLESS SLEEP.
Ha-Ha! True.
If it is a dream...
YES.
STARING FROM OVER THERE.
...like it or not, we'll wake up...
...when the rocks fall on us.
...I SEE.

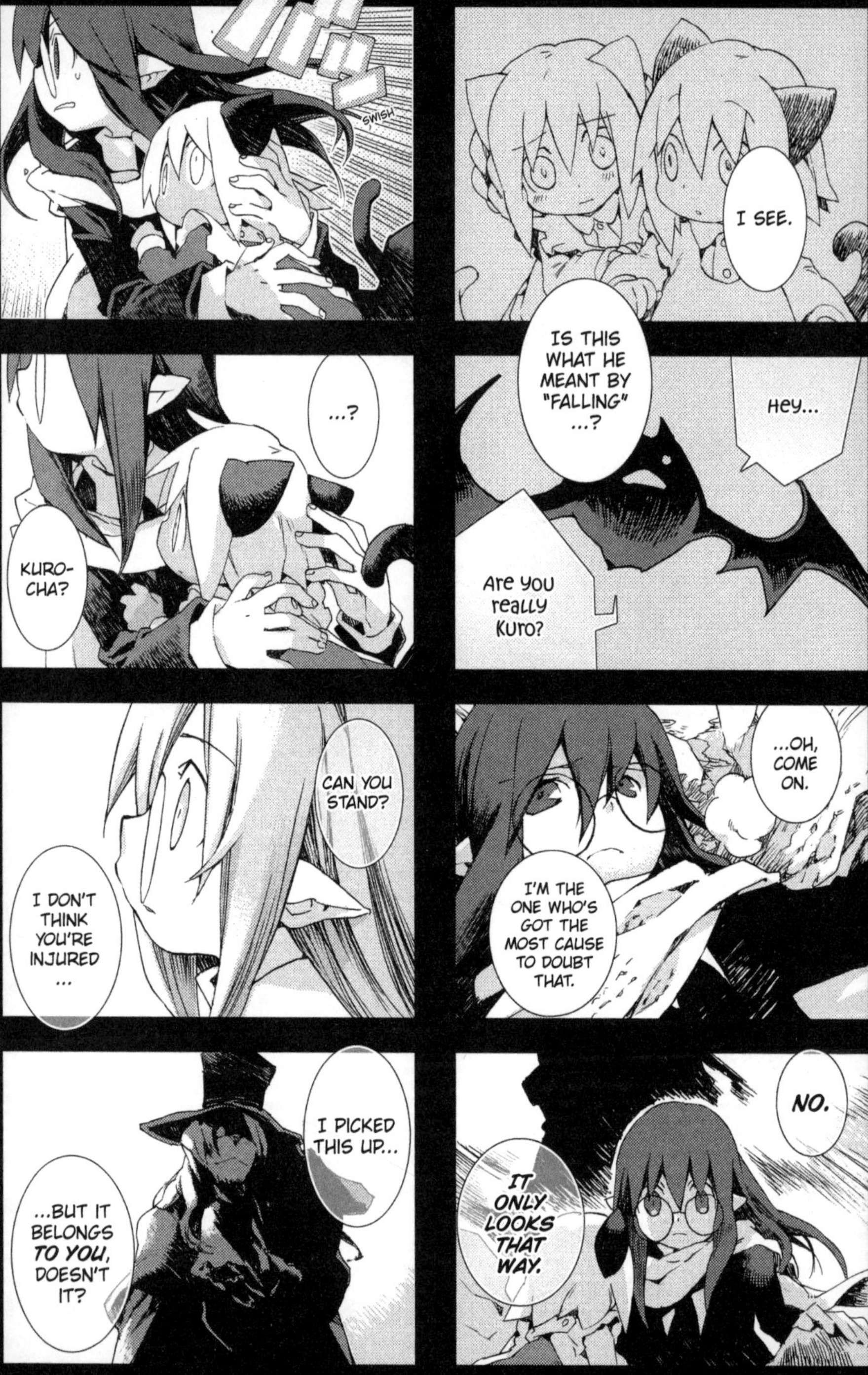
I SEE.
SWISH
IS THIS WHAT HE MEANT BY "FALLING" ...?
Hey...
Are you really Kuro?
...?
KURO-CHA?
...OH, COME ON.
I'M THE ONE WHO'S GOT THE MOST CAUSE TO DOUBT THAT.
CAN YOU STAND?
I DON'T THINK YOU'RE INJURED ...
NO.
IT ONLY LOOKS THAT WAY.
I PICKED THIS UP...
...BUT IT BELONGS *TO YOU,* DOESN'T IT?

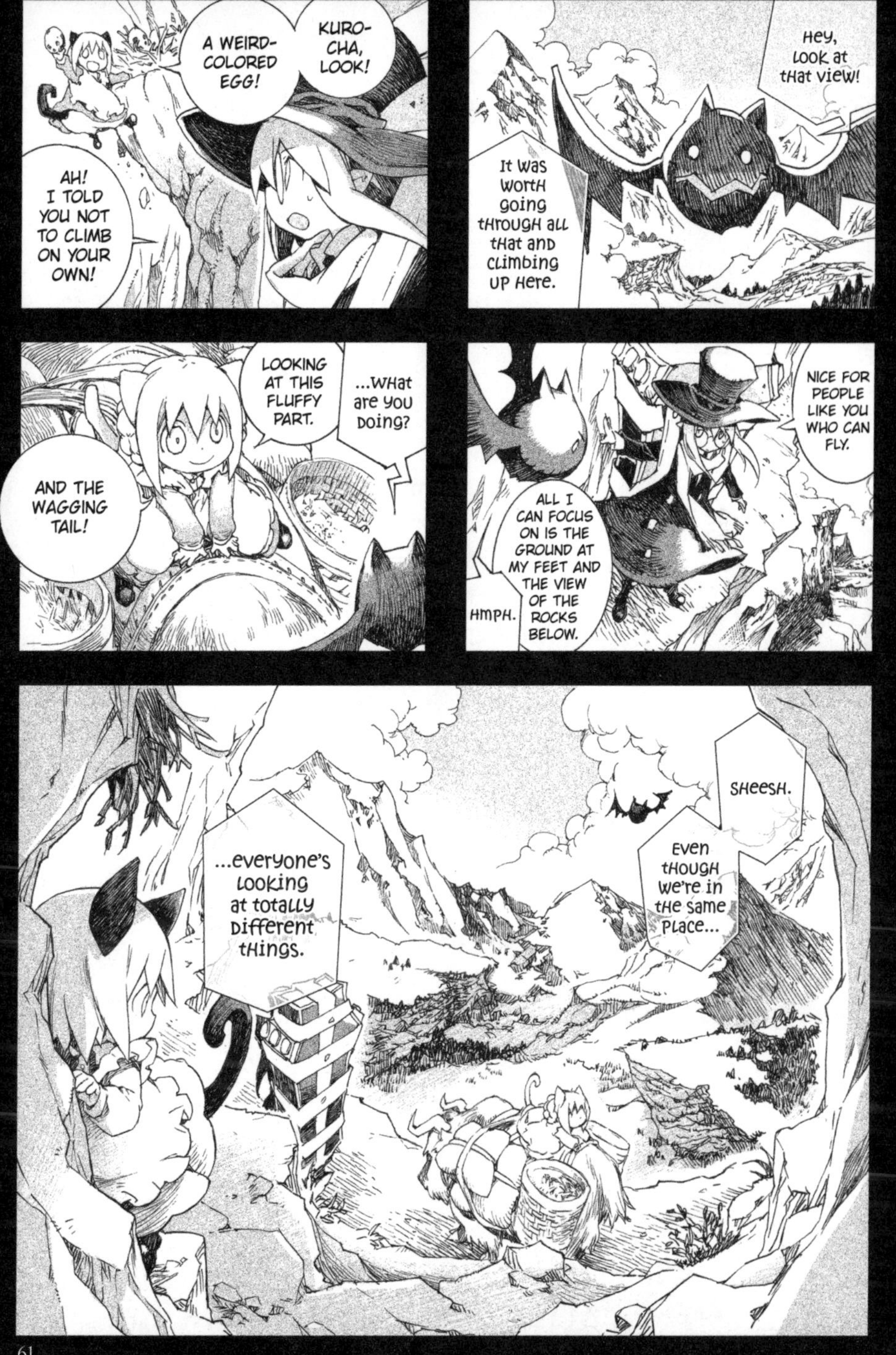
Hey, look at that view!
It was worth going through all that and climbing up here.
Kuro-cha, look!
A weird-colored egg!
Ah! I told you not to climb on your own!
Nice for people like you who can fly.
All I can focus on is the ground at my feet and the view of the rocks below.
Hmph.
...What are you doing?
Looking at this fluffy part.
And the wagging tail!
Sheesh.
Even though we're in the same place...
...everyone's looking at totally different things.

KURO-CHA, YOU DIDN'T FALL FROM ANYWHERE.

FELL?

I KNOW I FELL FROM THE BOTTOM OF THE VALLEY...

CAN YOU STAND UP?

FOR NOW...

...YOU SHOULD LEAVE THIS PLACE.

WHAT HAVE YOU HEARD ABOUT THIS PLACE?

HUH?

YOU SUDDENLY JUST COLLAPSED HERE.

....

YEAH...

HMM...

A LOCAL CALLED IT "PRIMEVAL VALLEY"...

THAT MAKES SENSE.

DID YOU FALL TOO?

UM...

WHAT ARE YOU DOING HERE AT THE VALLEY BOTTOM?

ACTUALLY, SOME TIME AGO...

...PEOPLE CALLED IT "VISION VALLEY."

...HUH!?

FALL FROM WHERE?

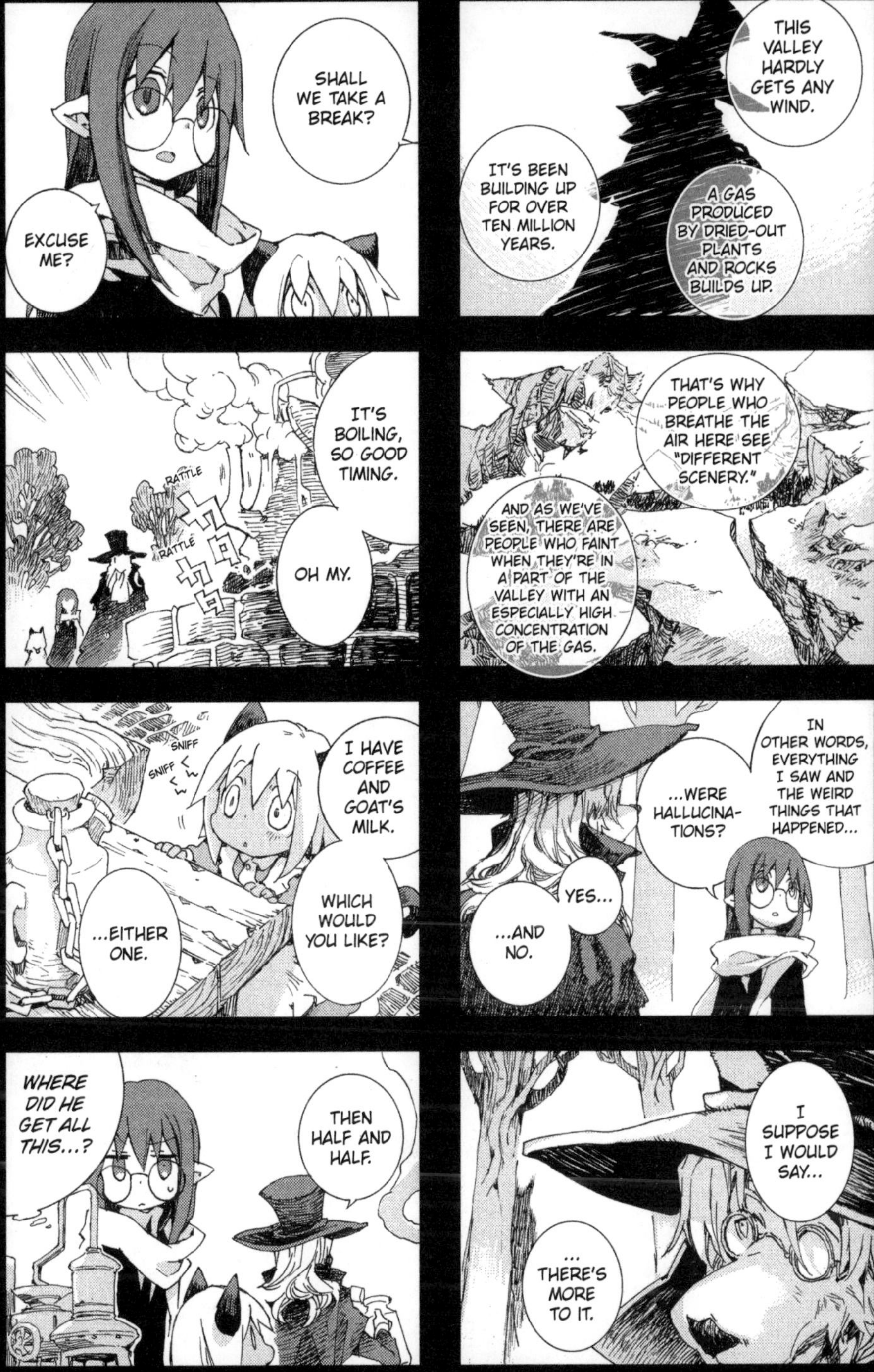
THIS VALLEY HARDLY GETS ANY WIND.
A GAS PRODUCED BY DRIED-OUT PLANTS AND ROCKS BUILDS UP.
IT'S BEEN BUILDING UP FOR OVER TEN MILLION YEARS.
SHALL WE TAKE A BREAK?
EXCUSE ME?
THAT'S WHY PEOPLE WHO BREATHE THE AIR HERE SEE "DIFFERENT SCENERY."
AND AS WE'VE SEEN, THERE ARE PEOPLE WHO FAINT WHEN THEY'RE IN A PART OF THE VALLEY WITH AN ESPECIALLY HIGH CONCENTRATION OF THE GAS.
IT'S BOILING, SO GOOD TIMING.
RATTLE
RATTLE
OH MY.
IN OTHER WORDS, EVERYTHING I SAW AND THE WEIRD THINGS THAT HAPPENED...
...WERE HALLUCINATIONS?
YES...
...AND NO.
I HAVE COFFEE AND GOAT'S MILK.
SNIFF
SNIFF
WHICH WOULD YOU LIKE?
...EITHER ONE.
I SUPPOSE I WOULD SAY...
...THERE'S MORE TO IT.
THEN HALF AND HALF.
WHERE DID HE GET ALL THIS...?

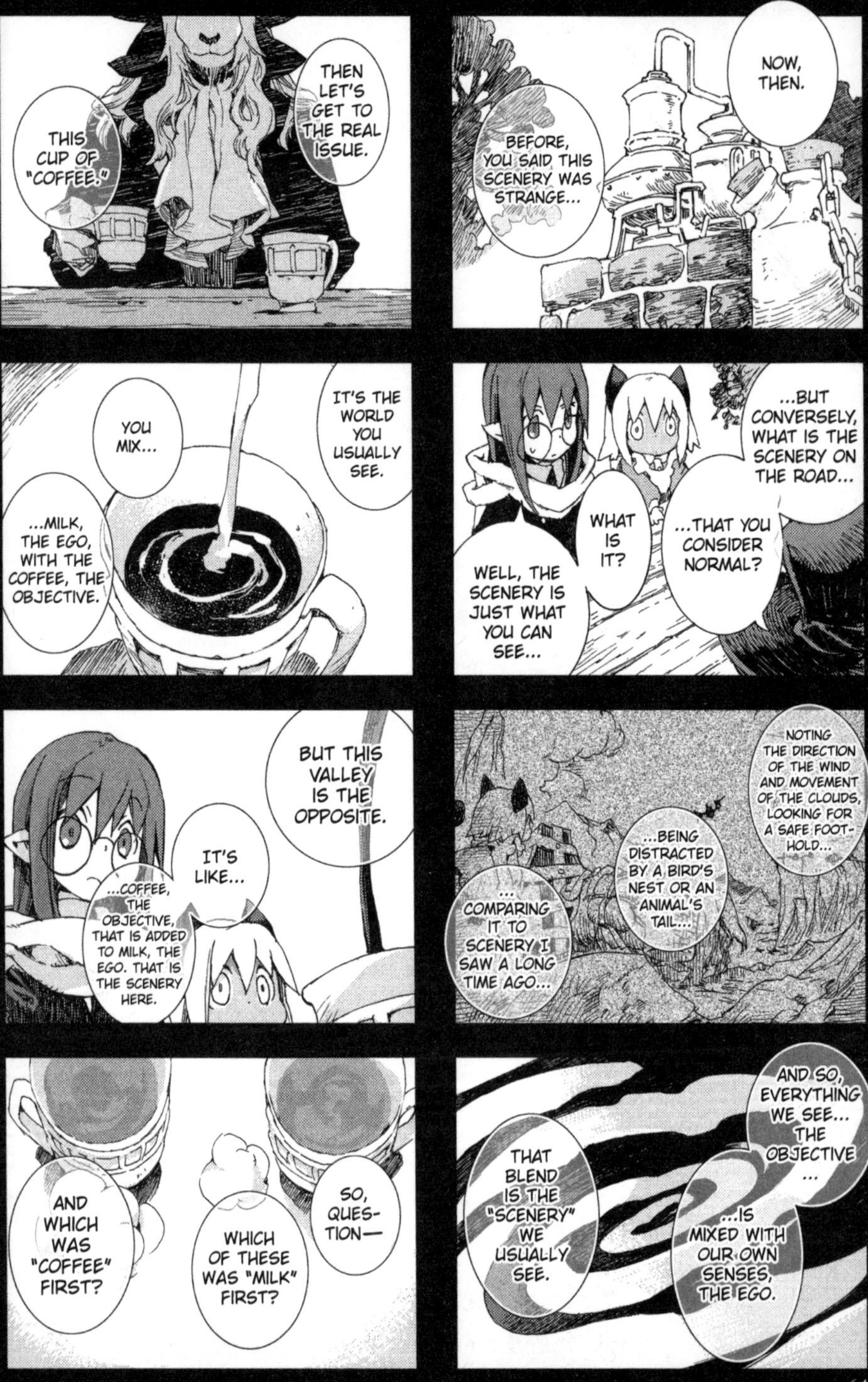
NOW, THEN.
BEFORE, YOU SAID THIS SCENERY WAS STRANGE...
THEN LET'S GET TO THE REAL ISSUE.
THIS CUP OF "COFFEE."
...BUT CONVERSELY, WHAT IS THE SCENERY ON THE ROAD...
...THAT YOU CONSIDER NORMAL?
WHAT IS IT?
WELL, THE SCENERY IS JUST WHAT YOU CAN SEE...
IT'S THE WORLD YOU USUALLY SEE.
YOU MIX...
...MILK, THE EGO, WITH THE COFFEE, THE OBJECTIVE.
NOTING THE DIRECTION OF THE WIND AND MOVEMENT OF THE CLOUDS, LOOKING FOR A SAFE FOOT-HOLD...
...BEING DISTRACTED BY A BIRD'S NEST OR AN ANIMAL'S TAIL...
...COMPARING IT TO SCENERY I SAW A LONG TIME AGO...
BUT THIS VALLEY IS THE OPPOSITE.
IT'S LIKE...
...COFFEE, THE OBJECTIVE, THAT IS ADDED TO MILK, THE EGO. THAT IS THE SCENERY HERE.
AND SO, EVERYTHING WE SEE... THE OBJECTIVE...
...IS MIXED WITH OUR OWN SENSES, THE EGO.
THAT BLEND IS THE "SCENERY" WE USUALLY SEE.
SO, QUES-TION—
WHICH OF THESE WAS "MILK" FIRST?
AND WHICH WAS "COFFEE" FIRST?

WELL...

IT CAN'T BE HELPED, YOU ENTERING THE VALLEY WITHOUT KNOWING ANYTHING ABOUT IT.

...WELL, YOU'RE A MERRY PERSON, KNOWING ABOUT THIS PLACE AND YET ENTERING IT.

FOR A PLEASANT PLACE LIKE THIS...

...I DON'T RECOMMEND YOU SET FOOT IN HERE THINKING IT WILL BE A SHORTCUT.

THAT'S BECAUSE THE CONTENTS ARE JUST ABOUT THE SAME.

INDEED.

BOTH OF THEM...

...TASTE ABOUT THE SAME.

WHAT? I JUST HAPPENED TO BE PASSING BY WHEN I WAS CALLED.

? BY WHOM?

THEY'RE THE SAME AND YET ALSO DIFFERENT.

IT'S UP TO YOU HOW TO TAKE IT.

....

THEM.

AS YOU GET OLDER, YOU COME TO ENJOY MORE COMPLICATED TASTES.

I ONLY LIKE THE WHITE DRINK.

IT SEEMS HE'S TALKING ABOUT THE HEART OF THE MATTER...

...BUT THEN IT'S LIKE HE GIVES ME THE SLIP.

HERE, IT SEEMS THE "PRIMEVAL" INSIDE OF YOU...

...THE PART THAT IS CLOSE TO THE "ROOT" OF YOURSELF... IS MADE VISIBLE.

IN THIS PLACE, YOUR VISUAL POINT IS CLOSE TO YOUR EGO.

YES.

YES.

THEM... AGAIN!

IN THE SPACE OF THAT EGO, THERE ARE INHABITANTS.

"THEY" ARE THE ONES WHO TAKE ON THE ROLE OF WEIGHING INSTINCTS WITH COEXISTENCE AND MEDIATION.

YOUR CONSCIENCE, THAT IS.

IT'S TAKEN ON A VERY INTERESTING FORM.

HUH!?

...THEN THE CLOSEST THING TO CALL THEM IS YOUR "CONSCIENCE."

THEY ESPECIALLY TRY TO STOP THE WARNING INSTINCT FROM GOING OUT OF CONTROL.

I THOUGHT IF YOU, THE CENTER OF THE EGO, ARE "INSTINCTS"...

BUT WHAT DO YOU MEAN, MY "CONSCIENCE" ...?

...I JUST... WOULD RATHER NOT GET ANY CLOSER.

IT'S ALL RIGHT. YOU CAN COME CLOSER.

IT WON'T BITE YOU.

THAT'S WHY IT'S NO WONDER YOU REJECTED THEM.

BY NATURE, YOU'RE CONTRARY TO EACH OTHER.

OH, IT JUST SEEMED TO FIT.

I DON'T KNOW IF THIS SERVES AS A SUITABLE REPRESENTATION THOUGH.

LIKE A WOMAN I SAW ONCE BEFORE.

BUT I FORGET FROM WHERE.

....

NIJUKU, WHAT DOES THAT LOOK LIKE TO YOU?

ESPECIALLY IN A SITUATION IN WHICH ITS EXISTENCE IS GIVEN RELATIVE WEIGHT BY TAKING ON "FORM."

TO INSTINCTS, THE "CONSCIENCE" IS OFTEN PERCEIVED AS THE FORM OF AN "OTHER" THAT IT IS ACQUAINTED WITH BUT NOT ITSELF.

RATTLE

NOT IN THE "COFFEE" WORLD.

BUT SOMETIMES HUMANS CREATE PEOPLE "INSIDE" THEM-SELVES.

BUT...

...I'VE NEVER ENCOUNTERED ANYTHING LIKE THIS BEFORE.

AH...MY COFFIN!

THAT'S RIGHT, THEY STOLE IT.

I ONCE SAW...

...SHAMANS OF A PRIMITIVE RELIGION IN ANOTHER COUNTRY...

...IMITATE THIS.

...YOU DROPPED THE COFFIN.

THEY SAY...

...WITH INSTINCTS, THAT IS, "NATURE," AREN'T YOU?

YOU YOURSELF ARE TRYING TO COEXIST...

OH YEAH.

THE EXIT IS RIGHT THROUGH THERE.

I CAN FEEL A BIT OF A WIND.

......

APPARENTLY THEY WERE RUNNING AFTER YOU IN AN ATTEMPT TO RETURN IT.

WE'RE DONE BEING TOGETHER?

AND THIS IS WHERE WE PART WAYS.

MY DES-TINATION LIES IN A DIFFERENT DIRECTION.

I WAS CON-VINCED...

OH, I NEARLY FORGOT.

I HAVE TO RETURN THIS TOO.

...BUT IF THAT'S NOT THE CASE...

...THEY'D STOLEN THE COFFIN...

HERE.

TRY NOT TO *DROP IT AGAIN.*

*...THEN MAYBE **I** ACTUALLY WANTED TO...*

...ABANDON THE COFFIN?

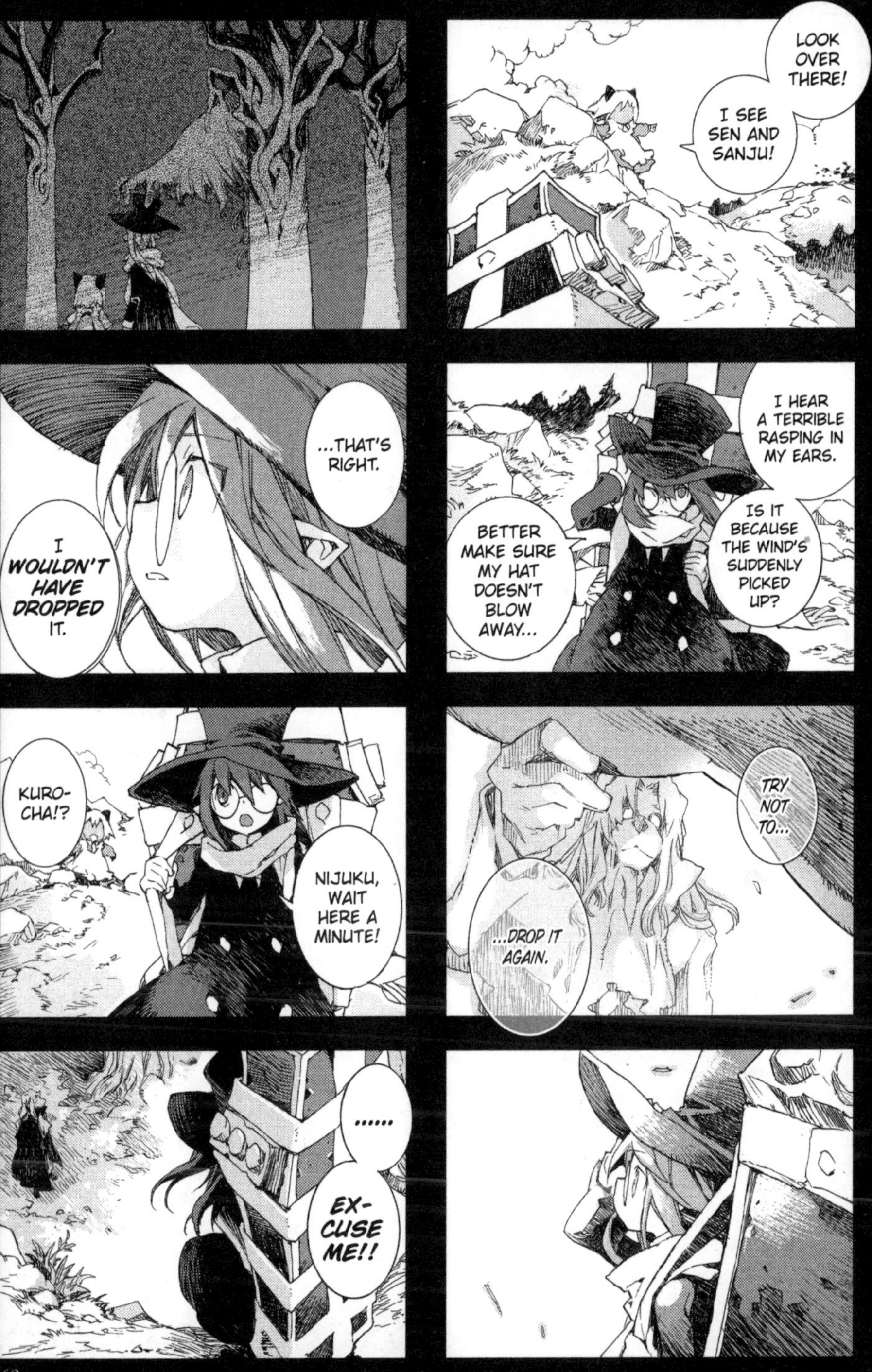
LOOK OVER THERE!
I SEE SEN AND SANJU!
I HEAR A TERRIBLE RASPING IN MY EARS.
IS IT BECAUSE THE WIND'S SUDDENLY PICKED UP?
BETTER MAKE SURE MY HAT DOESN'T BLOW AWAY...
...THAT'S RIGHT.
I *WOULDN'T HAVE DROPPED* IT.
TRY NOT TO...
...DROP IT AGAIN.
KURO-CHA!?
NIJUKU, WAIT HERE A MINUTE!
......
EX-CUSE ME!!

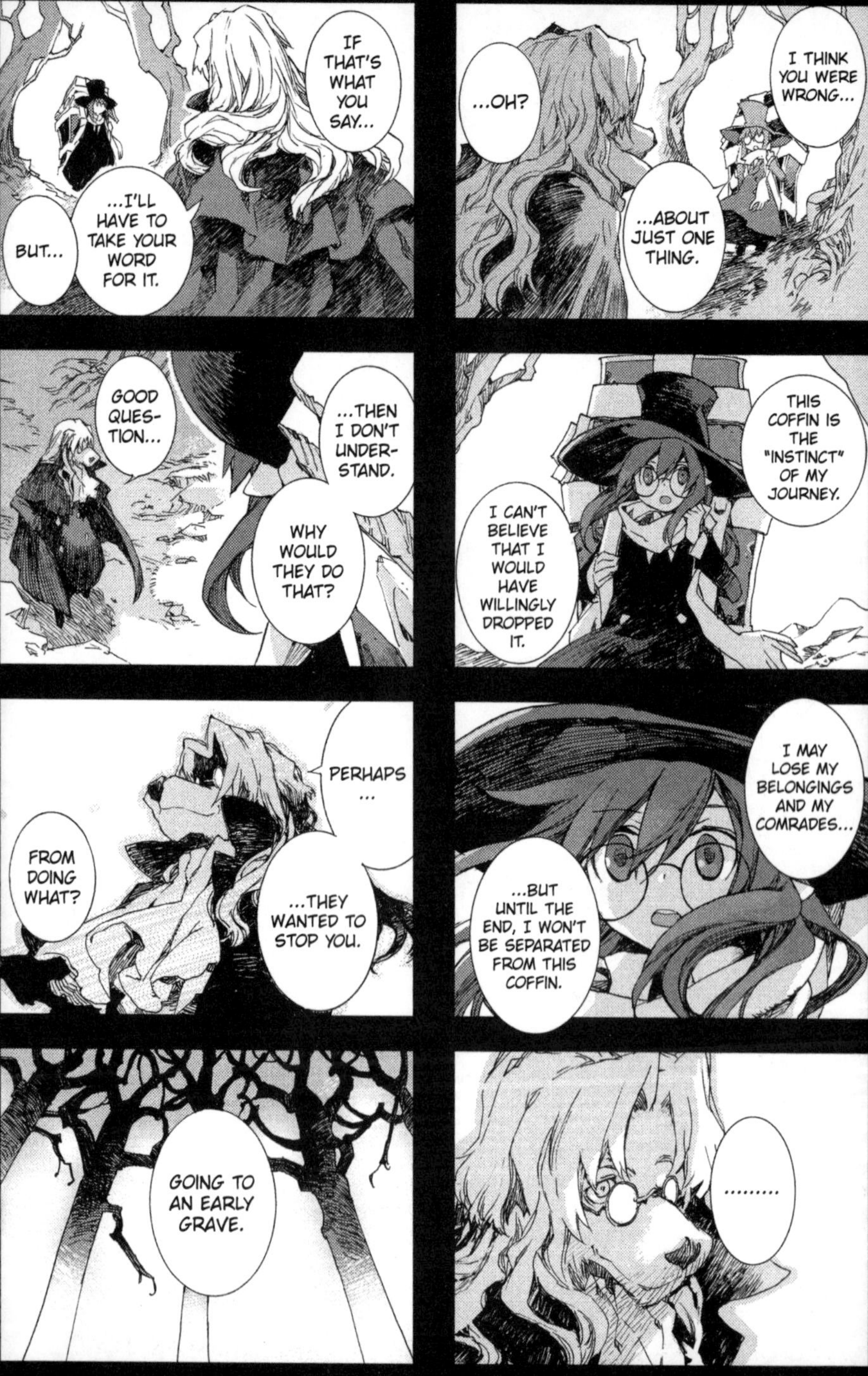
I THINK YOU WERE WRONG...
...ABOUT JUST ONE THING.
...OH?
IF THAT'S WHAT YOU SAY...
...I'LL HAVE TO TAKE YOUR WORD FOR IT.
BUT...
THIS COFFIN IS THE "INSTINCT" OF MY JOURNEY.
I CAN'T BELIEVE THAT I WOULD HAVE WILLINGLY DROPPED IT.
...THEN I DON'T UNDER-STAND.
WHY WOULD THEY DO THAT?
GOOD QUES-TION...
I MAY LOSE MY BELONGINGS AND MY COMRADES...
...BUT UNTIL THE END, I WON'T BE SEPARATED FROM THIS COFFIN.
PERHAPS ...
...THEY WANTED TO STOP YOU.
FROM DOING WHAT?
....
GOING TO AN EARLY GRAVE.

PEOPLE SAY...

...THAT DREAMS ARE A REPRESENTATION OF THE UNCONSCIOUS MIND'S TRUE CHARACTER.

THE PERSON WHO GAVE ME THIS HAT EARLIER... DID YOU KNOW HIM, NIJUKU?

YES, I KNEW HIM.

SO THAT'S WHY YOU LOOK UNCOMFORTABLE...

...EVEN THOUGH YOU CLAIM IT DIDN'T AFFECT YOU.

WHEN YOU HAVE AN UNBELIEVABLE DREAM THAT MAKES YOU WONDER WHY YOU'RE HAVING IT...

...YOU WAKE UP AND ARE LATER TORMENTED BY A SENSE OF GUILT.

I MET HIM BEFORE SOMEWHERE.

BUT I FORGET WHERE.

...I SEE.

IT WAS A DREAM...

...BUT IT WAS ALSO REALITY.

IT WAS A LIE...

...BUT IT WAS ALSO THE TRUTH.

UNTIL WE MET, NIJUKU HAD NEVER BEEN OUTSIDE.

SO I DON'T SEE HOW SHE COULD BE ACQUAINTED WITH HIM...

TWO OPPOSITE COLORS THAT CAN'T BE MIXED...

...BEING STIRRED ROUND AND ROUND IN THAT WORLD.

HE MAY HAVE BEEN AN IMAGE CONJURED UP BY MY OWN MIND.

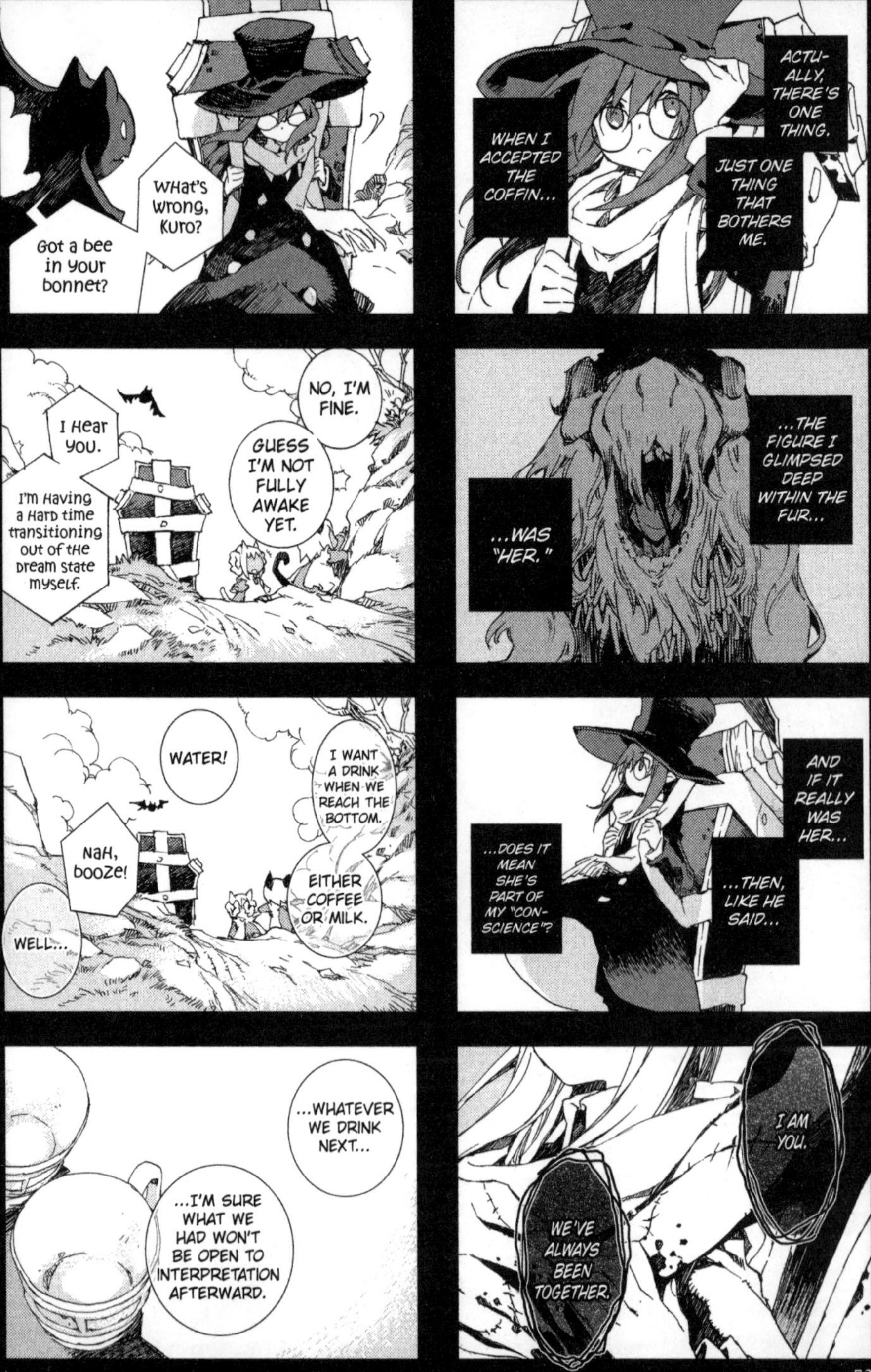
ACTUALLY, THERE'S ONE THING.
JUST ONE THING THAT BOTHERS ME.
WHEN I ACCEPTED THE COFFIN...
What's wrong, Kuro?
Got a bee in your bonnet?
...THE FIGURE I GLIMPSED DEEP WITHIN THE FUR...
...WAS "HER."
NO, I'M FINE.
GUESS I'M NOT FULLY AWAKE YET.
I Hear you.
I'm Having a Hard time transitioning out of the dream state myself.
AND IF IT REALLY WAS HER...
...THEN, LIKE HE SAID...
...DOES IT MEAN SHE'S PART OF MY "CONSCIENCE"?
I WANT A DRINK WHEN WE REACH THE BOTTOM.
EITHER COFFEE OR MILK.
WATER!
NaH, booze!
WELL...
I AM YOU.
WE'VE ALWAYS BEEN TOGETHER.
...WHATEVER WE DRINK NEXT...
...I'M SURE WHAT WE HAD WON'T BE OPEN TO INTERPRETATION AFTERWARD.

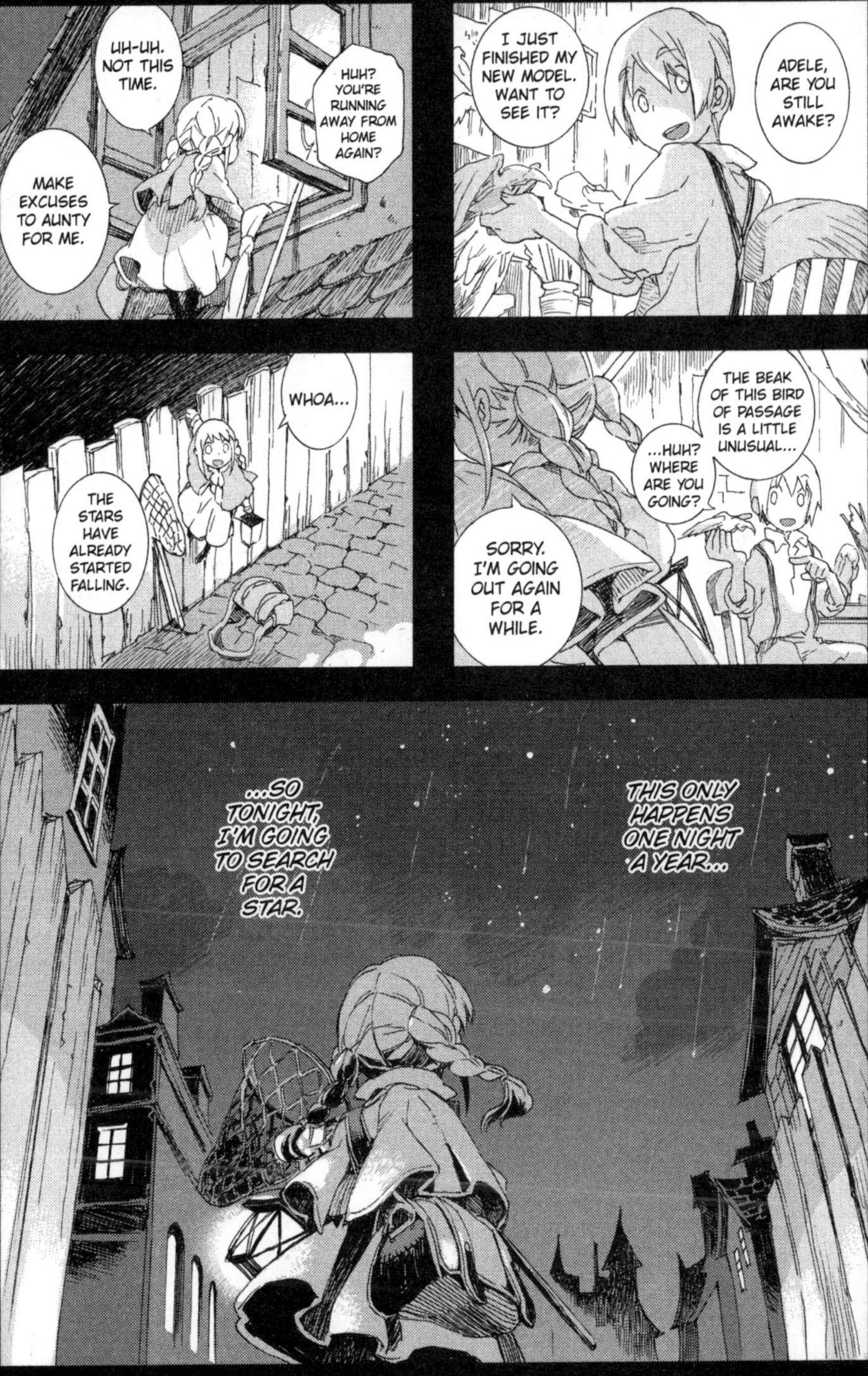
ADELE, ARE YOU STILL AWAKE?
I JUST FINISHED MY NEW MODEL. WANT TO SEE IT?
HUH? YOU'RE RUNNING AWAY FROM HOME AGAIN?
UH-UH. NOT THIS TIME.
MAKE EXCUSES TO AUNTY FOR ME.
THE BEAK OF THIS BIRD OF PASSAGE IS A LITTLE UNUSUAL...
...HUH? WHERE ARE YOU GOING?
SORRY. I'M GOING OUT AGAIN FOR A WHILE.
WHOA...
THE STARS HAVE ALREADY STARTED FALLING.
THIS ONLY HAPPENS ONE NIGHT A YEAR...
...SO TONIGHT, I'M GOING TO SEARCH FOR A STAR.

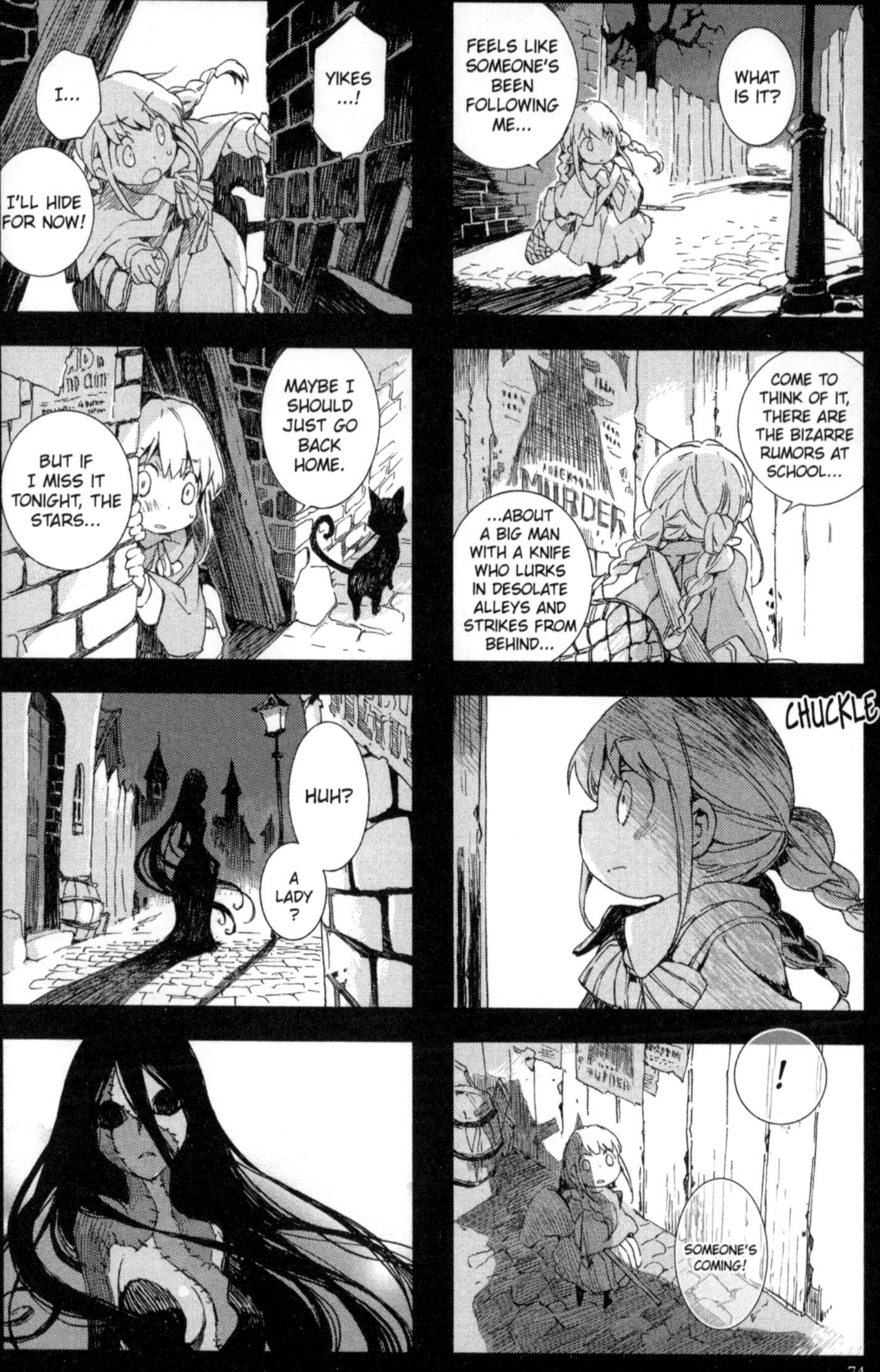
WHAT IS IT?
FEELS LIKE SOMEONE'S BEEN FOLLOWING ME...
YIKES ...!
I...
I'LL HIDE FOR NOW!
COME TO THINK OF IT, THERE ARE THE BIZARRE RUMORS AT SCHOOL...
MURDER
...ABOUT A BIG MAN WITH A KNIFE WHO LURKS IN DESOLATE ALLEYS AND STRIKES FROM BEHIND...
MAYBE I SHOULD JUST GO BACK HOME.
BUT IF I MISS IT TONIGHT, THE STARS...
CHUCKLE
HUH?
A LADY?
!
SOMEONE'S COMING!

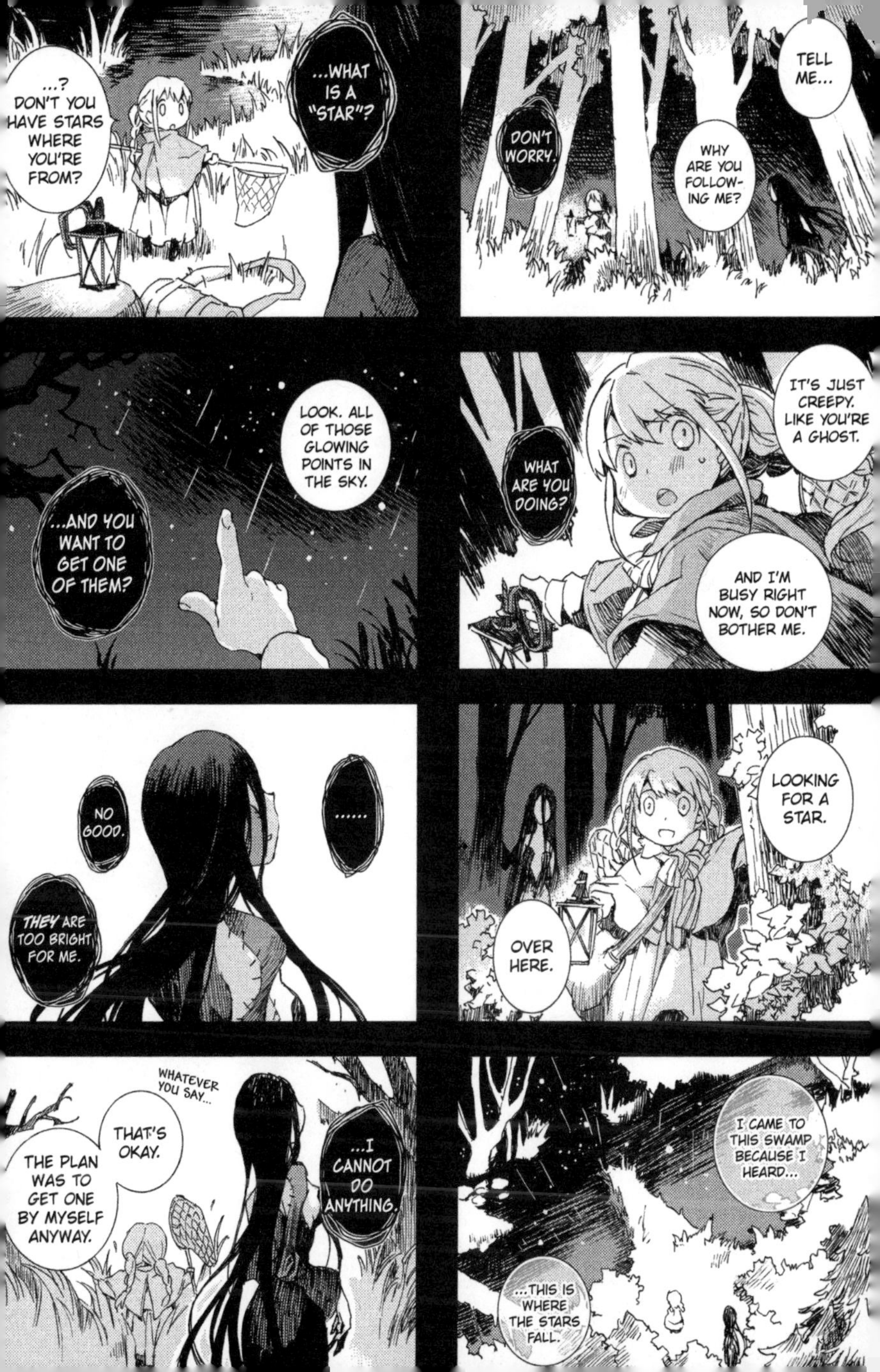
TELL ME...
WHY ARE YOU FOLLOWING ME?
DON'T WORRY.
IT'S JUST CREEPY. LIKE YOU'RE A GHOST.
WHAT ARE YOU DOING?
AND I'M BUSY RIGHT NOW, SO DON'T BOTHER ME.
LOOKING FOR A STAR.
OVER HERE.
I CAME TO THIS SWAMP BECAUSE I HEARD...
...THIS IS WHERE THE STARS FALL.
...WHAT IS A "STAR"?
...? DON'T YOU HAVE STARS WHERE YOU'RE FROM?
LOOK. ALL OF THOSE GLOWING POINTS IN THE SKY.
...AND YOU WANT TO GET ONE OF THEM?
......
NO GOOD.
THEY ARE TOO BRIGHT FOR ME.
...I CANNOT DO ANYTHING.
WHATEVER YOU SAY...
THAT'S OKAY.
THE PLAN WAS TO GET ONE BY MYSELF ANYWAY.

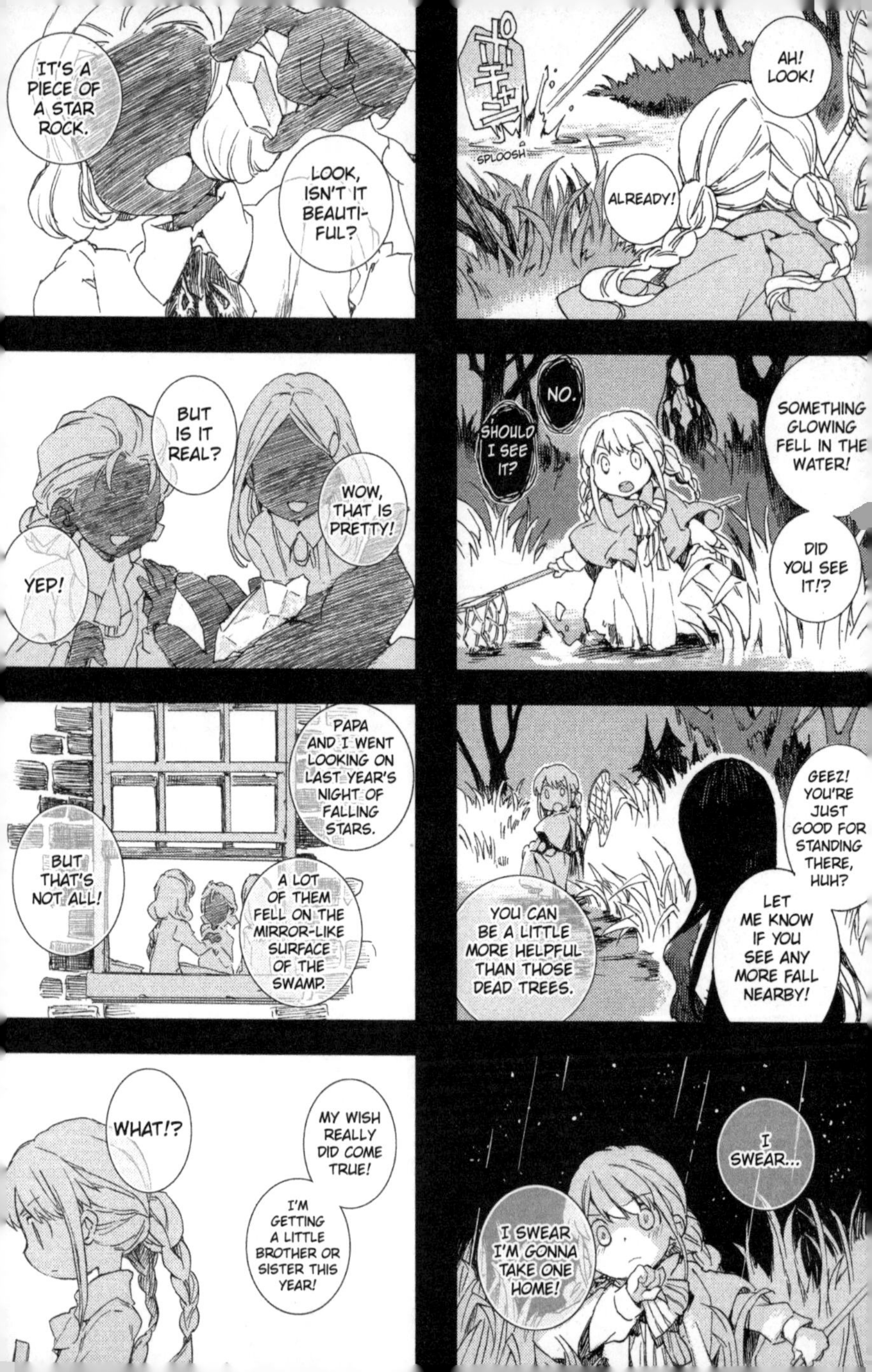
AH! LOOK!
SPLOOSH
ALREADY!
IT'S A PIECE OF A STAR ROCK.
LOOK, ISN'T IT BEAUTI-FUL?
SOMETHING GLOWING FELL IN THE WATER!
DID YOU SEE IT!?
NO.
SHOULD I SEE IT?
WOW, THAT IS PRETTY!
BUT IS IT REAL?
YEP!
GEEZ! YOU'RE JUST GOOD FOR STANDING THERE, HUH?
LET ME KNOW IF YOU SEE ANY MORE FALL NEARBY!
YOU CAN BE A LITTLE MORE HELPFUL THAN THOSE DEAD TREES.
PAPA AND I WENT LOOKING ON LAST YEAR'S NIGHT OF FALLING STARS.
A LOT OF THEM FELL ON THE MIRROR-LIKE SURFACE OF THE SWAMP.
BUT THAT'S NOT ALL!
I SWEAR...
I SWEAR I'M GONNA TAKE ONE HOME!
MY WISH REALLY DID COME TRUE!
I'M GETTING A LITTLE BROTHER OR SISTER THIS YEAR!
WHAT!?

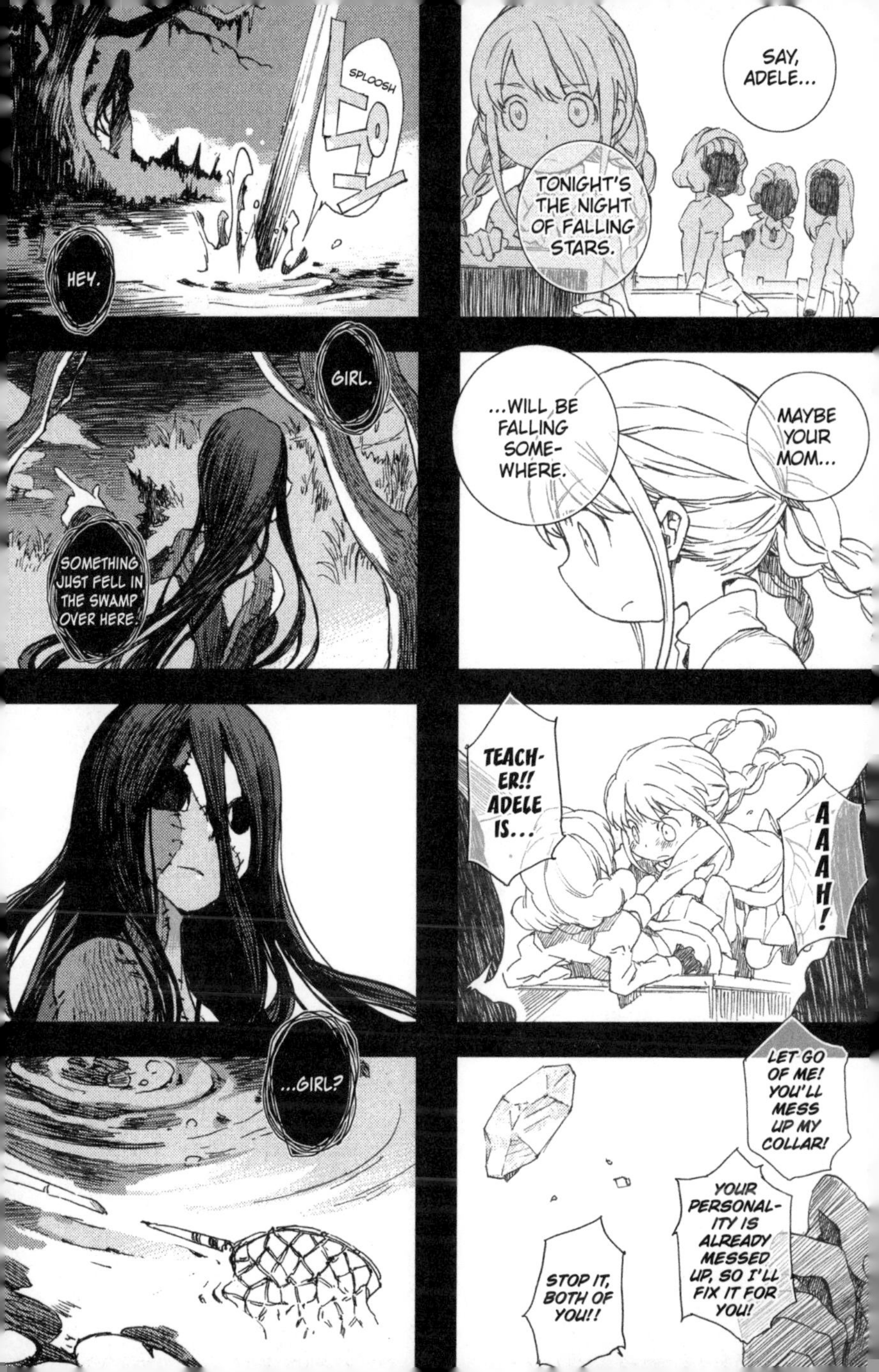
SAY, ADELE...
TONIGHT'S THE NIGHT OF FALLING STARS.
SPLOOSH
HEY.
MAYBE YOUR MOM...
...WILL BE FALLING SOMEWHERE.
GIRL.
SOMETHING JUST FELL IN THE SWAMP OVER HERE.
TEACHER!! ADELE IS...
AAAAH!
LET GO OF ME! YOU'LL MESS UP MY COLLAR!
YOUR PERSONALITY IS ALREADY MESSED UP, SO I'LL FIX IT FOR YOU!
STOP IT, BOTH OF YOU!!
...GIRL?

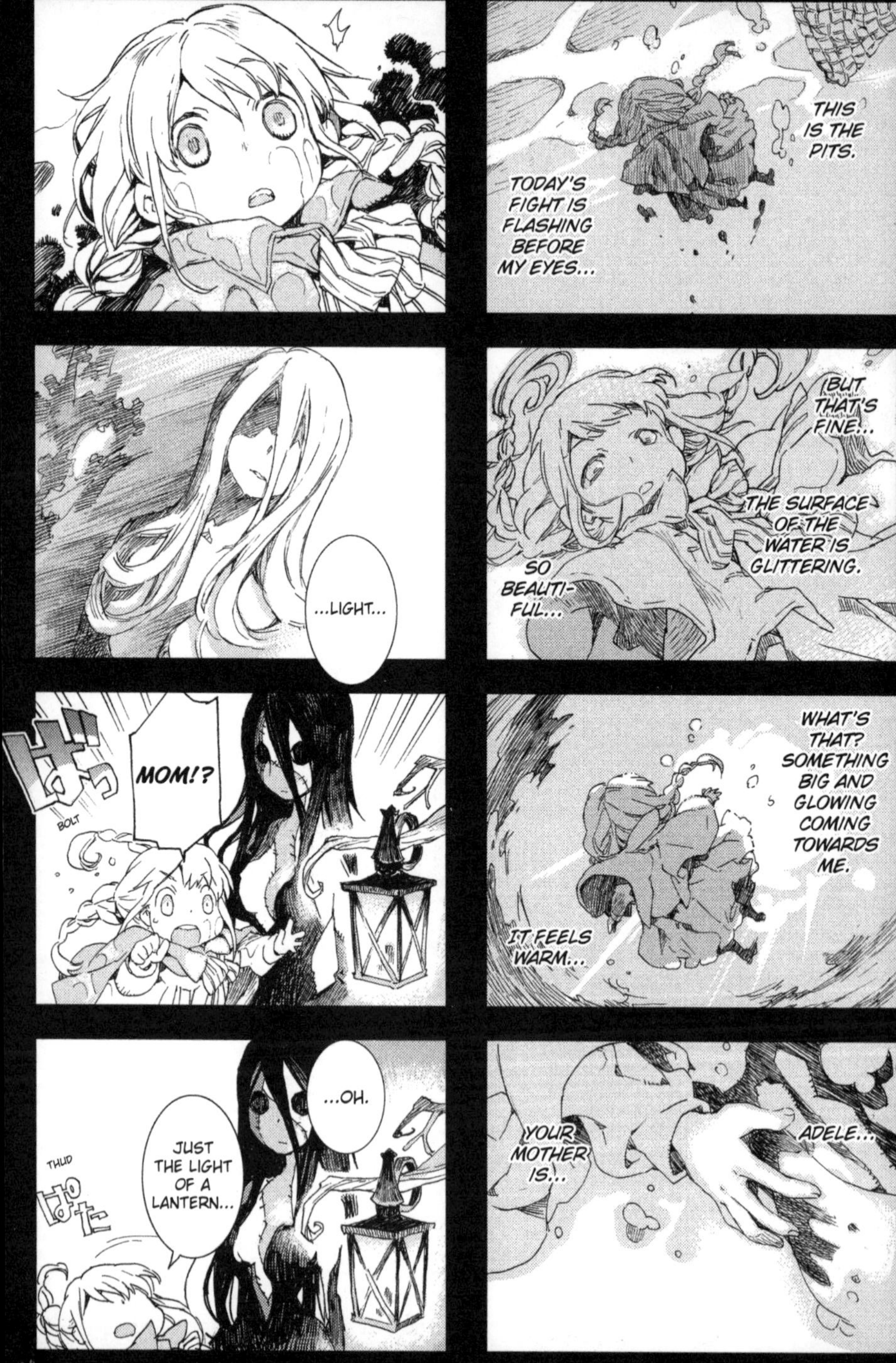
THIS IS THE PITS.
TODAY'S FIGHT IS FLASHING BEFORE MY EYES...
BUT THAT'S FINE...
THE SURFACE OF THE WATER IS GLITTERING.
SO BEAUTI-FUL...
...LIGHT...
WHAT'S THAT? SOMETHING BIG AND GLOWING COMING TOWARDS ME.
IT FEELS WARM...
MOM!?
BOLT
ADELE...
YOUR MOTHER IS...
...OH.
JUST THE LIGHT OF A LANTERN...
THUD

YOU WANT TO SEE...

...YOUR MOTHER?

...THEY TOLD ME MOM "BECAME A STAR."

WHEN I WAS LITTLE...

I CANNOT BRING YOU A STAR...

...BUT I MAY BE ABLE TO MANAGE THAT.

...BUT SHE'LL ALWAYS BE WATCHING OVER YOU FROM THE SKY ABOVE, ADELE.

YOU CAN'T SEE HER AGAIN...

I WILL SHARE SOME OF MY POWER WITH YOU.

HOW YOU USE IT IS UP TO YOU.

WHAT IS THAT?

IN THE END, YOU ARRIVE AT THE PREDE-TERMINED "REALITY"...

IT'S NOT FAIR.

PERHAPS YOUR WISH...

...WILL COME TRUE.

...SO WHAT'S THE POINT OF LETTING ME HOPE?

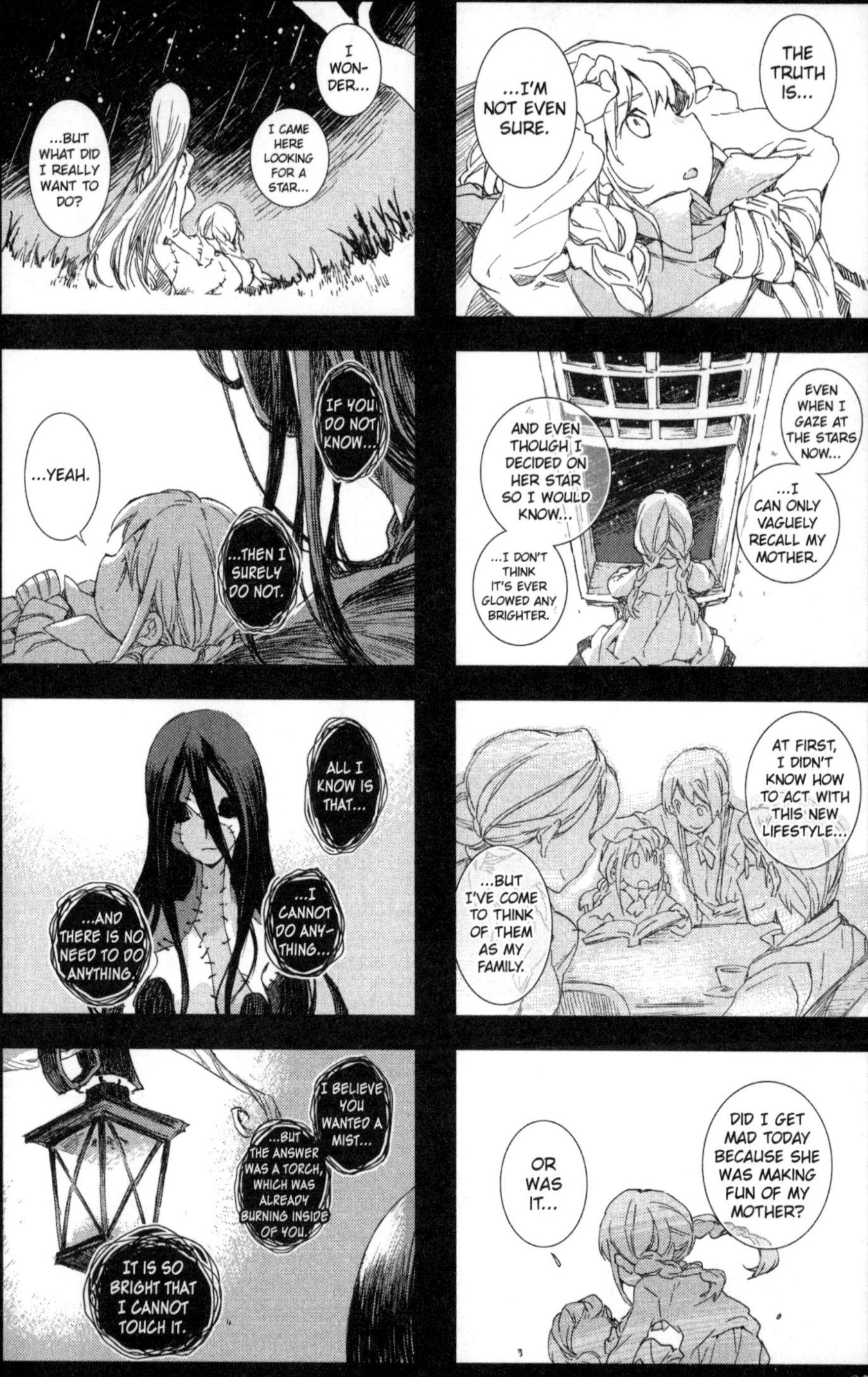
THE TRUTH IS...
...I'M NOT EVEN SURE.
I WONDER...
I CAME HERE LOOKING FOR A STAR...
...BUT WHAT DID I REALLY WANT TO DO?
EVEN WHEN I GAZE AT THE STARS NOW...
...I CAN ONLY VAGUELY RECALL MY MOTHER.
AND EVEN THOUGH I DECIDED ON HER STAR SO I WOULD KNOW...
...I DON'T THINK IT'S EVER GLOWED ANY BRIGHTER.
IF YOU DO NOT KNOW...
...YEAH.
...THEN I SURELY DO NOT.
AT FIRST, I DIDN'T KNOW HOW TO ACT WITH THIS NEW LIFESTYLE...
...BUT I'VE COME TO THINK OF THEM AS MY FAMILY.
ALL I KNOW IS THAT...
...I CANNOT DO ANYTHING...
...AND THERE IS NO NEED TO DO ANYTHING.
DID I GET MAD TODAY BECAUSE SHE WAS MAKING FUN OF MY MOTHER?
OR WAS IT...
I BELIEVE YOU WANTED A MIST...
...BUT THE ANSWER WAS A TORCH, WHICH WAS ALREADY BURNING INSIDE OF YOU.
IT IS SO BRIGHT THAT I CANNOT TOUCH IT.

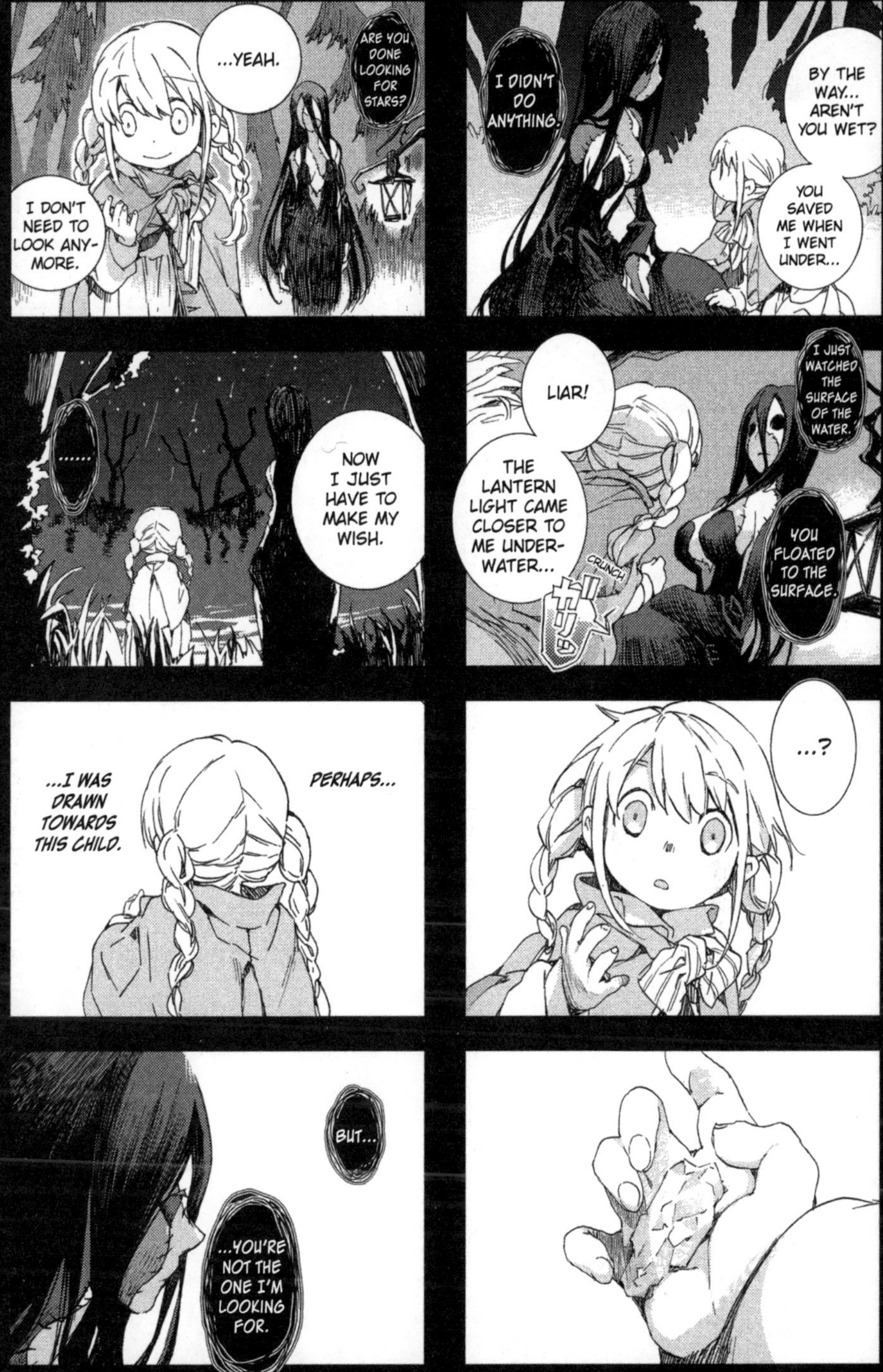
BY THE WAY... AREN'T YOU WET?
YOU SAVED ME WHEN I WENT UNDER...
I DIDN'T DO ANYTHING.
ARE YOU DONE LOOKING FOR STARS?
...YEAH.
I DON'T NEED TO LOOK ANY-MORE.
I JUST WATCHED THE SURFACE OF THE WATER.
LIAR!
THE LANTERN LIGHT CAME CLOSER TO ME UNDER-WATER...
YOU FLOATED TO THE SURFACE.
CRUNCH
NOW I JUST HAVE TO MAKE MY WISH.
......
...?
PERHAPS...
...I WAS DRAWN TOWARDS THIS CHILD.
BUT...
...YOU'RE NOT THE ONE I'M LOOKING FOR.

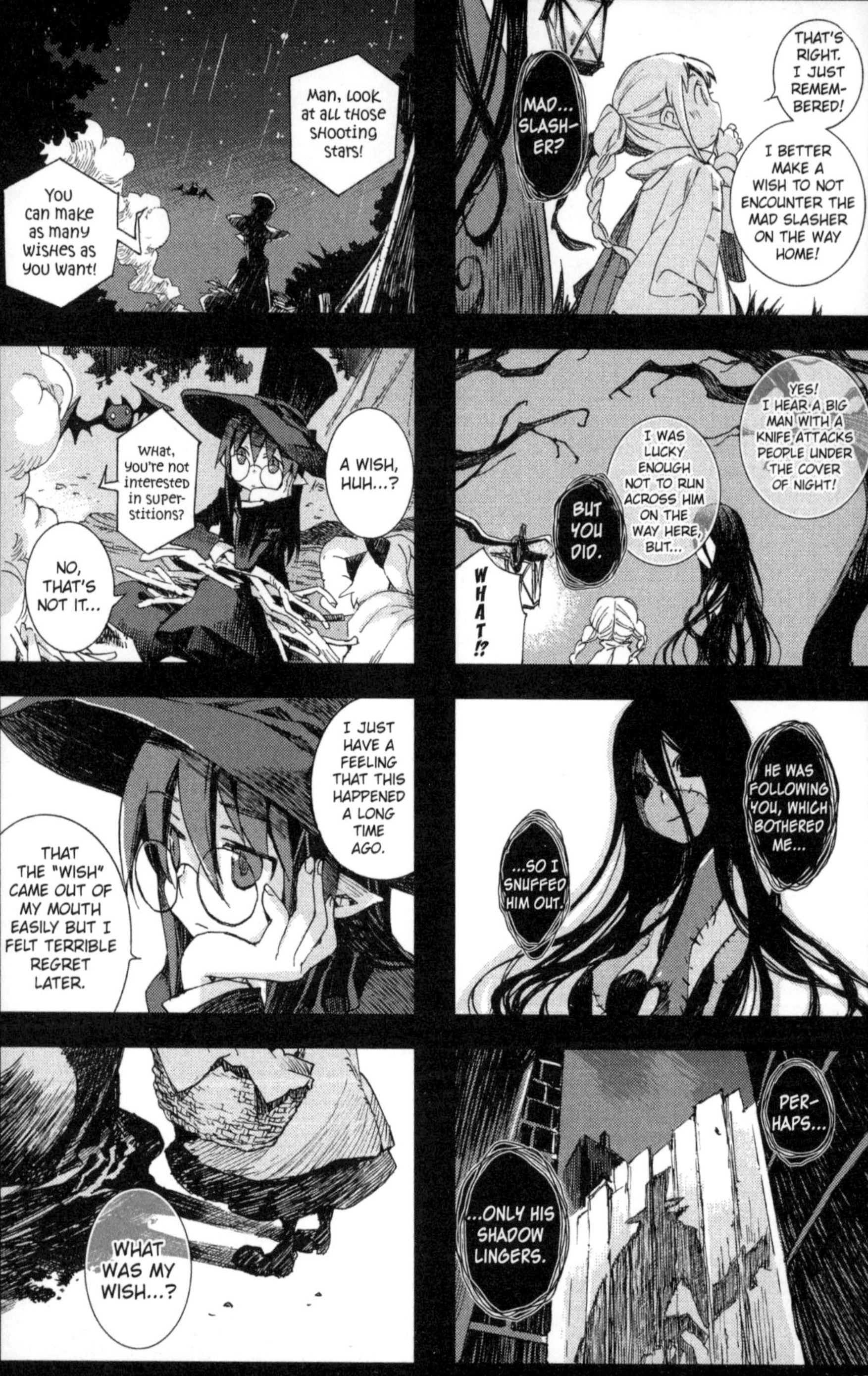
THAT'S RIGHT. I JUST REMEMBERED!
I BETTER MAKE A WISH TO NOT ENCOUNTER THE MAD SLASHER ON THE WAY HOME!
MAD... SLASHER?
YES! I HEAR A BIG MAN WITH A KNIFE ATTACKS PEOPLE UNDER THE COVER OF NIGHT!
I WAS LUCKY ENOUGH NOT TO RUN ACROSS HIM ON THE WAY HERE, BUT...
BUT YOU DID.
WHAT!?
HE WAS FOLLOWING YOU, WHICH BOTHERED ME...
...SO I SNUFFED HIM OUT.
PERHAPS...
...ONLY HIS SHADOW LINGERS.
Man, look at all those shooting stars!
You can make as many wishes as you want!
A WISH, HUH...?
What, you're not interested in superstitions?
NO, THAT'S NOT IT...
I JUST HAVE A FEELING THAT THIS HAPPENED A LONG TIME AGO.
THAT THE "WISH" CAME OUT OF MY MOUTH EASILY BUT I FELT TERRIBLE REGRET LATER.
WHAT WAS MY WISH...?

SAY...

AREN'T YOU GOING TO WISH FOR SOME-THING?

MM?

A FALLING METEOR?

BONK

AH! OW!

YEAH.

WISH?

I'M SURE EVEN YOU HAVE SOMETHING YOU'D LIKE TO COME TRUE, RIGHT?

NO...LOOK OVER THERE. A FLOCK OF GRAY HERONS.

SHOOT. SO THE METEOR SHOWER WAS JUST ROCKS FALLING OUT OF THEIR MOUTHS?

IN THAT CASE...

...I SUP-POSE.

MAYBE THEY...

...BUT I WONDER WHAT LAND THEY BROUGHT THIS STUFF FROM.

APPARENTLY THEY GATHER ALL KINDS OF SHINY ROCKS, FROM ROCK SALT TO CRYSTAL...

...I WISH TO MEET HER...

...SOON.

...REALLY DID CARRY IT FROM THE STARS.

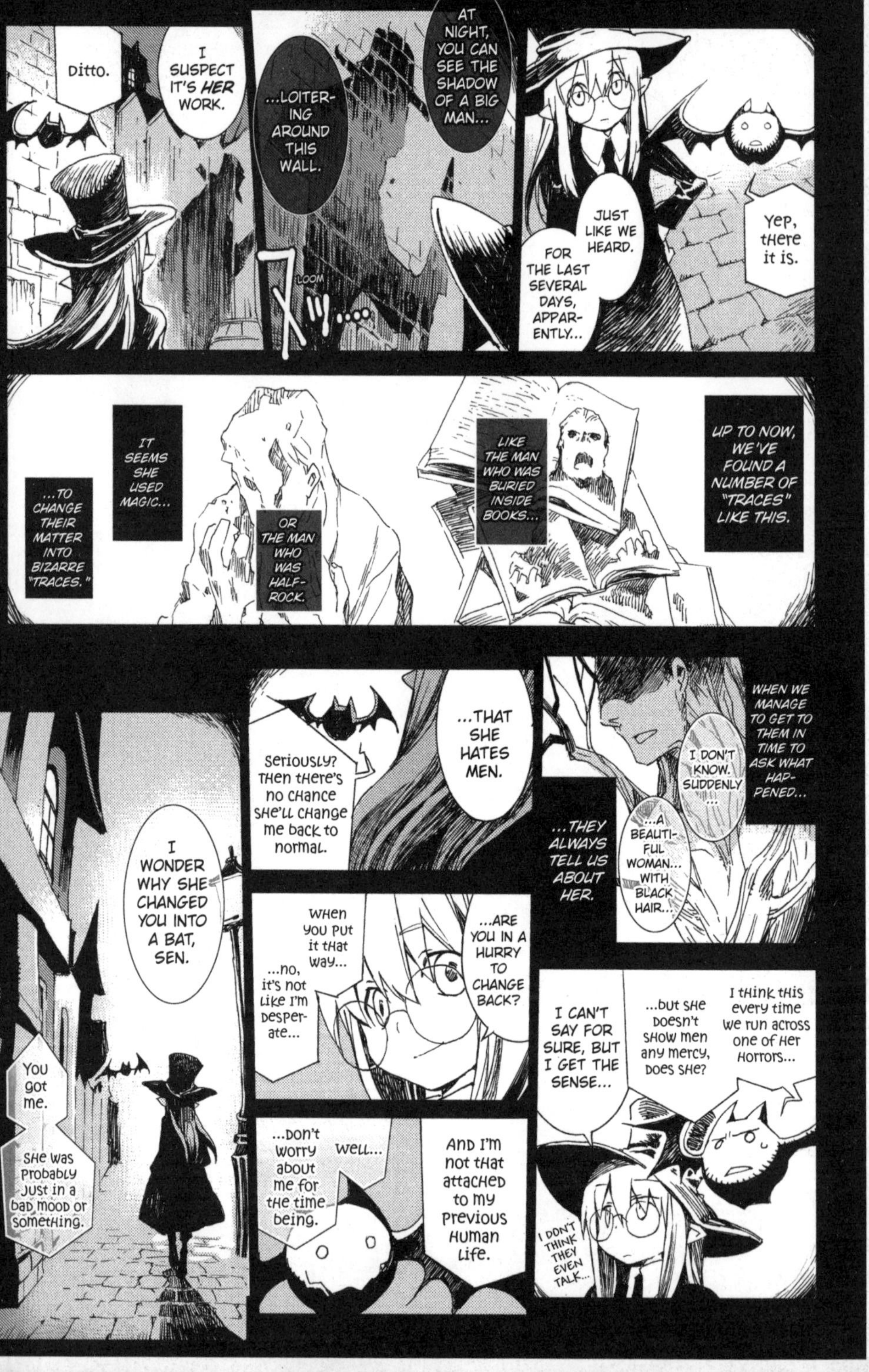
Yep, there it is.
JUST LIKE WE HEARD.
FOR THE LAST SEVERAL DAYS, APPARENTLY...
AT NIGHT, YOU CAN SEE THE SHADOW OF A BIG MAN...
...LOITERING AROUND THIS WALL.
LOOM
I SUSPECT IT'S HER WORK.
Ditto.
UP TO NOW, WE'VE FOUND A NUMBER OF "TRACES" LIKE THIS.
LIKE THE MAN WHO WAS BURIED INSIDE BOOKS...
OR THE MAN WHO WAS HALF-ROCK.
IT SEEMS SHE USED MAGIC...
...TO CHANGE THEIR MATTER INTO BIZARRE "TRACES."
WHEN WE MANAGE TO GET TO THEM IN TIME TO ASK WHAT HAPPENED...
I DON'T KNOW. SUDDENLY...
...A BEAUTIFUL WOMAN... WITH BLACK HAIR...
...THEY ALWAYS TELL US ABOUT HER.
I think this every time we run across one of her Horrors...
...but she doesn't show men any mercy, does she?
I CAN'T SAY FOR SURE, BUT I GET THE SENSE...
I DON'T THINK THEY EVEN TALK...
...THAT SHE HATES MEN.
Seriously? Then there's no chance she'll change me back to normal.
...ARE YOU IN A HURRY TO CHANGE BACK?
When you put it that way...
...no, it's not like I'm desperate...
And I'm not that attached to my previous human life.
Well...
...don't worry about me for the time being.
I WONDER WHY SHE CHANGED YOU INTO A BAT, SEN.
You got me.
She was probably just in a bad mood or something.

Shoulder-a-Coffin Kuro by Satoko Kiyuduki

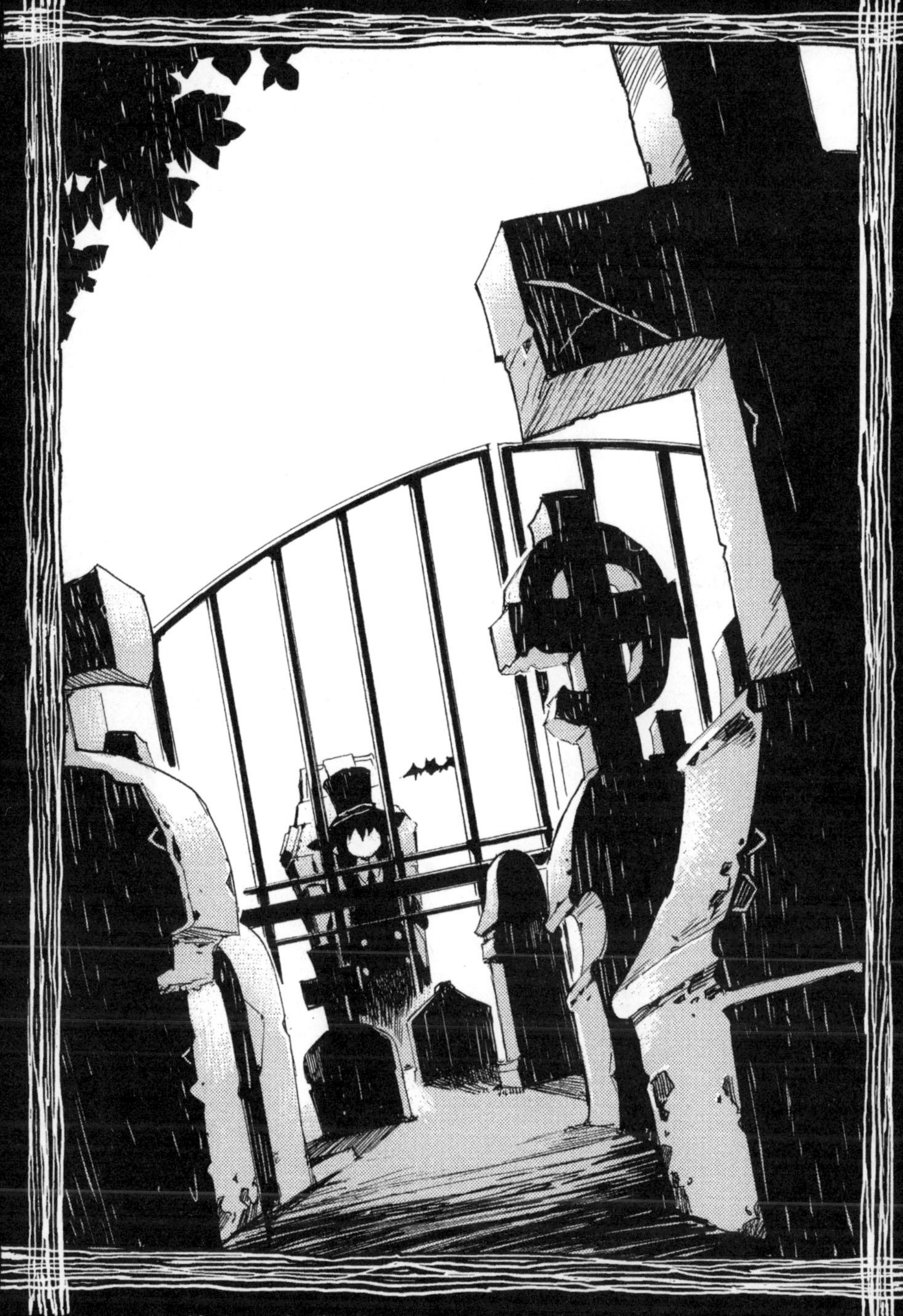

At every destination, the travelers search for "traces" that the witch left behind. And sometimes they even encounter their past or future "selves."

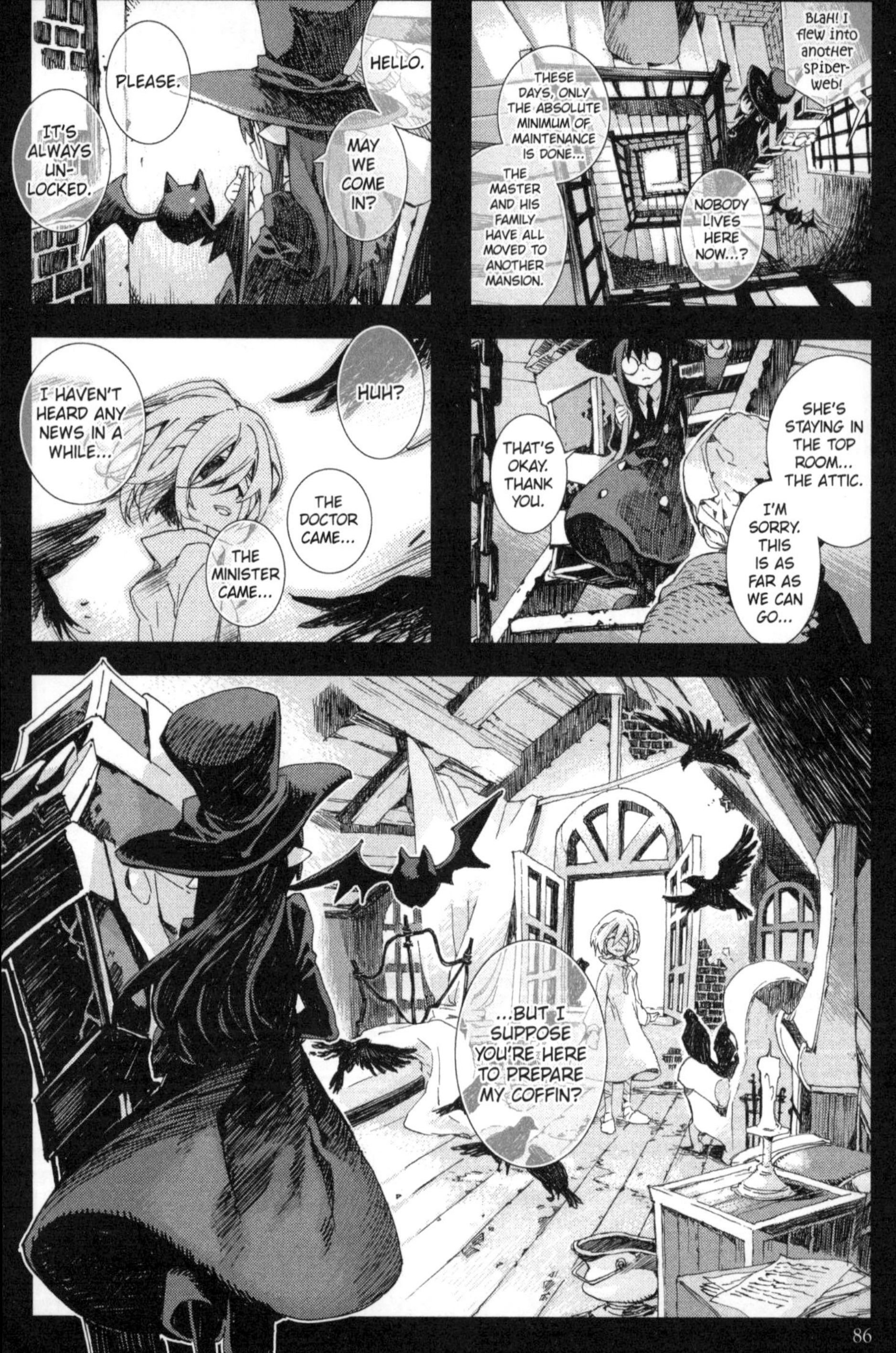
Blah! I flew into another spider-web!
These days, only the absolute minimum of maintenance is done...
Nobody lives here now...?
The master and his family have all moved to another mansion.
Hello.
Please.
May we come in?
It's always un-locked.
She's staying in the top room... the attic.
I'm sorry. This is as far as we can go...
That's okay. Thank you.
Huh?
I haven't heard any news in a while...
The doctor came...
The minister came...
...But I suppose you're here to prepare my coffin?

...ME AND MILLY.

I THOUGHT IT WAS ONLY...

OH YEAH. YOU HAVE THE SAME THING.

WHAT DO YOU THINK, KURO?

THERE'S NO DOUBT.

...YEAH.

YOU MET THE "WITCH"... DIDN'T YOU?

WE'RE ON A JOURNEY TO FIND A WAY TO RETURN TO NORMAL.

WILL YOU TELL US YOUR STORY?

SHE'S LIKE US.

THAT WITCH CURSED HER.

WE DIDN'T TELL OUR STEPMOTHER THAT WE WENT TO THE CEMETERY.

...IT WAS ABOUT FOUR YEARS AGO.

WE WANTED TO PUT NEW FLOWERS ON OUR MOTHER'S GRAVE.

SORRY TO BARGE IN ON YOU. WE'RE TRAVELERS.

WE CAME TO MEET YOU AFTER HEARING RUMORS.

TRAVELERS...?

BUT ALONG THE WAY...

...WE RAN INTO HER.

THEY'VE ALWAYS BEEN CROWS.

NO IDEA WHAT YOU'RE TALKING ABOUT. BUT...

SHE TRANS-FORMED YOU TOO, DIDN'T SHE?

AND I FEEL SORRY FOR YOU TWO...

CAW

CAW

HAVE YOU EVER MET SOMEBODY LIKE US IN OTHER PLACES YOU'VE BEEN TO?

...SOME.

IS THIS WHAT YOU USED TO LOOK LIKE?

YOU'VE... CHANGED A LOT.

NO, NO. HALF OF IT'S DUE TO SIDE EFFECTS FROM THE MEDICINE.

WERE ANY OF THEM CURED?

OF COURSE...

...IF THEY WERE, YOU WOULDN'T BE HERE.

......

THEY SUBJECTED ME TO ALL KINDS OF MEDICINE AND MAGIC, ANYTHING THAT HAD A SHOT AT CURING THIS.

I THINK ONLY ONE MEDICINE WAS ABLE TO KEEP THE SYMPTOMS IN CHECK.

...THERE'S SOMEONE WHO CAN USE "MAGIC" WELL.

I KEEP HOPING...

IT MIGHT HAVE BEEN SOME NEW INFECTIOUS DISEASE DRUG FROM ANOTHER COUNTRY.

IT WORKED FOR ABOUT A YEAR...

...BUT THEN THEY COULDN'T GET ANY MORE OF IT.

MAGIC?

....

NOT CURSES?

THANKS TO THAT THOUGH, THEY'VE BEEN TREATING IT LIKE A VIRUS.

IS SHE A ZOMBIE INSTEAD OF A WITCH?

MEDICINE FOR AN INFECTIOUS DISEASE...

88

...YOU'RE GOING?

YEAH.

THANK YOU FOR TALKING TO US.

NO MATTER HOW MUCH I'D LIKE TO FORGET IT...

OF COURSE.

DO YOU REMEM-BER...

...EVERY-THING THAT HAPPENED WHEN YOU ENCOUN-TERED THE WITCH?

I...

...MAY NEVER SEE YOU AGAIN, HUH?

WELL...

LIKE-WISE.

....

WAIT...

COME TO THINK OF IT, THERE IS SOMETHING I'VE FORGOT-TEN.

WHAT HAPPENED RIGHT BEFORE AND AFTER SHE CAST THE CURSE...

...I MADE A BET OR SOME KIND OF AGREEMENT WITH HER.

I THINK...

BUT I CAN'T REMEMBER WHAT IT WAS.

...I THOUGHT MAYBE MAGIC CHANGED INTO A CURSE...

SINCE I CAN'T REMEM-BER...

...AND THIS IS THE RESULT.

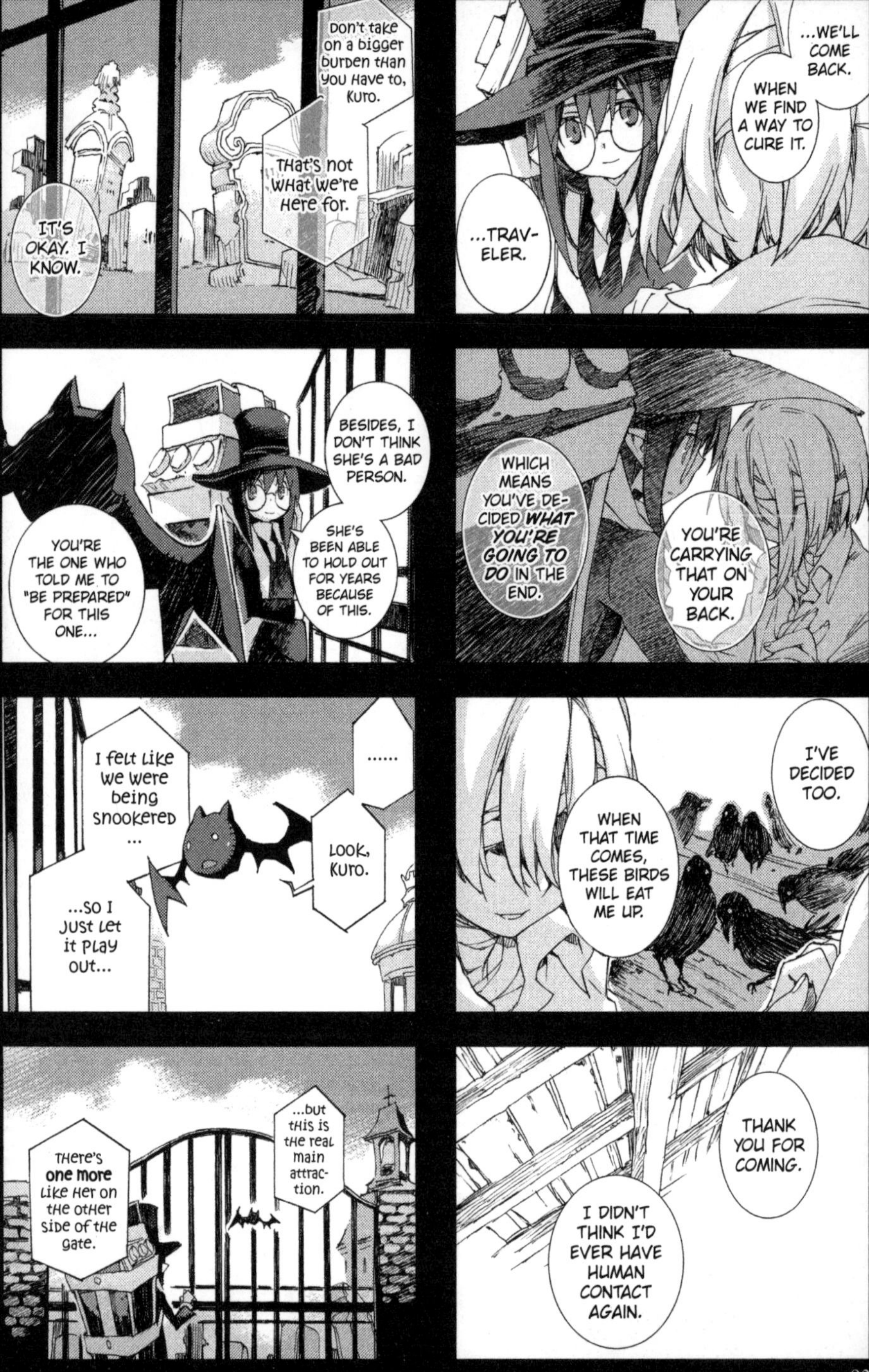
...WE'LL COME BACK.
WHEN WE FIND A WAY TO CURE IT.
...TRAVELER.
Don't take on a bigger burden than you have to, Kuro.
That's not what we're here for.
IT'S OKAY. I KNOW.
YOU'RE CARRYING THAT ON YOUR BACK.
WHICH MEANS YOU'VE DECIDED ***WHAT YOU'RE GOING TO DO*** IN THE END.
BESIDES, I DON'T THINK SHE'S A BAD PERSON.
SHE'S BEEN ABLE TO HOLD OUT FOR YEARS BECAUSE OF THIS.
YOU'RE THE ONE WHO TOLD ME TO "BE PREPARED" FOR THIS ONE...
I'VE DECIDED TOO.
WHEN THAT TIME COMES, THESE BIRDS WILL EAT ME UP.
......
Look, Kuro.
I felt like we were being snookered...
...so I just let it play out...
THANK YOU FOR COMING.
I DIDN'T THINK I'D EVER HAVE HUMAN CONTACT AGAIN.
...but this is the real main attraction.
There's **one more** like her on the other side of the gate.

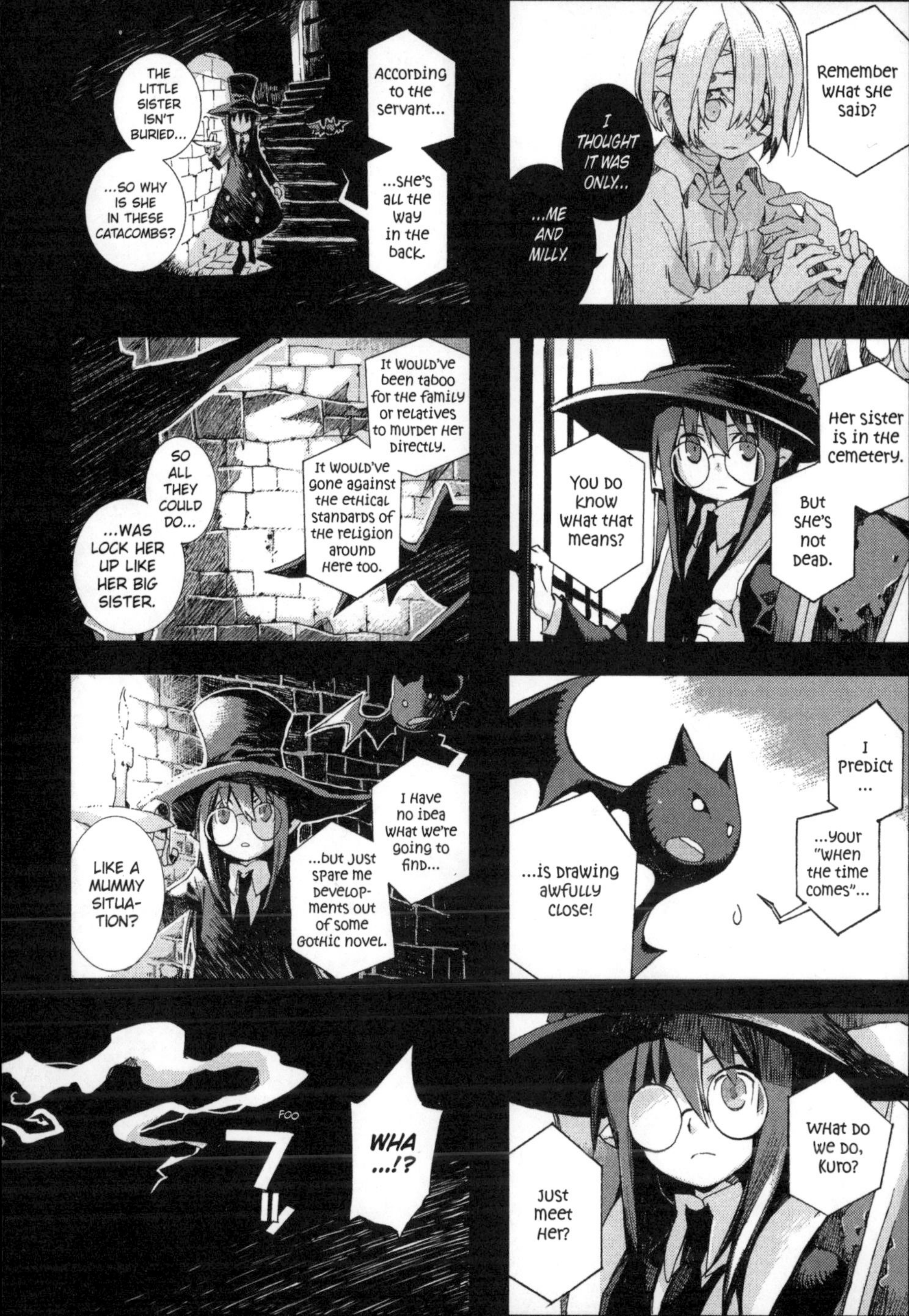

Remember what she said?
I thought it was only...
...me and Milly.
According to the servant...
...she's all the way in the back.
The little sister isn't buried...
...so why is she in these catacombs?
Her sister is in the cemetery.
But she's not dead.
You do know what that means?
It would've been taboo for the family or relatives to murder her directly.
It would've gone against the ethical standards of the religion around here too.
So all they could do...
...was lock her up like her big sister.
I predict...
...your "when the time comes"...
...is drawing awfully close!
I have no idea what we're going to find...
...but just spare me developments out of some Gothic novel.
Like a mummy situation?
What do we do, Kuro?
Just meet her?
WHA ...!?
FOO

......

ARE YOU...

...MILLY?

WHAT HAPPENED?

I BUMPED INTO SOMETHING...

THE CANDLE WENT OUT.

IN FACT, THE CANDLE'S GONE.

CALM DOWN.

IT'S OKAY. I WON'T RUN AWAY.

SLIDE

WOULD YOU LIKE TO LEAVE HERE?

I DON'T KNOW...

It wasn't a signal for us to "get out"?

SHOOT. GUESS I DROPPED MY HAT TOO.

...I SEE.

YOU WANT ME TO **END IT.**

BUT...

FOR SOMEONE WHO'S GOT THE FORM OF A BAT, YOU'RE PRETTY USELESS.

I can't see anything in this darkness.

DIDN'T YOU DROP IT OVER THERE?

...THERE'S NO GUARANTEE THAT IT'LL BE ANY BRIGHTER...

...WHERE I TAKE YOU.

SPLAT

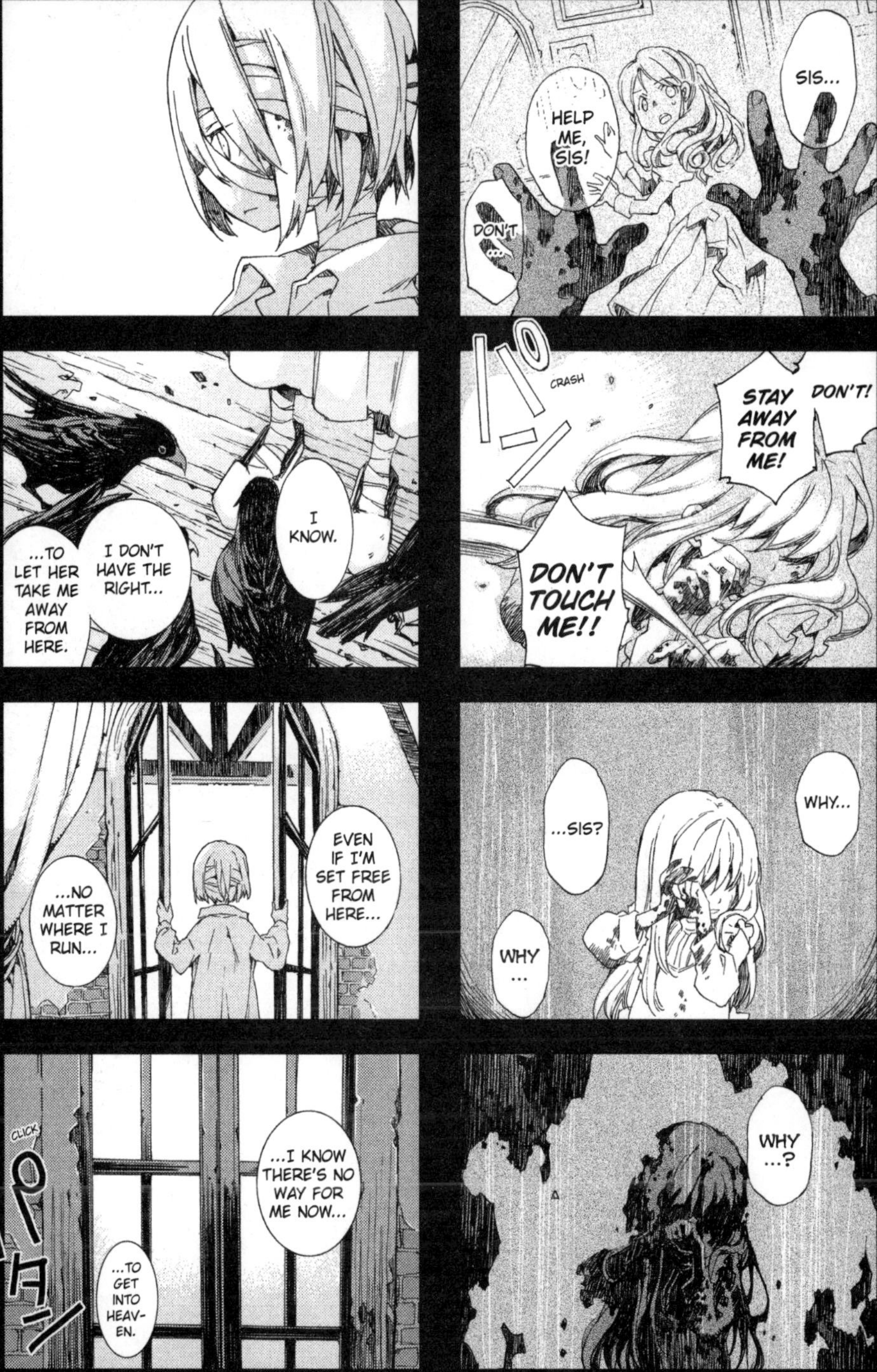
SIS...
HELP ME, SIS!
DON'T ...
CRASH
DON'T!
STAY AWAY FROM ME!
DON'T TOUCH ME!!
I KNOW.
I DON'T HAVE THE RIGHT...
...TO LET HER TAKE ME AWAY FROM HERE.
WHY...
...SIS?
WHY ...
EVEN IF I'M SET FREE FROM HERE...
...NO MATTER WHERE I RUN...
WHY ...?
CLICK
...I KNOW THERE'S NO WAY FOR ME NOW...
...TO GET INTO HEAV- EN.

THE NEXT DAY...

KURO-CHA, WELCOME BACK!

AH!

...KURO-CHAN WOKE UP BEFORE US AS USUAL...

...AND GOT READY TO GO OUT AS USUAL.

HUH?

MM?

HUH? KURO-CHA...

GOOD MORNING, KURO-CHAN.

.... SORRY.

IT'S STILL LIGHT OUTSIDE, KURO-CHAN.

KURO-CHA?

YOUR HANDS...

...ARE DIFFERENT.

...I WANT TO SLEEP A BIT.

RIGHT NOW, I DON'T FEEL GOOD AT ALL.

94

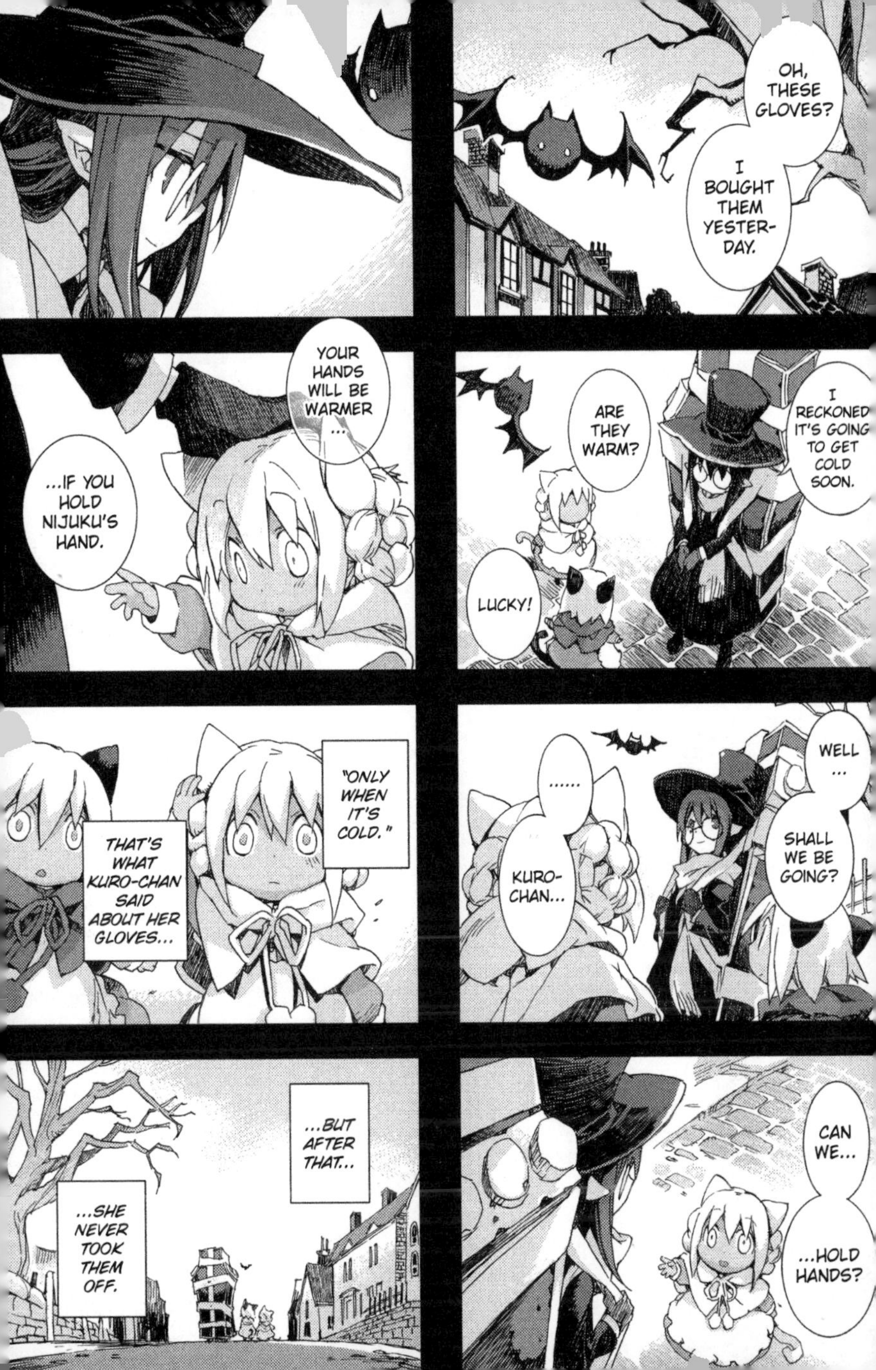
OH, THESE GLOVES?
I BOUGHT THEM YESTER-DAY.
I RECKONED IT'S GOING TO GET COLD SOON.
ARE THEY WARM?
LUCKY!
YOUR HANDS WILL BE WARMER ...
...IF YOU HOLD NIJUKU'S HAND.
WELL ...
SHALL WE BE GOING?
......
KURO-CHAN...
"ONLY WHEN IT'S COLD."
THAT'S WHAT KURO-CHAN SAID ABOUT HER GLOVES...
CAN WE...
...HOLD HANDS?
...BUT AFTER THAT...
...SHE NEVER TOOK THEM OFF.

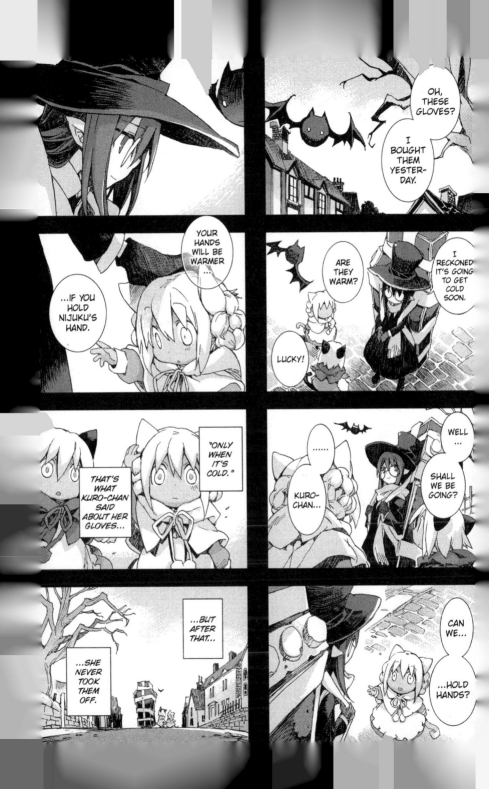

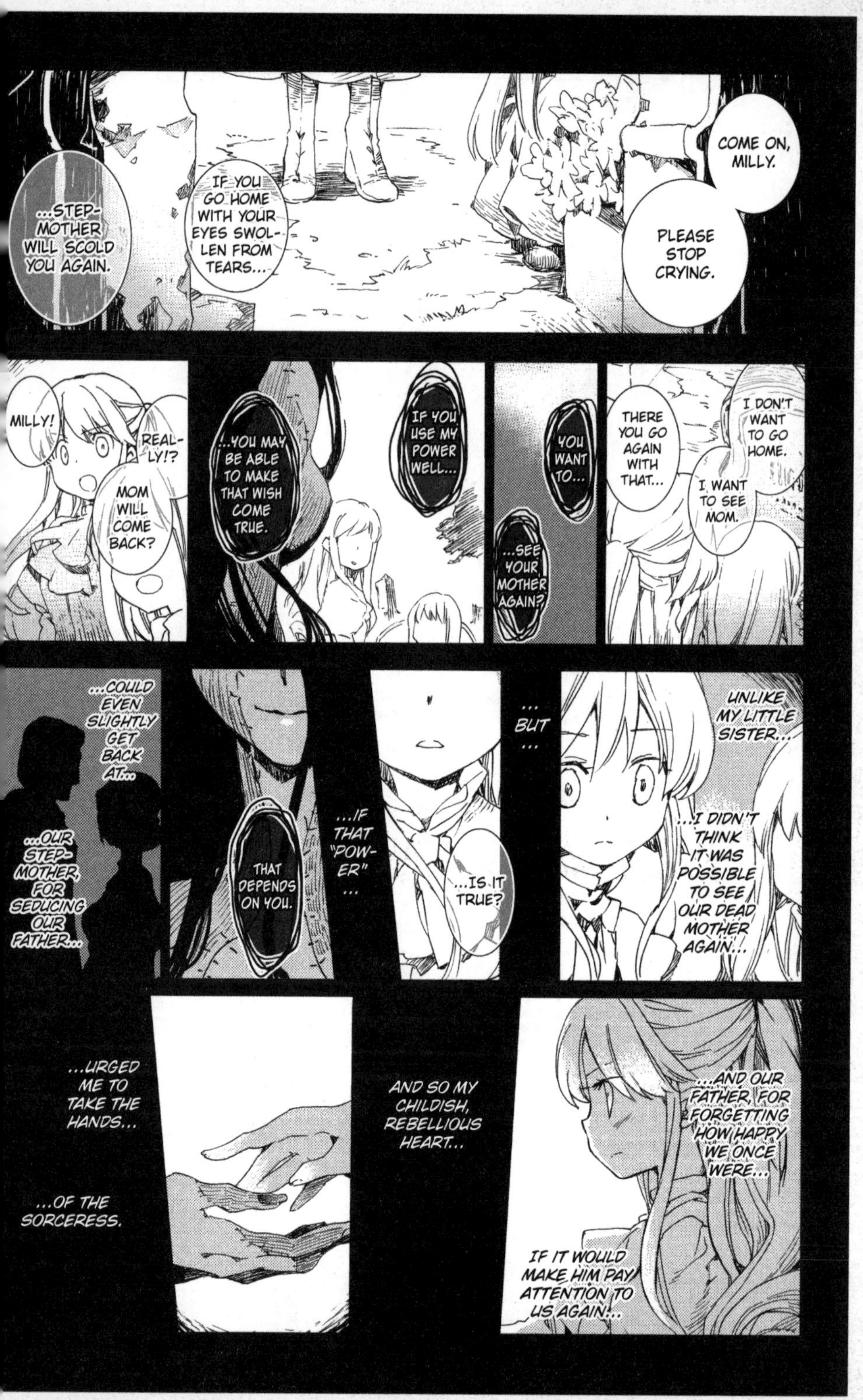
COME ON, MILLY.
PLEASE STOP CRYING.
IF YOU GO HOME WITH YOUR EYES SWOLLEN FROM TEARS...
...STEPMOTHER WILL SCOLD YOU AGAIN.
I DON'T WANT TO GO HOME.
I WANT TO SEE MOM.
THERE YOU GO AGAIN WITH THAT...
YOU WANT TO...
...SEE YOUR MOTHER AGAIN?
IF YOU USE MY POWER WELL...
...YOU MAY BE ABLE TO MAKE THAT WISH COME TRUE.
REALLY!?
MOM WILL COME BACK?
MILLY!
UNLIKE MY LITTLE SISTER...
...I DIDN'T THINK IT WAS POSSIBLE TO SEE OUR DEAD MOTHER AGAIN...
...BUT...
...IS IT TRUE?
...IF THAT "POWER"...
THAT DEPENDS ON YOU.
...COULD EVEN SLIGHTLY GET BACK AT...
...OUR STEPMOTHER, FOR SEDUCING OUR FATHER...
...AND OUR FATHER, FOR FORGETTING HOW HAPPY WE ONCE WERE...
IF IT WOULD MAKE HIM PAY ATTENTION TO US AGAIN...
AND SO MY CHILDISH, REBELLIOUS HEART...
...URGED ME TO TAKE THE HANDS...
...OF THE SORCERESS.

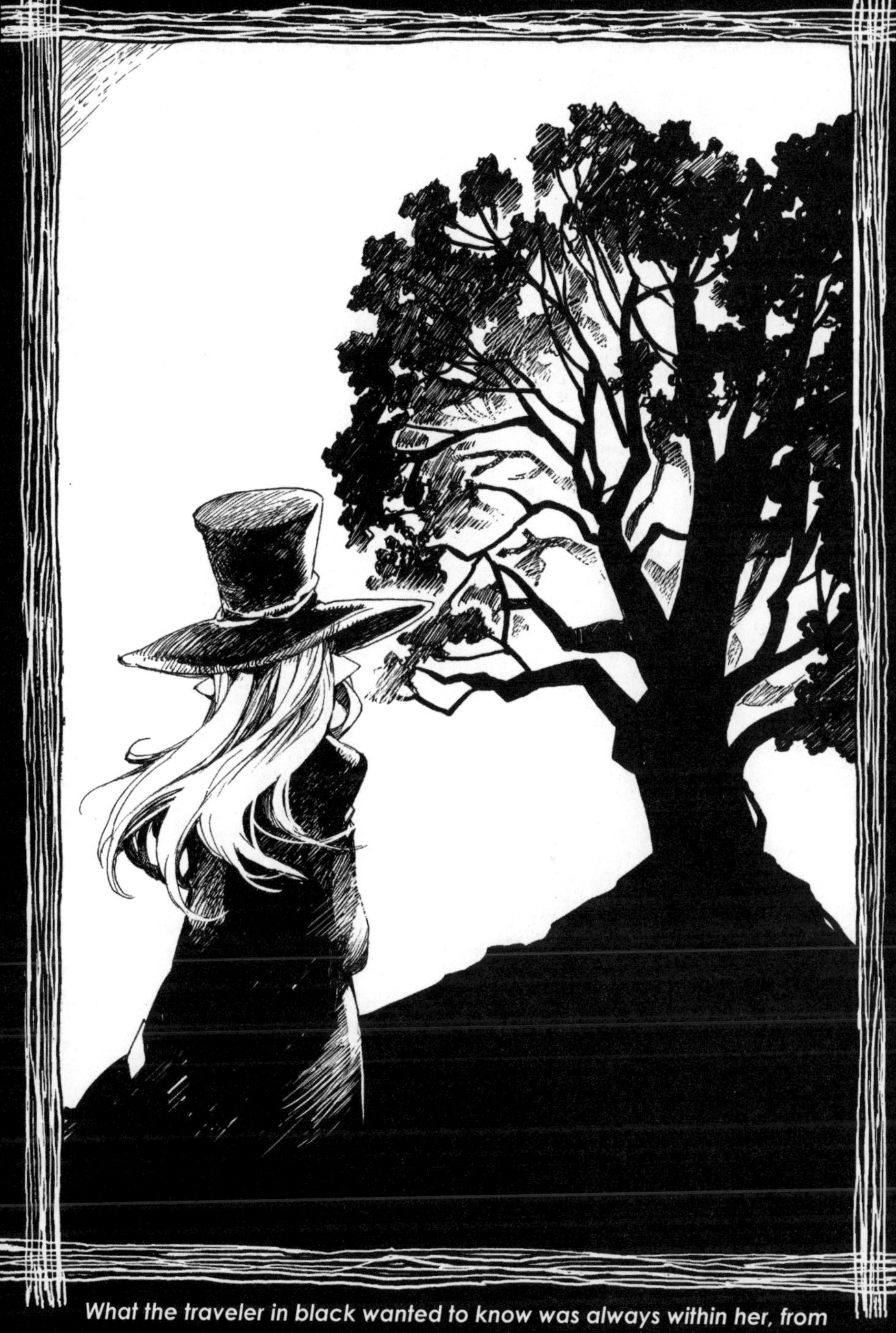

What the traveler in black wanted to know was always within her, from the start. But she had the feeling that she'd sealed it off deep inside because to reveal it would make her not a traveler, but a witch.

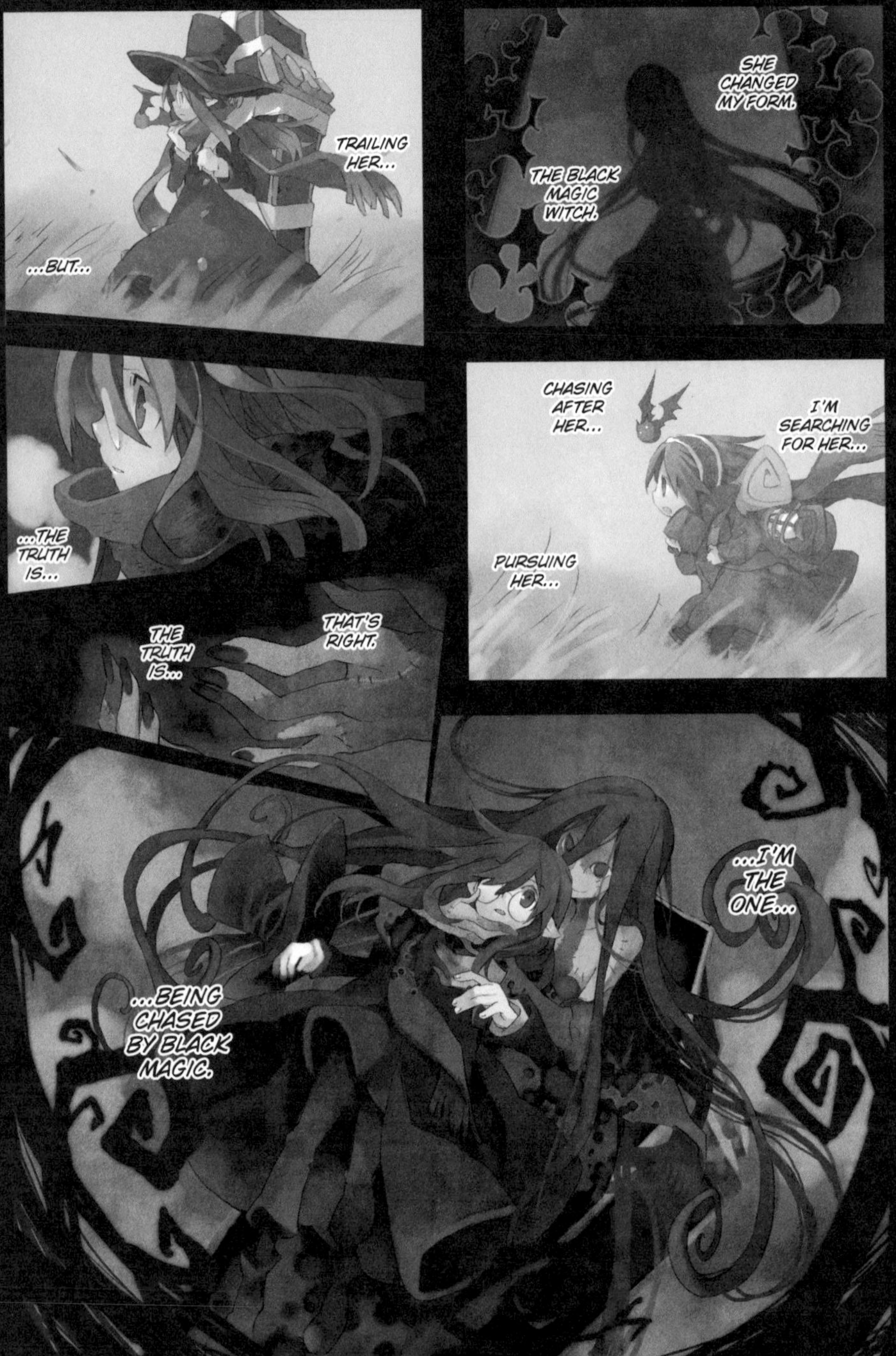
SHE CHANGED MY FORM.
THE BLACK MAGIC WITCH.
TRAILING HER...
...BUT...
I'M SEARCHING FOR HER...
CHASING AFTER HER...
PURSUING HER...
...THE TRUTH IS...
THAT'S RIGHT.
THE TRUTH IS...
...I'M THE ONE...
...BEING CHASED BY BLACK MAGIC.

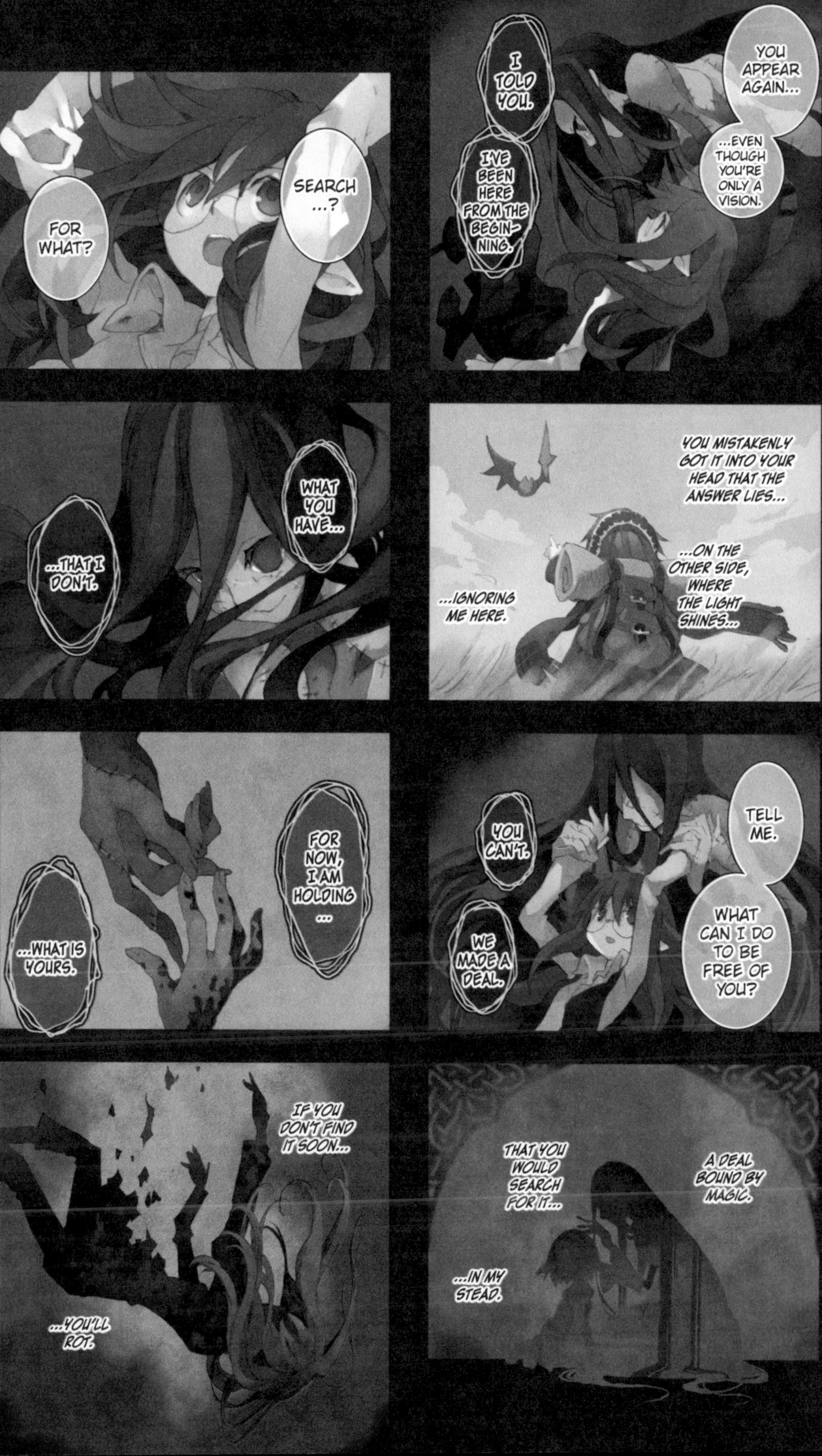
YOU APPEAR AGAIN...
...EVEN THOUGH YOU'RE ONLY A VISION.
I TOLD YOU.
I'VE BEEN HERE FROM THE BEGIN-NING.
SEARCH ...?
FOR WHAT?
YOU MISTAKENLY GOT IT INTO YOUR HEAD THAT THE ANSWER LIES...
...ON THE OTHER SIDE, WHERE THE LIGHT SHINES...
...IGNORING ME HERE.
WHAT YOU HAVE...
...THAT I DON'T.
TELL ME.
WHAT CAN I DO TO BE FREE OF YOU?
YOU CAN'T.
WE MADE A DEAL.
FOR NOW, I AM HOLDING ...
...WHAT IS YOURS.
A DEAL BOUND BY MAGIC.
THAT YOU WOULD SEARCH FOR IT...
...IN MY STEAD.
IF YOU DON'T FIND IT SOON...
...YOU'LL ROT.

THE ONLY ROUTES TO OUR HARBOR TOWN DESTINATION ARE BY BOAT...

...OR VIA THIS LONG LAND BRIDGE.

THAT'S UNUSUAL.

....

...BUT RIGHT NOW, BY ORDER OF THE SECOND SECURITY CODE... STRANGERS ARE NOT ALLOWED ON THE BRIDGE.

I BEG YOUR PARDON, TRAVELERS...

KURO CRASHING INTO THINGS BECAUSE SHE'S STILL HALF-ASLEEP...

ARE YOU AWAKE?

YOU FELL?

...WHEN SHE CALLED OUT TO US.

UNEXPECTEDLY BLOCKED, WE WERE THINKING ABOUT WHAT TO DO...

YON TRAVELERS.

WE HAVE TO MOVE THESE BARRELS.

SLAP

SLAP

COME ON, SNAP TO IT!

IF SO... I MAY BE ABLE TO HELP YOU!

DO YOU HAVE BUSINESS IN THE HARBOR TOWN?

AND YOU DO WANT A LIFT TO TOWN, RIGHT?

I'M NOT PULLING OUT TODAY.

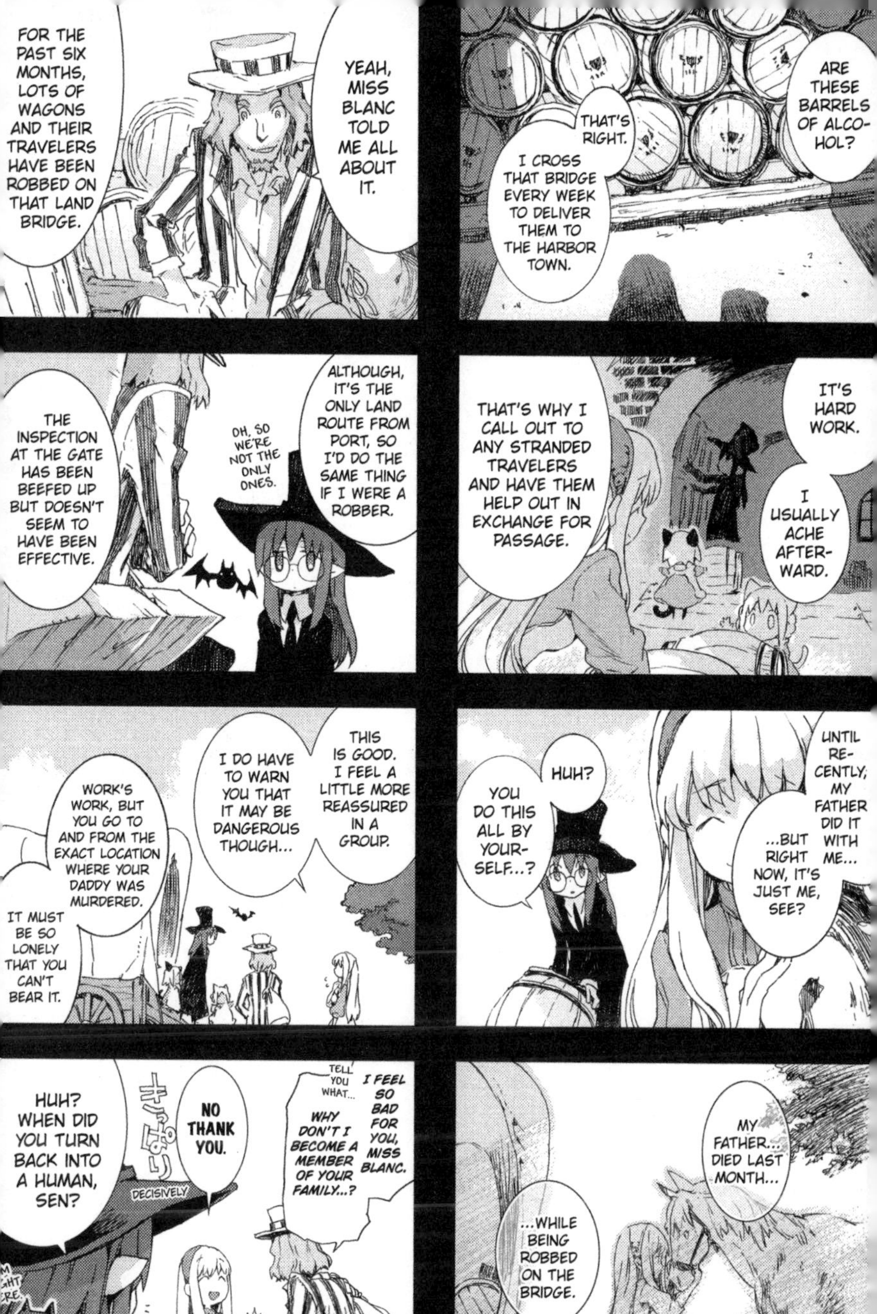
ARE THESE BARRELS OF ALCO-HOL?
THAT'S RIGHT.
I CROSS THAT BRIDGE EVERY WEEK TO DELIVER THEM TO THE HARBOR TOWN.
YEAH, MISS BLANC TOLD ME ALL ABOUT IT.
FOR THE PAST SIX MONTHS, LOTS OF WAGONS AND THEIR TRAVELERS HAVE BEEN ROBBED ON THAT LAND BRIDGE.
IT'S HARD WORK.
I USUALLY ACHE AFTER-WARD.
THAT'S WHY I CALL OUT TO ANY STRANDED TRAVELERS AND HAVE THEM HELP OUT IN EXCHANGE FOR PASSAGE.
ALTHOUGH, IT'S THE ONLY LAND ROUTE FROM PORT, SO I'D DO THE SAME THING IF I WERE A ROBBER.
OH, SO WE'RE NOT THE ONLY ONES.
THE INSPECTION AT THE GATE HAS BEEN BEEFED UP BUT DOESN'T SEEM TO HAVE BEEN EFFECTIVE.
UNTIL RE-CENTLY, MY FATHER DID IT WITH ME...
...BUT RIGHT NOW, IT'S JUST ME, SEE?
HUH?
YOU DO THIS ALL BY YOUR-SELF...?
THIS IS GOOD. I FEEL A LITTLE MORE REASSURED IN A GROUP.
I DO HAVE TO WARN YOU THAT IT MAY BE DANGEROUS THOUGH...
WORK'S WORK, BUT YOU GO TO AND FROM THE EXACT LOCATION WHERE YOUR DADDY WAS MURDERED.
IT MUST BE SO LONELY THAT YOU CAN'T BEAR IT.
MY FATHER... DIED LAST MONTH...
...WHILE BEING ROBBED ON THE BRIDGE.
I FEEL SO BAD FOR YOU, MISS BLANC.
TELL YOU WHAT...
WHY DON'T I BECOME A MEMBER OF YOUR FAMILY...?
NO THANK YOU.
DECISIVELY
HUH? WHEN DID YOU TURN BACK INTO A HUMAN, SEN?

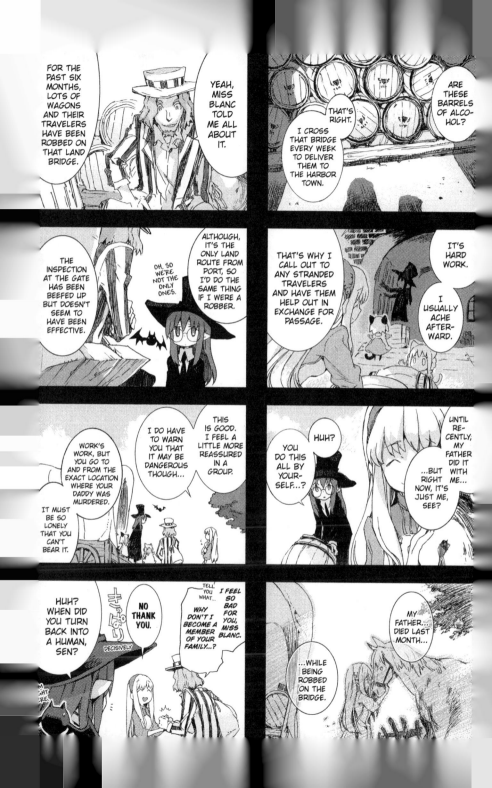

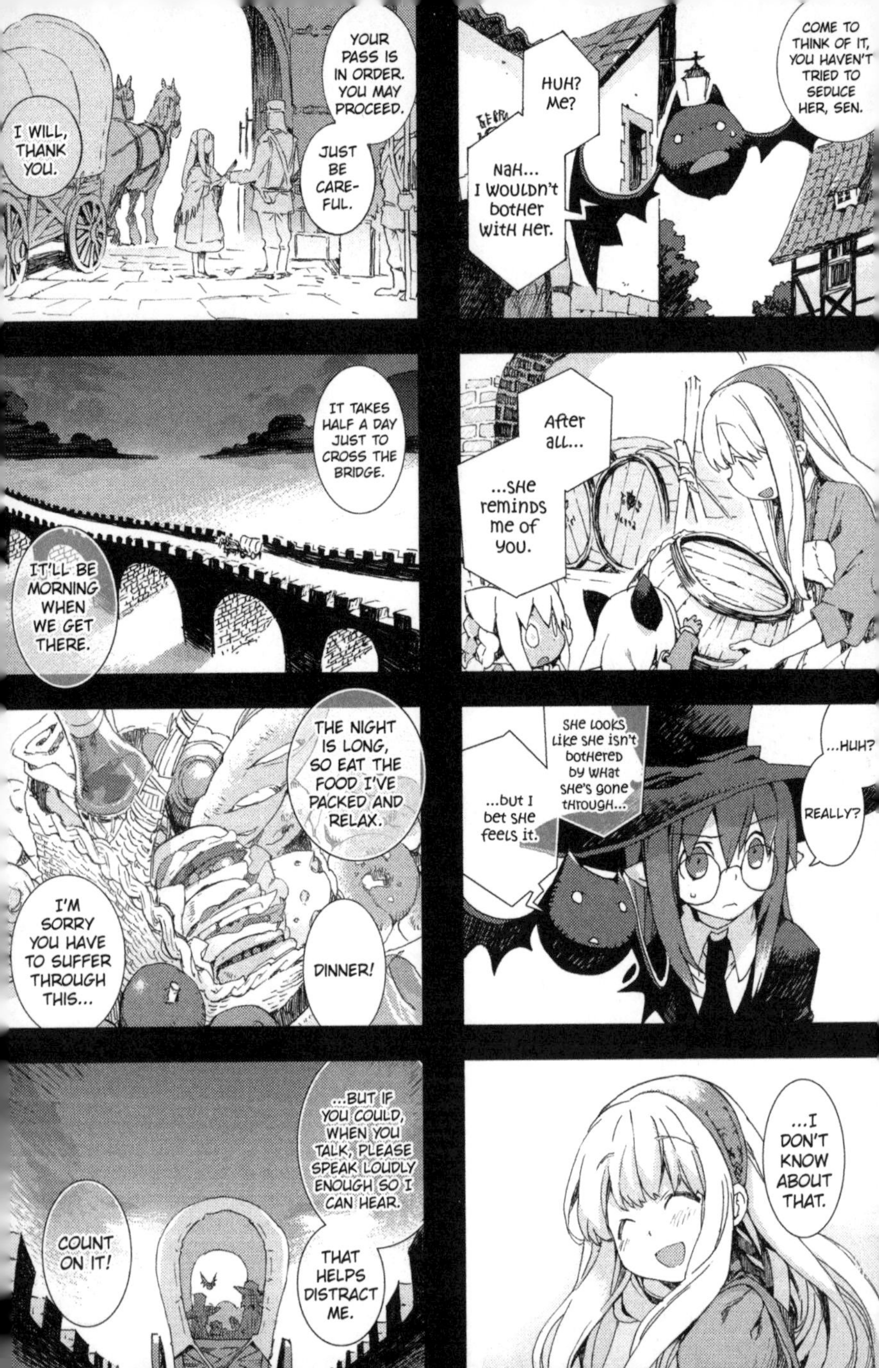
COME TO THINK OF IT, YOU HAVEN'T TRIED TO SEDUCE HER, SEN.
HUH? Me?
NaH... I WOULDN'T bother WITH Her.
YOUR PASS IS IN ORDER. YOU MAY PROCEED.
JUST BE CARE-FUL.
I WILL, THANK YOU.
After all...
...SHE reminds me of YOU.
IT TAKES HALF A DAY JUST TO CROSS THE BRIDGE.
IT'LL BE MORNING WHEN WE GET THERE.
...HUH?
REALLY?
SHE LOOKS LIKE SHE ISN'T bothered by WHAT SHE'S gone THROUGH...
...but I bet SHE feels it.
THE NIGHT IS LONG, SO EAT THE FOOD I'VE PACKED AND RELAX.
DINNER!
I'M SORRY YOU HAVE TO SUFFER THROUGH THIS...
...I DON'T KNOW ABOUT THAT.
...BUT IF YOU COULD, WHEN YOU TALK, PLEASE SPEAK LOUDLY ENOUGH SO I CAN HEAR.
THAT HELPS DISTRACT ME.
COUNT ON IT!

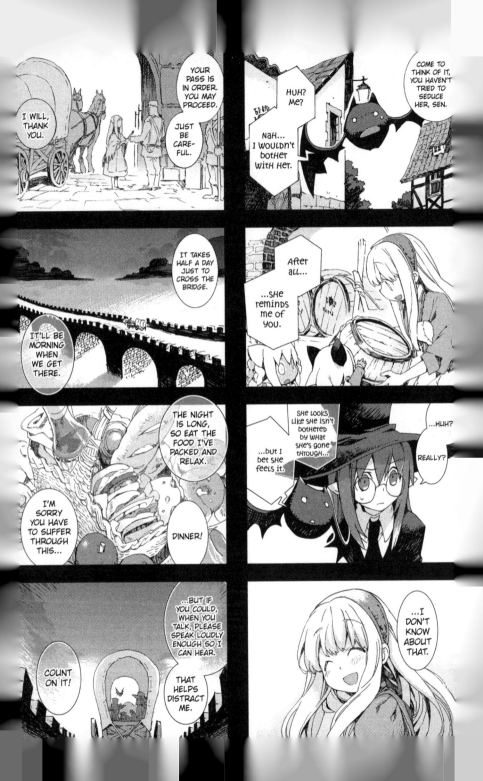

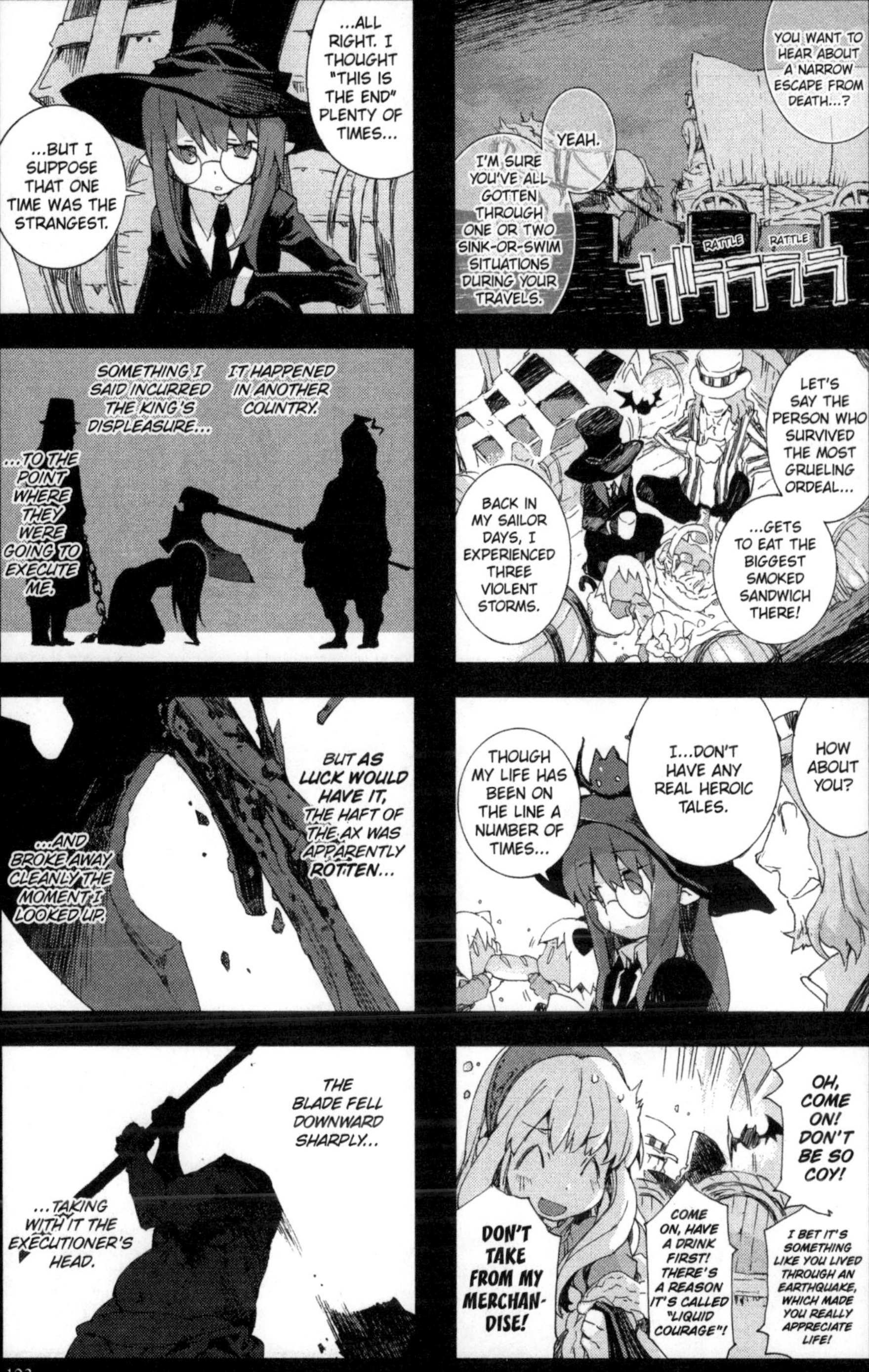
YOU WANT TO HEAR ABOUT A NARROW ESCAPE FROM DEATH...?
YEAH.
I'M SURE YOU'VE ALL GOTTEN THROUGH ONE OR TWO SINK-OR-SWIM SITUATIONS DURING YOUR TRAVELS.
RATTLE
RATTLE
...ALL RIGHT. I THOUGHT "THIS IS THE END" PLENTY OF TIMES...
...BUT I SUPPOSE THAT ONE TIME WAS THE STRANGEST.
LET'S SAY THE PERSON WHO SURVIVED THE MOST GRUELING ORDEAL...
...GETS TO EAT THE BIGGEST SMOKED SANDWICH THERE!
BACK IN MY SAILOR DAYS, I EXPERIENCED THREE VIOLENT STORMS.
IT HAPPENED IN ANOTHER COUNTRY.
SOMETHING I SAID INCURRED THE KING'S DISPLEASURE...
...TO THE POINT WHERE THEY WERE GOING TO EXECUTE ME.
HOW ABOUT YOU?
I...DON'T HAVE ANY REAL HEROIC TALES.
THOUGH MY LIFE HAS BEEN ON THE LINE A NUMBER OF TIMES...
BUT AS LUCK WOULD HAVE IT, THE HAFT OF THE AX WAS APPARENTLY ROTTEN...
...AND BROKE AWAY CLEANLY THE MOMENT I LOOKED UP.
OH, COME ON! DON'T BE SO COY!
I BET IT'S SOMETHING LIKE YOU LIVED THROUGH AN EARTHQUAKE, WHICH MADE YOU REALLY APPRECIATE LIFE!
COME ON, HAVE A DRINK FIRST! THERE'S A REASON IT'S CALLED "LIQUID COURAGE"!
DON'T TAKE FROM MY MERCHANDISE!
THE BLADE FELL DOWNWARD SHARPLY...
...TAKING WITH IT THE EXECUTIONER'S HEAD.

WELL, IF WE'RE TALKING ABOUT SURVIVING TERRIBLE ORDEALS...

...YOU WOULD QUALIFY TOO, BLANC.

DID THAT REALLY HAPPEN?

IT SOUNDS MADE-UP.

OR STILL GOING THROUGH IT...

I THINK WE'RE ABOUT HALFWAY THERE.

YAWN...

TH-THANK YOU.

BUT I'M FINE. YOU EAT IT, KURO-SAN.

YOU DESERVE THE SMOKED SANDWICH THE MOST!

THAT'S RIGHT! YOU'RE OUR WINNER, BLANC!

RIDE THROUGH THE TRAGEDY OF LOSING YOUR FATHER!!

AH...

A LIGHT'S COMING THIS WAY.

I APPRECIATE IT...

THAT'S...

BURP

I SHOULD'VE FIGURED THIS WOULD HAPPEN...

NO...

HUH? YOU'RE DONE ALREADY!?

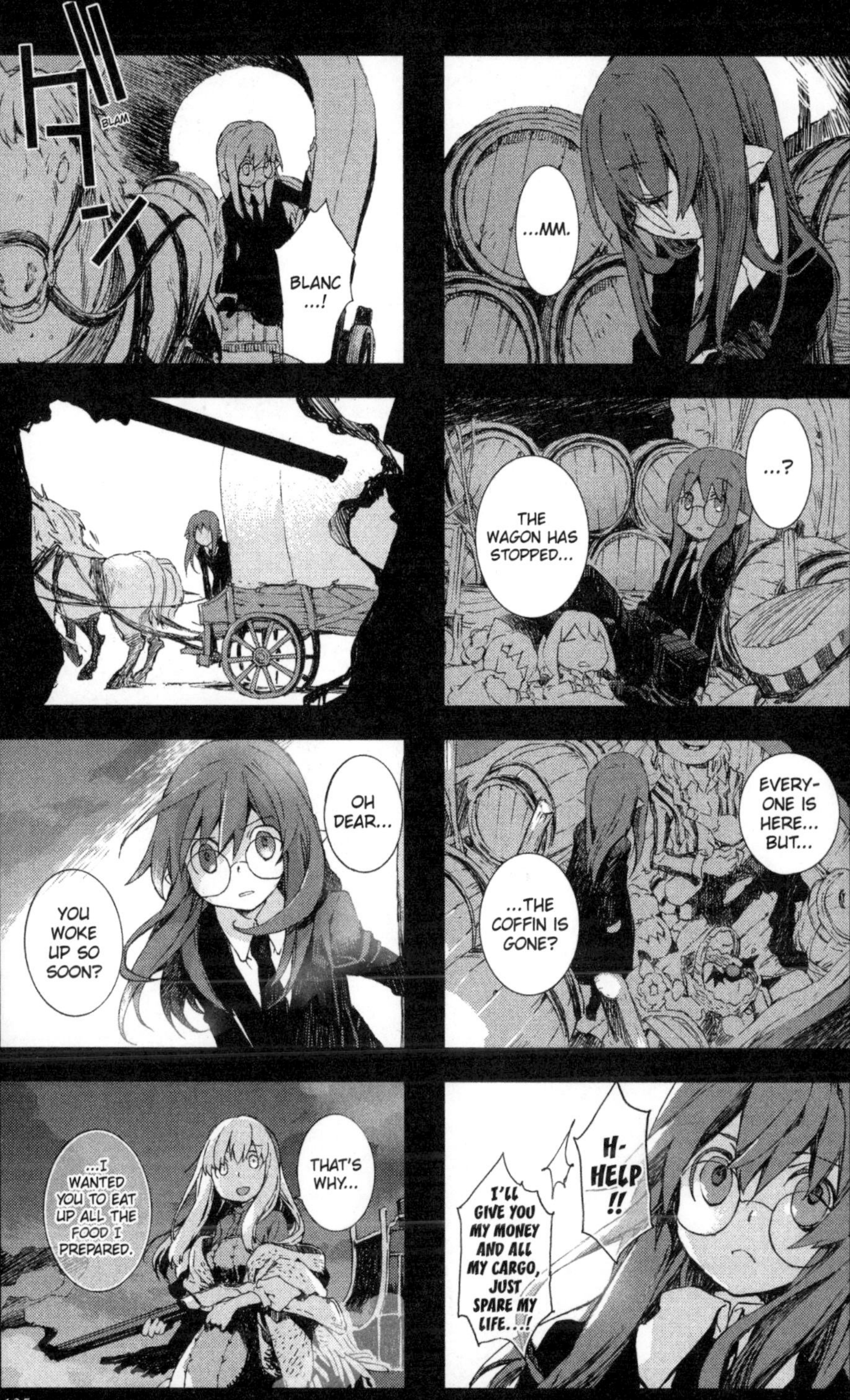
...MM.
BLAM
BLANC ...!
...?
THE WAGON HAS STOPPED...
EVERY-ONE IS HERE... BUT...
...THE COFFIN IS GONE?
OH DEAR...
YOU WOKE UP SO SOON?
H-HELP!!
I'LL GIVE YOU MY MONEY AND ALL MY CARGO, JUST SPARE MY LIFE...!
THAT'S WHY...
...I WANTED YOU TO EAT UP ALL THE FOOD I PREPARED.

...IF YOU'RE GOING TO DO IT, MAKE SURE YOU FINISH THE JOB.

THERE'S NOTHING WORSE THAN BEING CLOSE TO DEATH.

SHOOT. IT REALLY IS A PAIN HAVING TO BE A BANDIT ALONE.

NOT THAT I HAD MUCH CHOICE AFTER MY PARTNER SCREWED UP AND GOT HIMSELF KILLED.

I KNOW.

AND SO YOU WON'T BE LONELY, I'LL SEND YOUR COMRADES ALONG RIGHT AFTER YOU.

SADLY, I COULDN'T FIND ANYTHING VALUABLE...

...AMONG YOUR OR THE OLD MAN'S THINGS.

IF YOU'D JUST SLEPT ALL THE WAY TO TOWN, YOU'D HAVE BEEN SAFE AND NONE THE WISER.

GOOD-BYE...

...KURO-SAN.

...THIS IS THE ONLY THING I CAN DO.

BUT NOW THAT YOU KNOW...

YOU UNDERSTAND?

BLAM

ハ°
ア
ン

A COFFIN THAT'S JUST BEEN EMPTIED...

...NEEDS TO BE FILLED WITH SOMETHING.

106

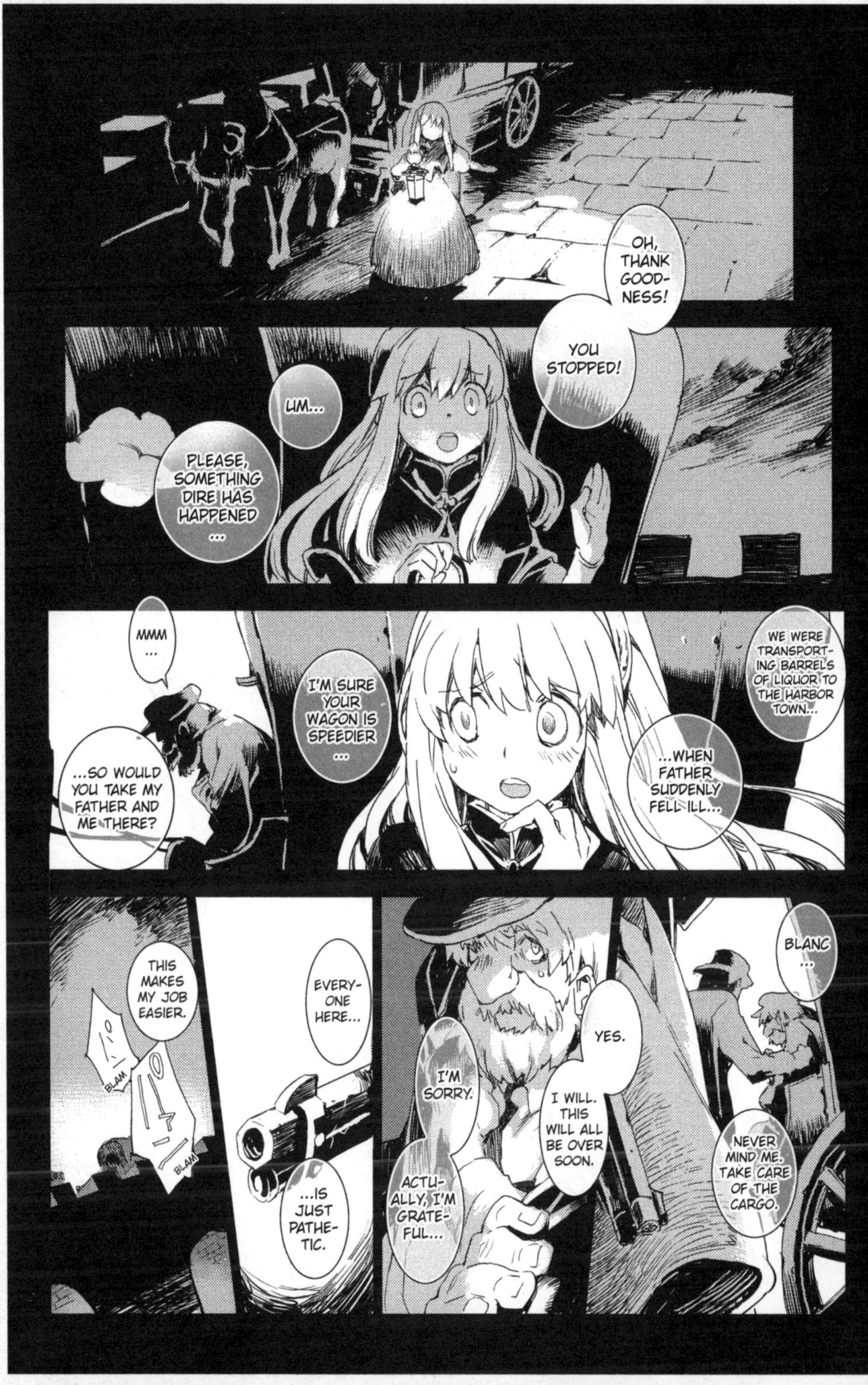
OH, THANK GOODNESS!
YOU STOPPED!
UM...
PLEASE, SOMETHING DIRE HAS HAPPENED ...
WE WERE TRANSPORTING BARRELS OF LIQUOR TO THE HARBOR TOWN...
...WHEN FATHER SUDDENLY FELL ILL...
I'M SURE YOUR WAGON IS SPEEDIER ...
MMM ...
...SO WOULD YOU TAKE MY FATHER AND ME THERE?
BLANC ...
YES.
NEVER MIND ME. TAKE CARE OF THE CARGO.
I'M SORRY.
I WILL. THIS WILL ALL BE OVER SOON.
ACTUALLY, I'M GRATEFUL...
EVERYONE HERE...
...IS JUST PATHETIC.
THIS MAKES MY JOB EASIER.
BLAM
BLAM

...ISN'T FEAR OF DEATH.

THIS MUDDLED SENSATION...

I'M GETTING THAT SENSATION AGAIN.

AHHH...

GOOD-BYE...

...KURO-SAN.

IT'S ATTACH-MENT...

...TO LIFE.

THEN THERE'S A SCARY, DARK FEELING.

FOR AN INSTANT, EVERY-THING GOES WHITE.

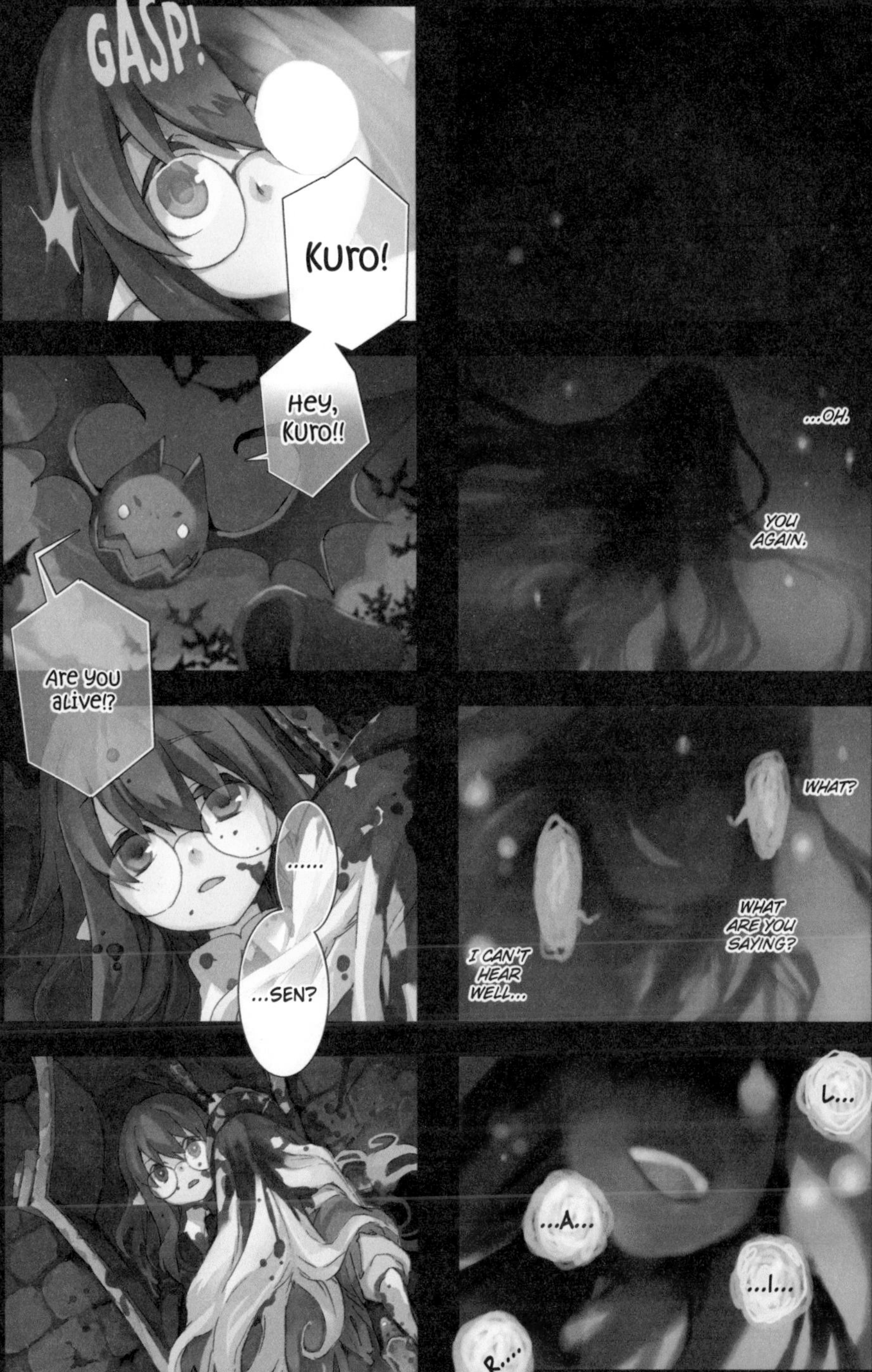
GASP!
Kuro!
...OH.
YOU AGAIN.
Hey, Kuro!!
Are you alive!?
WHAT?
WHAT ARE YOU SAYING?
I CAN'T HEAR WELL...
......
...SEN?
L...
...A...
...I...
...R....

SO...

...I'M ASKING YOU AGAIN.

....

YEAH.

WHAT DO YOU HAVE TO SAY TO ME THIS TIME...

...HI-FUMI?

IT SEEMS HER WOODEN GUN BARREL WAS ROTTEN...

...WHICH CAUSED THE HAMMER TO SUDDENLY GO OFF.

I'M OKAY.

......

YOU'RE...

...NOT HER.

...I DON'T WANT THEM TO SEE THIS.

BUT I DON'T THINK THERE'S AN EASY WAY TO EXPLAIN THIS AWAY.

WHERE ARE NIJUKU AND SANJU...?

STILL SLEEPING IN THE WAGON.

SKREE

SKREE

SKREE

BLANC...!?

...SORRY.

I'M EX-HAUSTED.

JUST LET ME SLEEP A LITTLE LONGER...

110

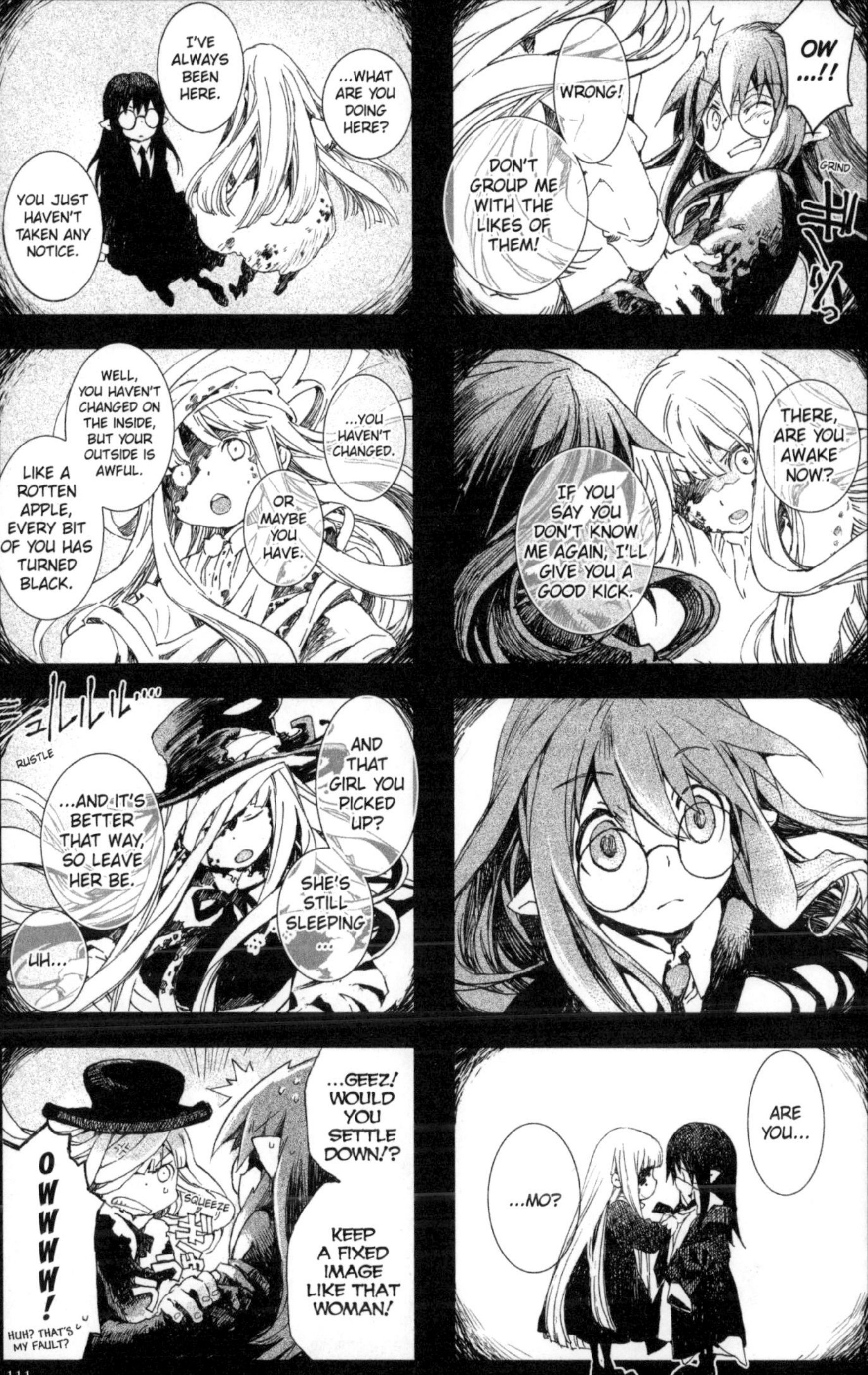
OW ...!!
WRONG!
DON'T GROUP ME WITH THE LIKES OF THEM!
GRIND
...WHAT ARE YOU DOING HERE?
I'VE ALWAYS BEEN HERE.
YOU JUST HAVEN'T TAKEN ANY NOTICE.
THERE, ARE YOU AWAKE NOW?
IF YOU SAY YOU DON'T KNOW ME AGAIN, I'LL GIVE YOU A GOOD KICK.
...YOU HAVEN'T CHANGED.
OR MAYBE YOU HAVE.
WELL, YOU HAVEN'T CHANGED ON THE INSIDE, BUT YOUR OUTSIDE IS AWFUL.
LIKE A ROTTEN APPLE, EVERY BIT OF YOU HAS TURNED BLACK.
AND THAT GIRL YOU PICKED UP?
SHE'S STILL SLEEPING...
...AND IT'S BETTER THAT WAY, SO LEAVE HER BE.
RUSTLE
UH...
ARE YOU...
...MO?
...GEEZ! WOULD YOU SETTLE DOWN!?
KEEP A FIXED IMAGE LIKE THAT WOMAN!
SQUEEZE
OWWWWW!
HUH? THAT'S MY FAULT?

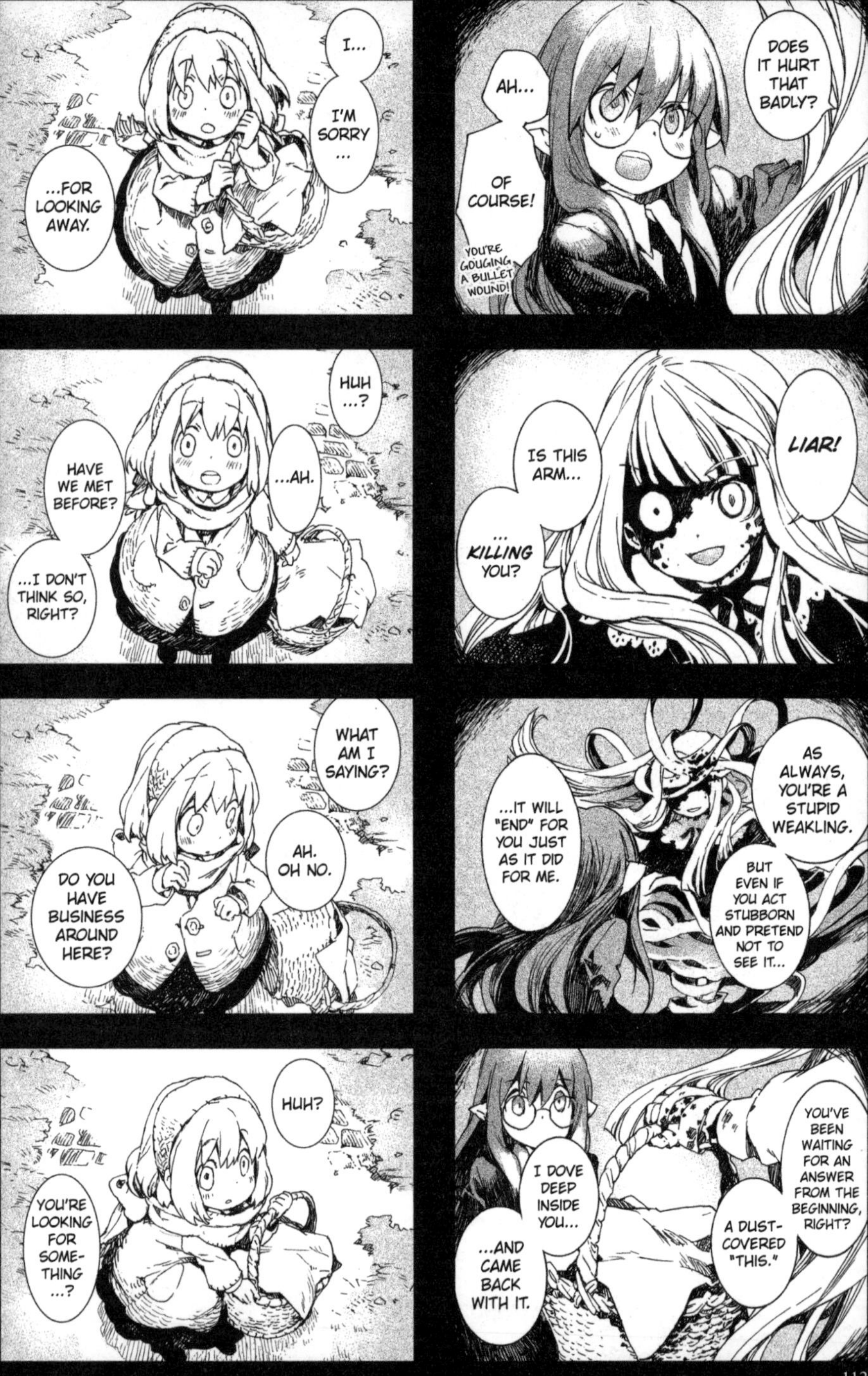
DOES IT HURT THAT BADLY?
AH...
OF COURSE!
YOU'RE GOUGING A BULLET WOUND!
I...
I'M SORRY ...
...FOR LOOKING AWAY.
LIAR!
IS THIS ARM...
... KILLING YOU?
HUH ...?
...AH.
HAVE WE MET BEFORE?
...I DON'T THINK SO, RIGHT?
AS ALWAYS, YOU'RE A STUPID WEAKLING.
BUT EVEN IF YOU ACT STUBBORN AND PRETEND NOT TO SEE IT...
...IT WILL "END" FOR YOU JUST AS IT DID FOR ME.
WHAT AM I SAYING?
AH. OH NO.
DO YOU HAVE BUSINESS AROUND HERE?
YOU'VE BEEN WAITING FOR AN ANSWER FROM THE BEGINNING, RIGHT?
A DUST-COVERED "THIS."
I DOVE DEEP INSIDE YOU...
...AND CAME BACK WITH IT.
HUH?
YOU'RE LOOKING FOR SOME-THING ...?

AND I STILL DON'T BELIEVE IT, BUT IF BLANC WAS THE ONE ALL ALONG, AS YOU INSIST...

...THEN THIS SHOULD RESOLVE THE SPATE OF ROBBERIES.

ALL RIGHT.

IN THE END, THERE WASN'T ENOUGH DEFINITIVE INFORMATION TO REACH A CONCLUSION, SO IT LOOKS LIKE THE CASE WILL BE FILED AS "UNSOLVED."

HI.

...YEAH.

WELL, EITHER WAY, I'M GLAD YOU'RE ALIVE.

THE MOMENT I SAW YOU IN THE COFFIN IN A PUDDLE OF BLOOD, I THOUGHT YOU WERE ALREADY DEAD.

YOU UP?

......

...?

I'M NOT GOING TO DIE.

MAYBE I CAN'T DIE.

HUH?

...... FLAP

SEN...

I CAN'T HEAR YOU.

WHAT?

FLAP

SHE TOOK IT...

...FROM ME LONG AGO.

YOU LIAR...

SHE WASN'T LIKE ME AFTER ALL...

....

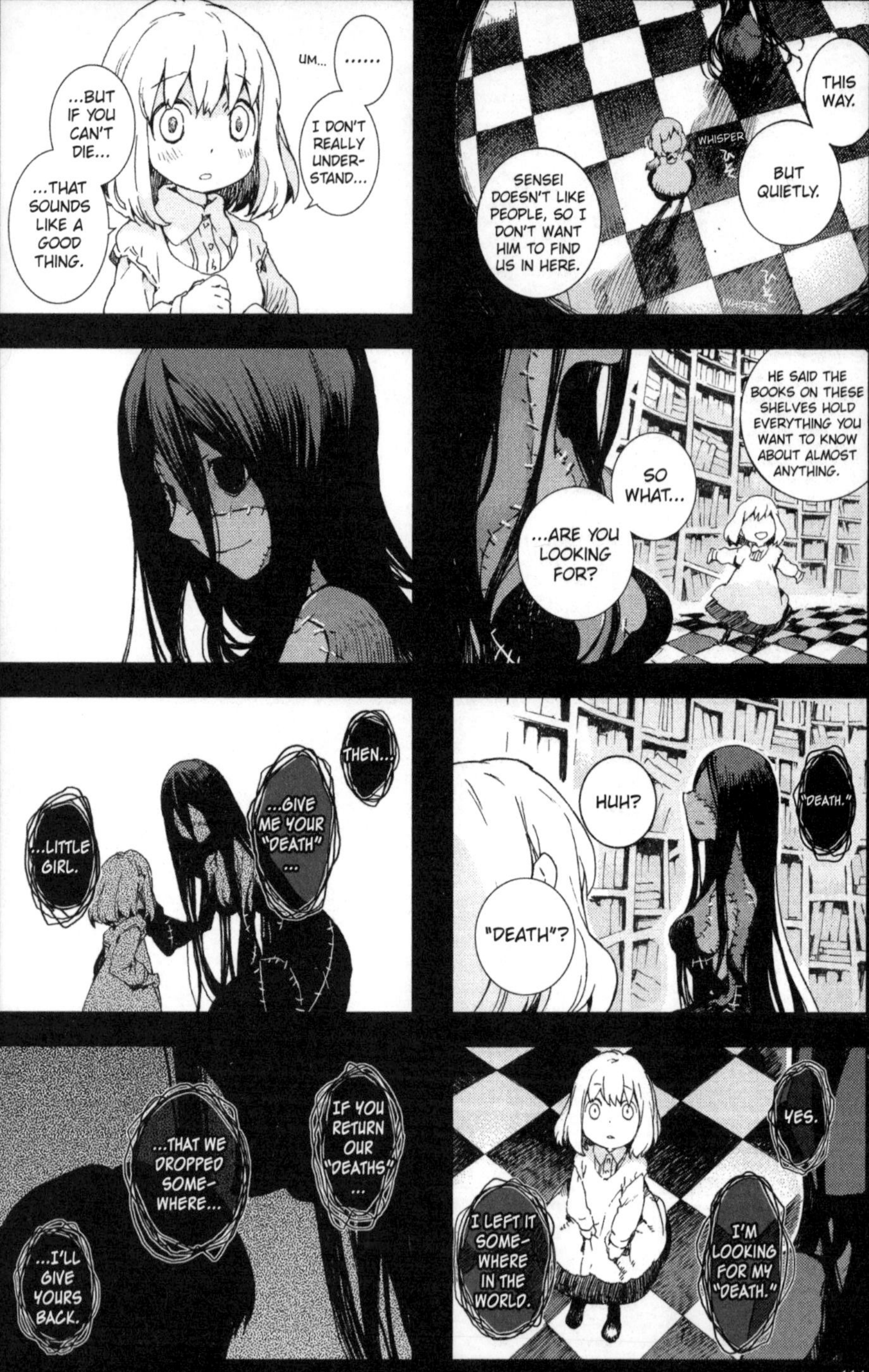
THIS WAY.
BUT QUIETLY.
WHISPER
SENSEI DOESN'T LIKE PEOPLE, SO I DON'T WANT HIM TO FIND US IN HERE.
WHISPER
......
UM...
I DON'T REALLY UNDER-STAND...
...BUT IF YOU CAN'T DIE...
...THAT SOUNDS LIKE A GOOD THING.
HE SAID THE BOOKS ON THESE SHELVES HOLD EVERYTHING YOU WANT TO KNOW ABOUT ALMOST ANYTHING.
SO WHAT...
...ARE YOU LOOKING FOR?
"DEATH."
HUH?
"DEATH"?
THEN...
...GIVE ME YOUR "DEATH"...
...LITTLE GIRL.
YES.
I'M LOOKING FOR MY "DEATH."
I LEFT IT SOME-WHERE IN THE WORLD.
IF YOU RETURN OUR "DEATHS"...
...THAT WE DROPPED SOME-WHERE...
...I'LL GIVE YOURS BACK.

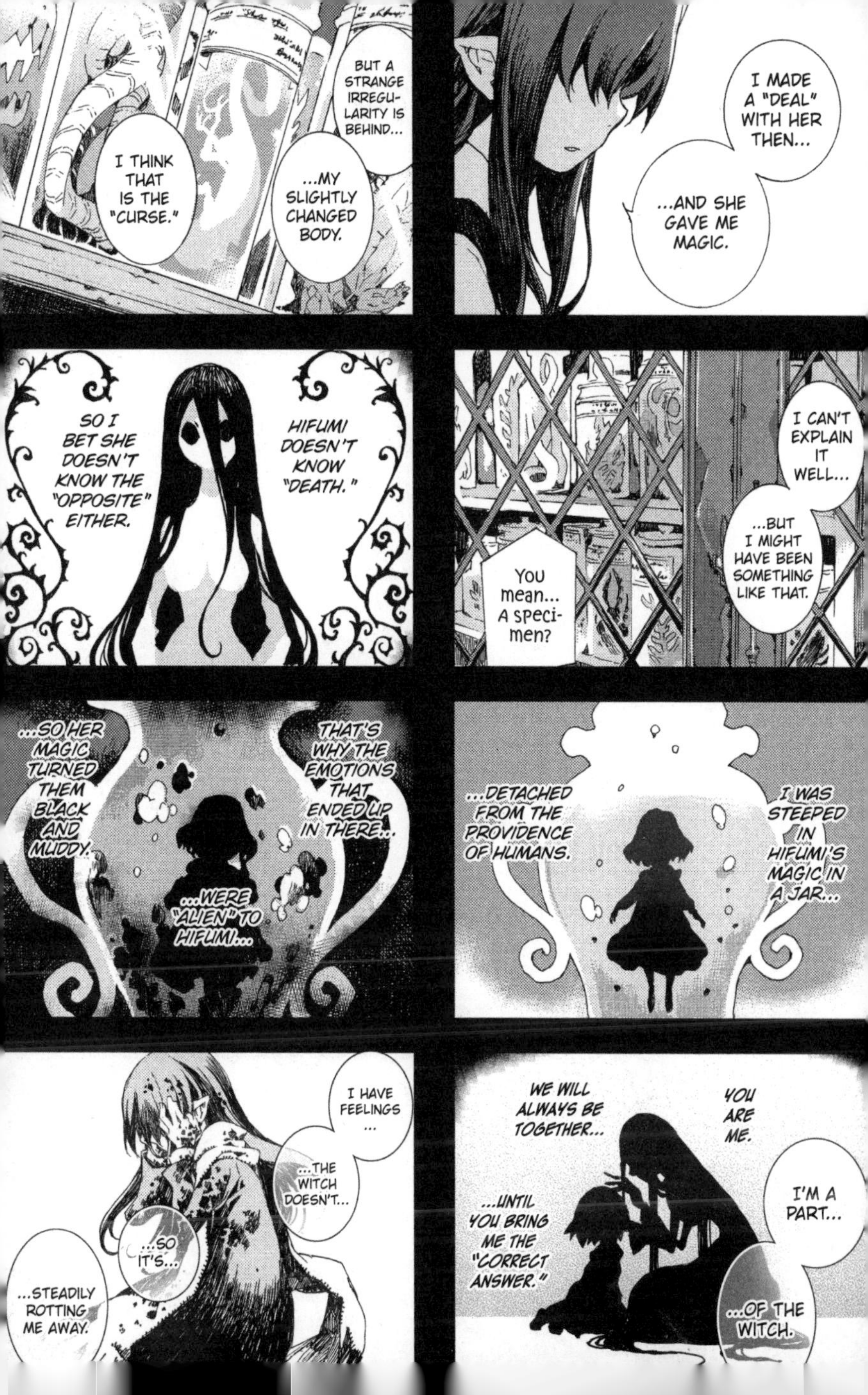
I MADE A "DEAL" WITH HER THEN...
...AND SHE GAVE ME MAGIC.
BUT A STRANGE IRREGULARITY IS BEHIND...
...MY SLIGHTLY CHANGED BODY.
I THINK THAT IS THE "CURSE."
I CAN'T EXPLAIN IT WELL...
...BUT I MIGHT HAVE BEEN SOMETHING LIKE THAT.
You mean... A specimen?
HIFUMI DOESN'T KNOW "DEATH."
SO I BET SHE DOESN'T KNOW THE "OPPOSITE" EITHER.
I WAS STEEPED IN HIFUMI'S MAGIC IN A JAR...
...DETACHED FROM THE PROVIDENCE OF HUMANS.
THAT'S WHY THE EMOTIONS THAT ENDED UP IN THERE...
...WERE "ALIEN" TO HIFUMI...
...SO HER MAGIC TURNED THEM BLACK AND MUDDY.
YOU ARE ME.
WE WILL ALWAYS BE TOGETHER...
I'M A PART...
...UNTIL YOU BRING ME THE "CORRECT ANSWER."
...OF THE WITCH.
I HAVE FEELINGS...
...THE WITCH DOESN'T...
...SO IT'S...
...STEADILY ROTTING ME AWAY.

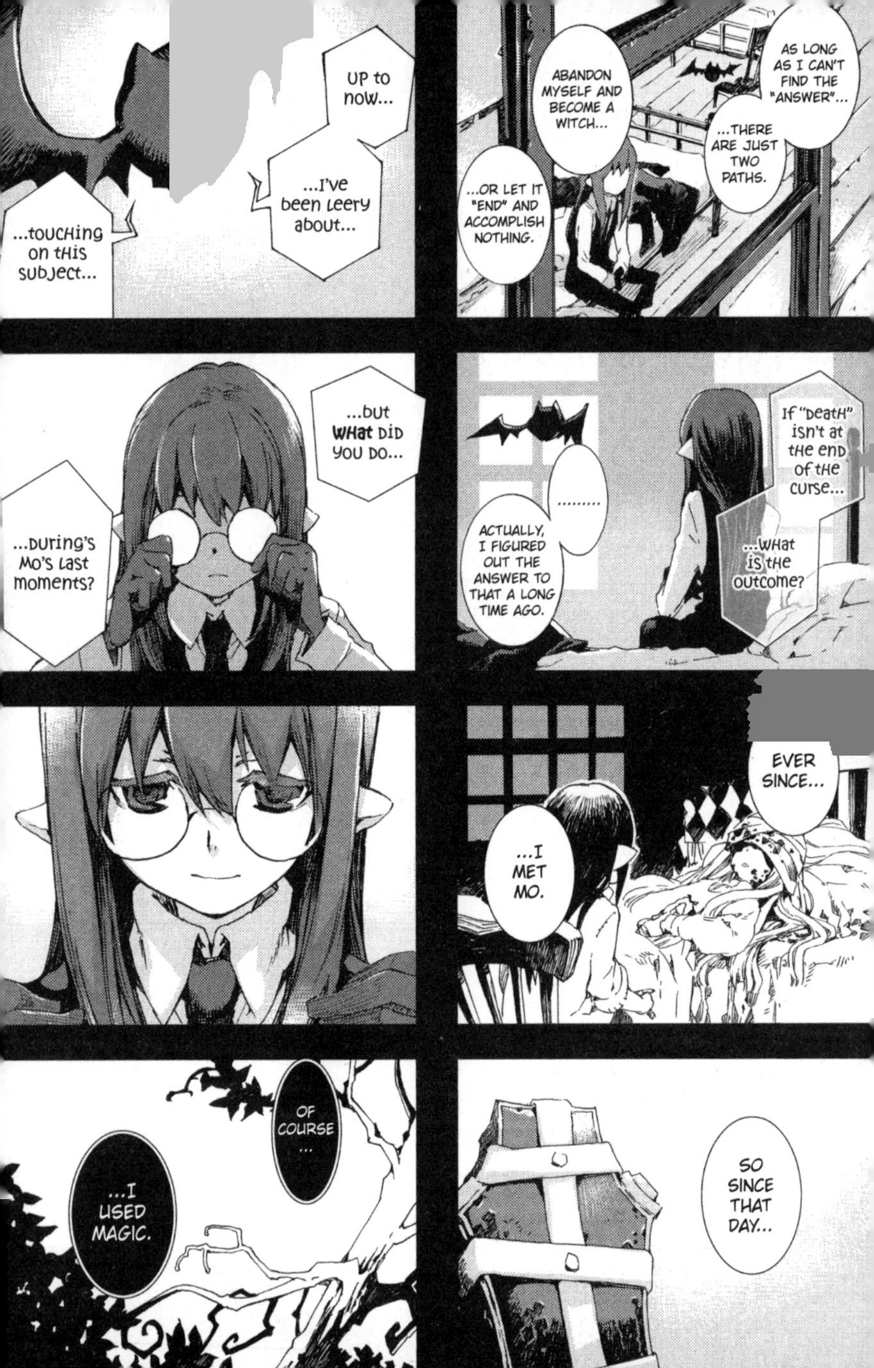
AS LONG AS I CAN'T FIND THE "ANSWER"...
...THERE ARE JUST TWO PATHS.
ABANDON MYSELF AND BECOME A WITCH...
...OR LET IT "END" AND ACCOMPLISH NOTHING.
UP to now...
...I've been leery about...
...touching on this subject...
If "Death" isn't at the end of the curse...
...What is the outcome?
....
ACTUALLY, I FIGURED OUT THE ANSWER TO THAT A LONG TIME AGO.
...but **WHAT** did you do...
...During's Mo's last moments?
EVER SINCE...
...I MET MO.
SO SINCE THAT DAY...
OF COURSE...
...I USED MAGIC.

AH... HE'S STILL ALIVE.

After I found you, he drove the wagon to town and got help.

THAT'S a COLD WAY to PUT it.

IS YOUR ARM OKAY?

YEAH.

GOOD AS NEW.

YEAH, A FEW MINUTES AGO.

BUT THAT ASIDE...

THIS HAS BEEN A DISASTER FOR ALL OF US.

DID THEY JUST LET YOU OUT?

REALLY? THANK YOU.

THE POLICE STILL HAVE CUSTODY OF THE COFFIN AND OUR THINGS.

NOT TO MENTION NIJUKU AND SANJU...

AH... I SEE.

...WHO KILLED BLANC, AREN'T YOU?

...YOU'RE THE ONE...

STILL, STEEL YOURSELF FOR A CERTAIN AMOUNT OF INTERROGATING.

I GUESS WE WERE FORTUNATE WE HAD KIDS WITH US. THAT MUST'VE DAMPENED THE COPS' SKEPTICISM.

THAT'S RIGHT.

......

YEAH.

HEY.

ULP...

SHIVER

GRAB

DAM- MIT...

...TO HELL...

WHAT THE HELL!?

... DAM- MIT.

...!

WHY !?

SHE WAS A GOOD GIRL!

IF I DIDN'T DO THAT JUST NOW, I DON'T THINK I COULD'VE HELD BACK.

IF HE'D RATTLED ME, I WOULD'VE BEEN SWALLOWED UP BY HIFUMI'S MAGIC.

... SOR- RY.

...WHY DID YOU HAVE TO AGITATE HIM LIKE THAT?

...SHE FAILED TO KILL ME.

EVEN THOUGH I BEGGED HER TO FINISH ME OFF...

THAT'S RIGHT. SHE WAS A KIND PERSON.

... THERE'S NOTHING WORSE THAN BEING CLOSE TO DEATH.

THAT'S WHY I SAID BEFORE...

...WITHOUT HESITATION, EVEN IF IT MEANS SACRIFICING YOURSELF?

HOW ABOUT YOU?

WILL YOU DESTROY THIS CLINGING BLACK CURSE...

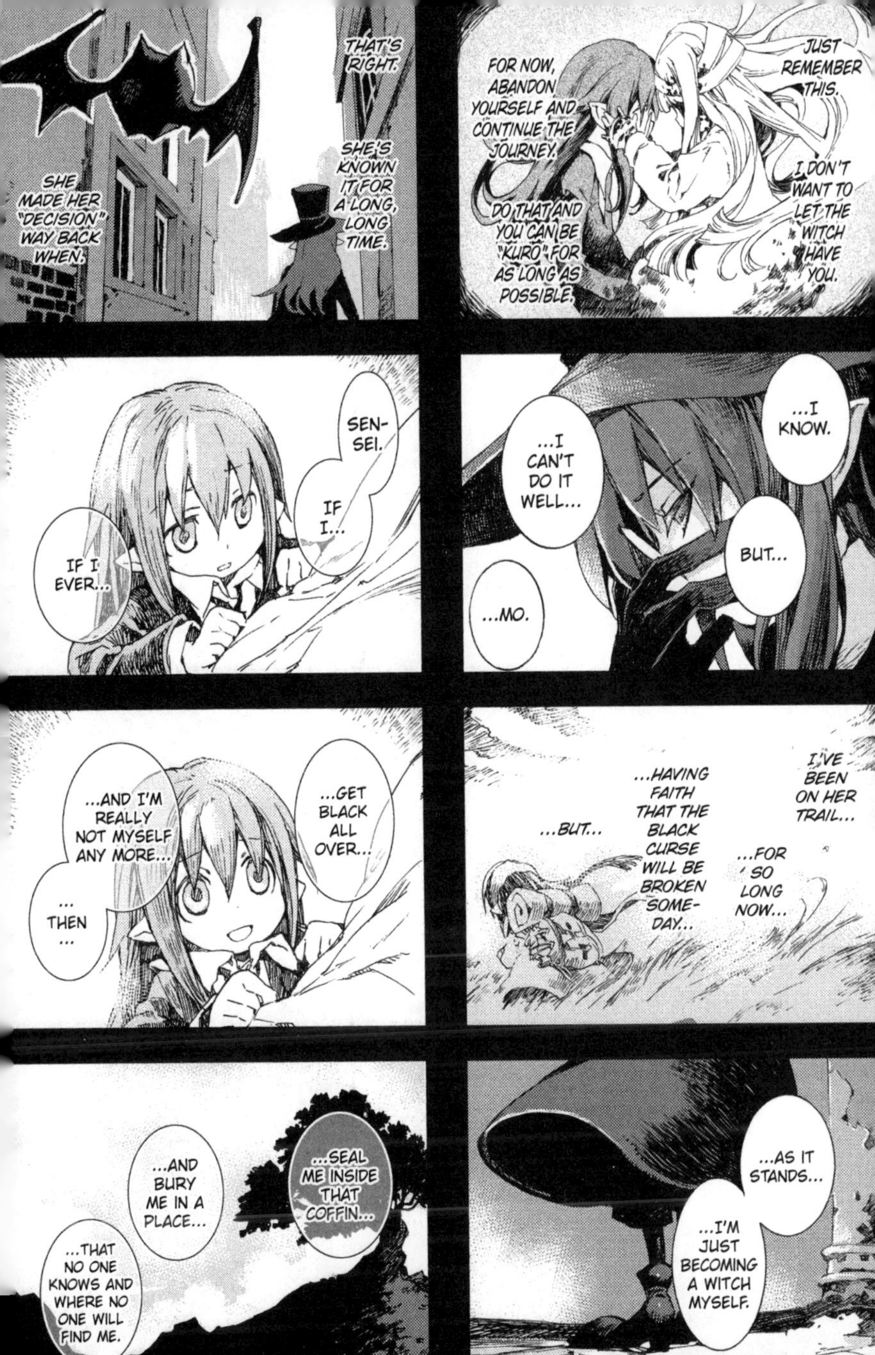
JUST REMEMBER THIS.
I DON'T WANT TO LET THE WITCH HAVE YOU.
FOR NOW, ABANDON YOURSELF AND CONTINUE THE JOURNEY.
DO THAT AND YOU CAN BE "KURO" FOR AS LONG AS POSSIBLE.
THAT'S RIGHT.
SHE'S KNOWN IT FOR A LONG, LONG TIME.
SHE MADE HER "DECISION" WAY BACK WHEN.
...I KNOW.
...I CAN'T DO IT WELL...
BUT...
...MO.
SEN-SEI.
IF I...
IF I EVER...
I'VE BEEN ON HER TRAIL...
...FOR SO LONG NOW...
...HAVING FAITH THAT THE BLACK CURSE WILL BE BROKEN SOME-DAY...
...BUT...
...GET BLACK ALL OVER...
...AND I'M REALLY NOT MYSELF ANY MORE...
...THEN...
...AS IT STANDS...
...I'M JUST BECOMING A WITCH MYSELF.
...SEAL ME INSIDE THAT COFFIN...
...AND BURY ME IN A PLACE...
...THAT NO ONE KNOWS AND WHERE NO ONE WILL FIND ME.

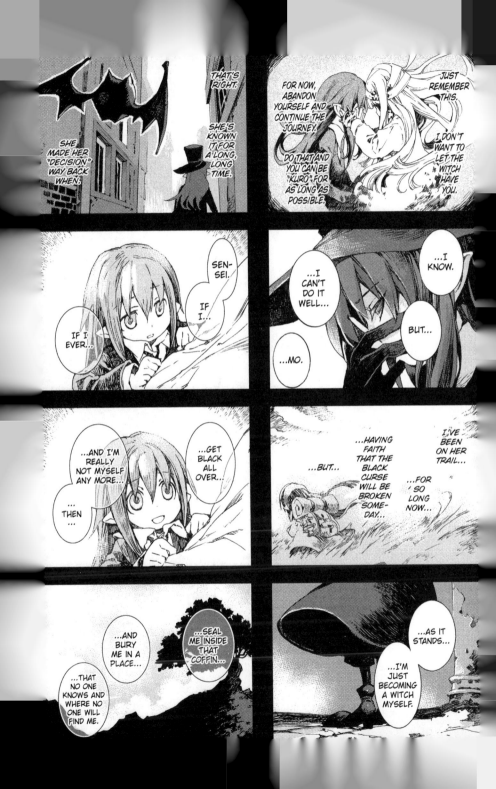

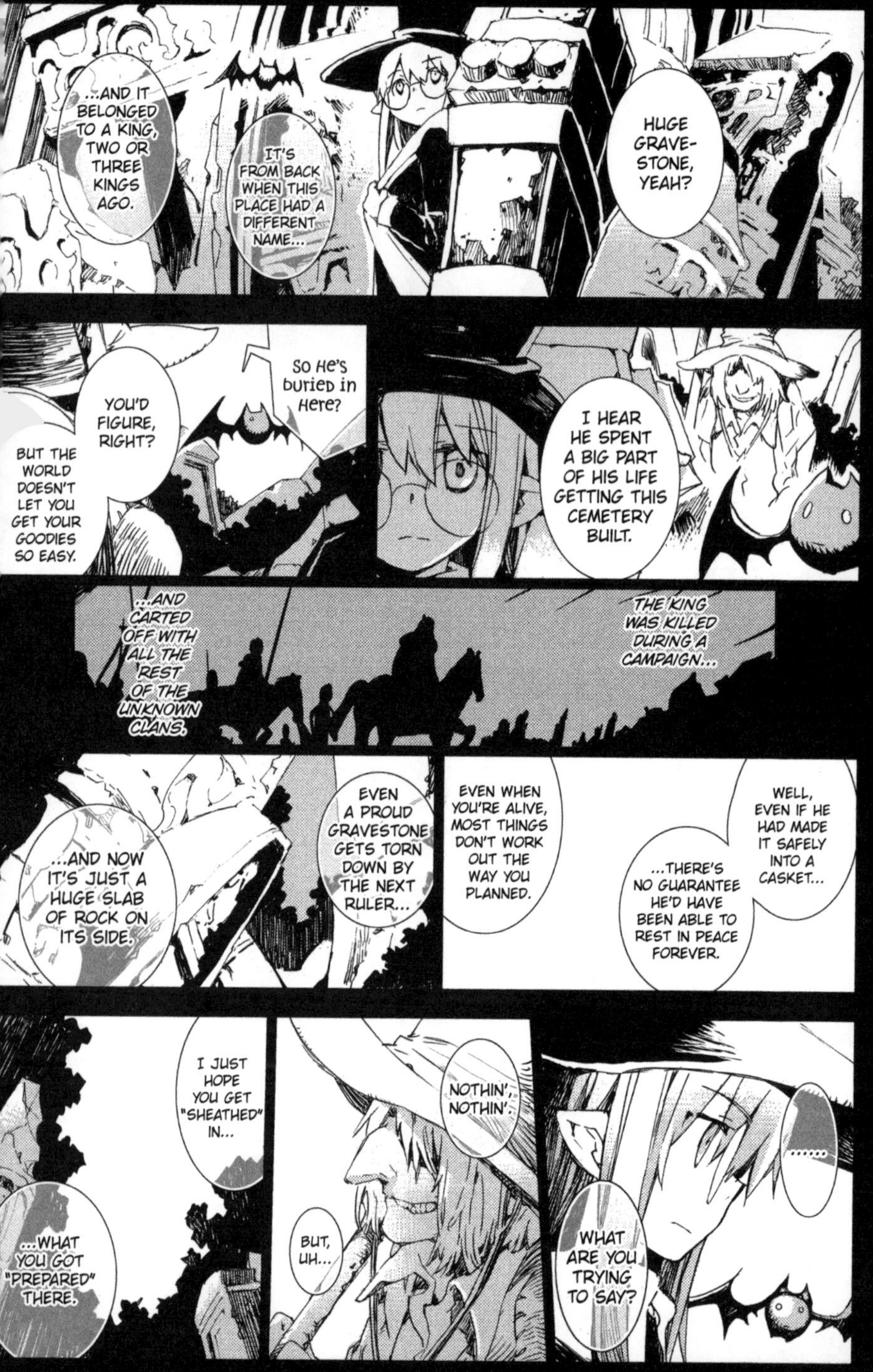
HUGE GRAVE-STONE, YEAH?
IT'S FROM BACK WHEN THIS PLACE HAD A DIFFERENT NAME...
...AND IT BELONGED TO A KING, TWO OR THREE KINGS AGO.
I HEAR HE SPENT A BIG PART OF HIS LIFE GETTING THIS CEMETERY BUILT.
So He's buried in Here?
YOU'D FIGURE, RIGHT?
BUT THE WORLD DOESN'T LET YOU GET YOUR GOODIES SO EASY.
THE KING WAS KILLED DURING A CAMPAIGN...
...AND CARTED OFF WITH ALL THE REST OF THE UNKNOWN CLANS.
WELL, EVEN IF HE HAD MADE IT SAFELY INTO A CASKET...
...THERE'S NO GUARANTEE HE'D HAVE BEEN ABLE TO REST IN PEACE FOREVER.
EVEN WHEN YOU'RE ALIVE, MOST THINGS DON'T WORK OUT THE WAY YOU PLANNED.
EVEN A PROUD GRAVESTONE GETS TORN DOWN BY THE NEXT RULER...
...AND NOW IT'S JUST A HUGE SLAB OF ROCK ON ITS SIDE.
......
WHAT ARE YOU TRYING TO SAY?
NOTHIN', NOTHIN'.
BUT, UH...
I JUST HOPE YOU GET "SHEATHED" IN...
...WHAT YOU GOT "PREPARED" THERE.

THANK YOU VERY MUCH FOR JOINING US FOR THE FIFTH
VOLUME OF *SHOULDER-A-COFFIN KURO*.

2015 SATOKO KIYUDUKI

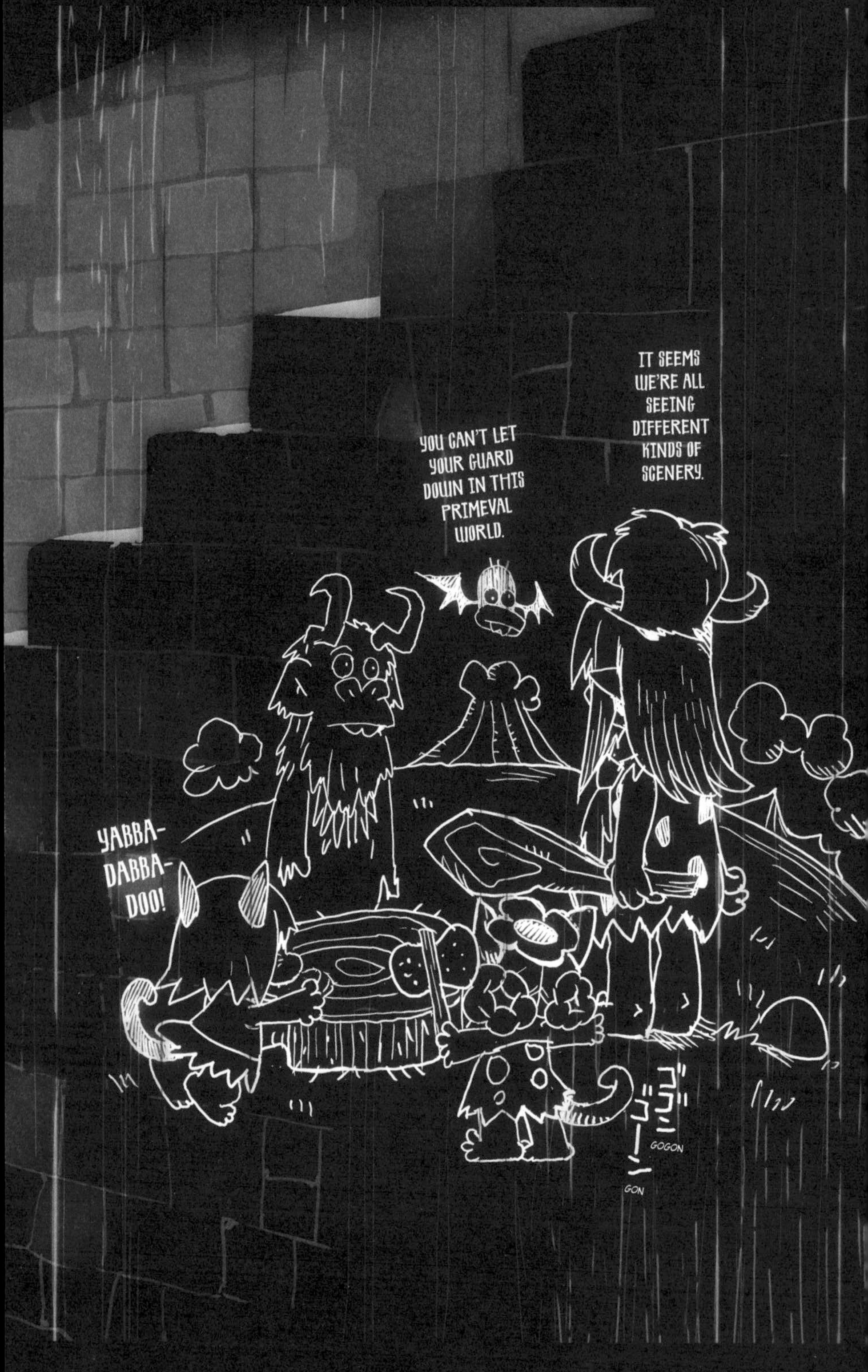
IT SEEMS WE'RE ALL SEEING DIFFERENT KINDS OF SCENERY.
YOU CAN'T LET YOUR GUARD DOWN IN THIS PRIMEVAL WORLD.
GOGON
GON
YABBA-DABBA-DOO!

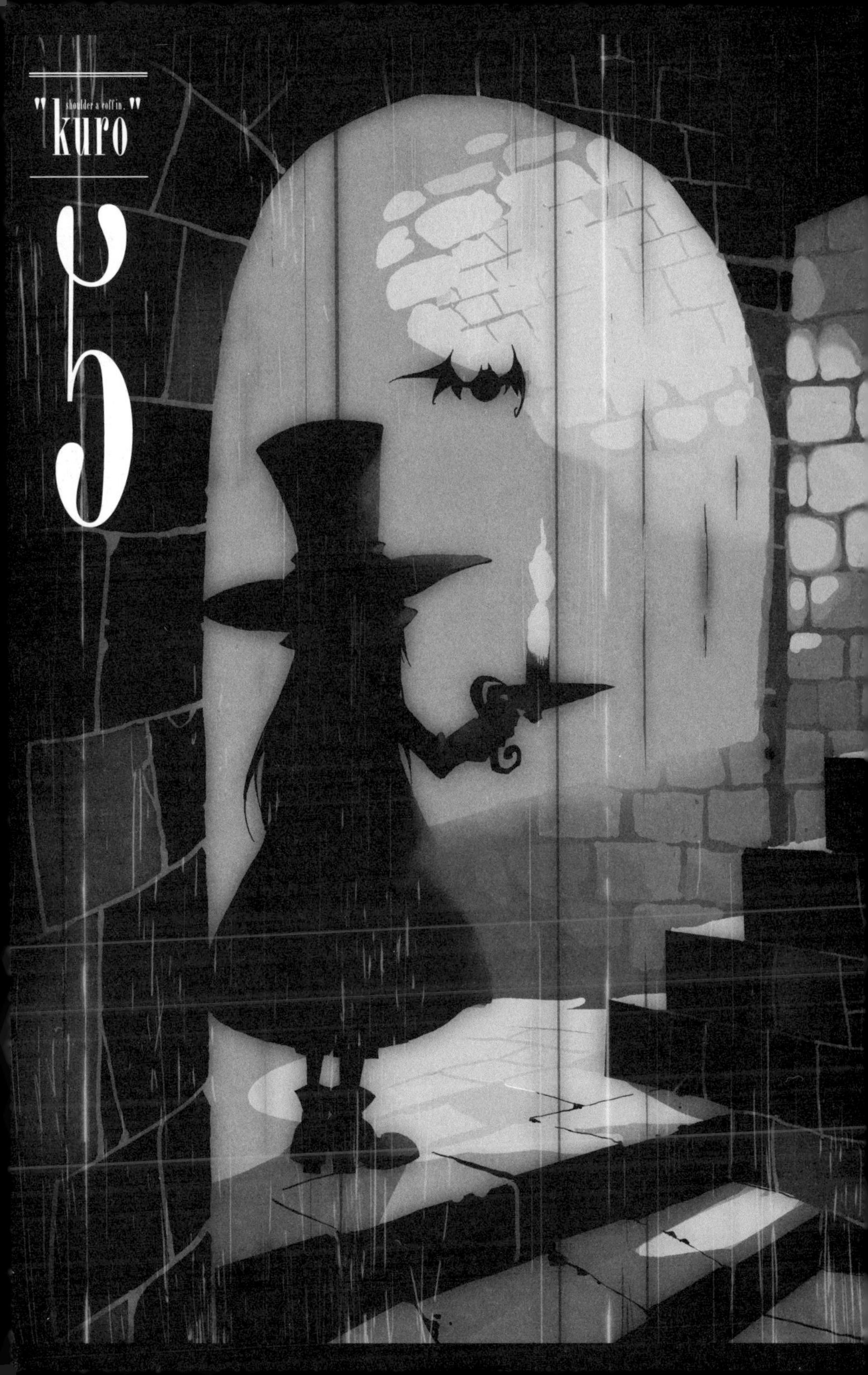
"shoulder a coffin."
kuro
5

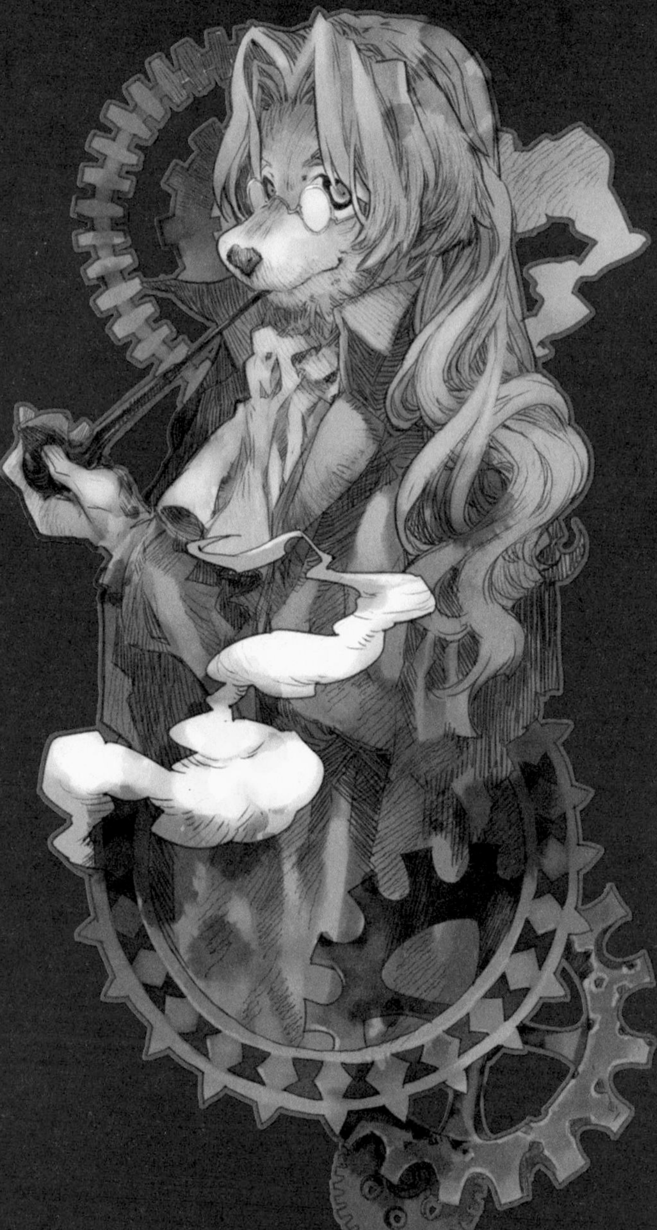

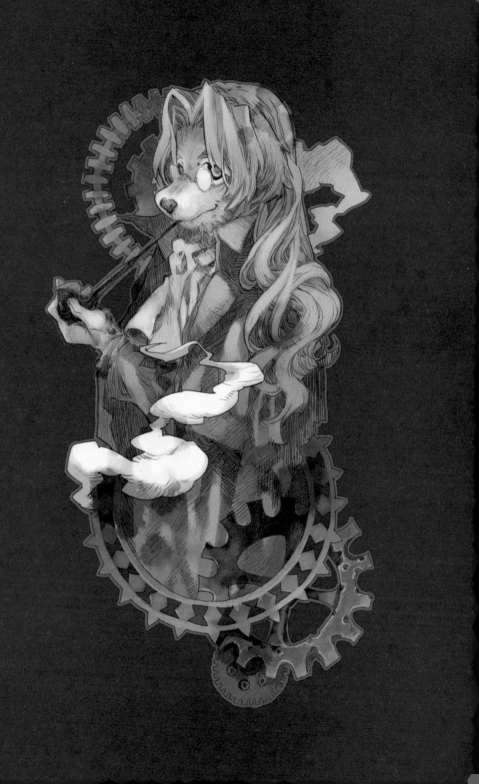

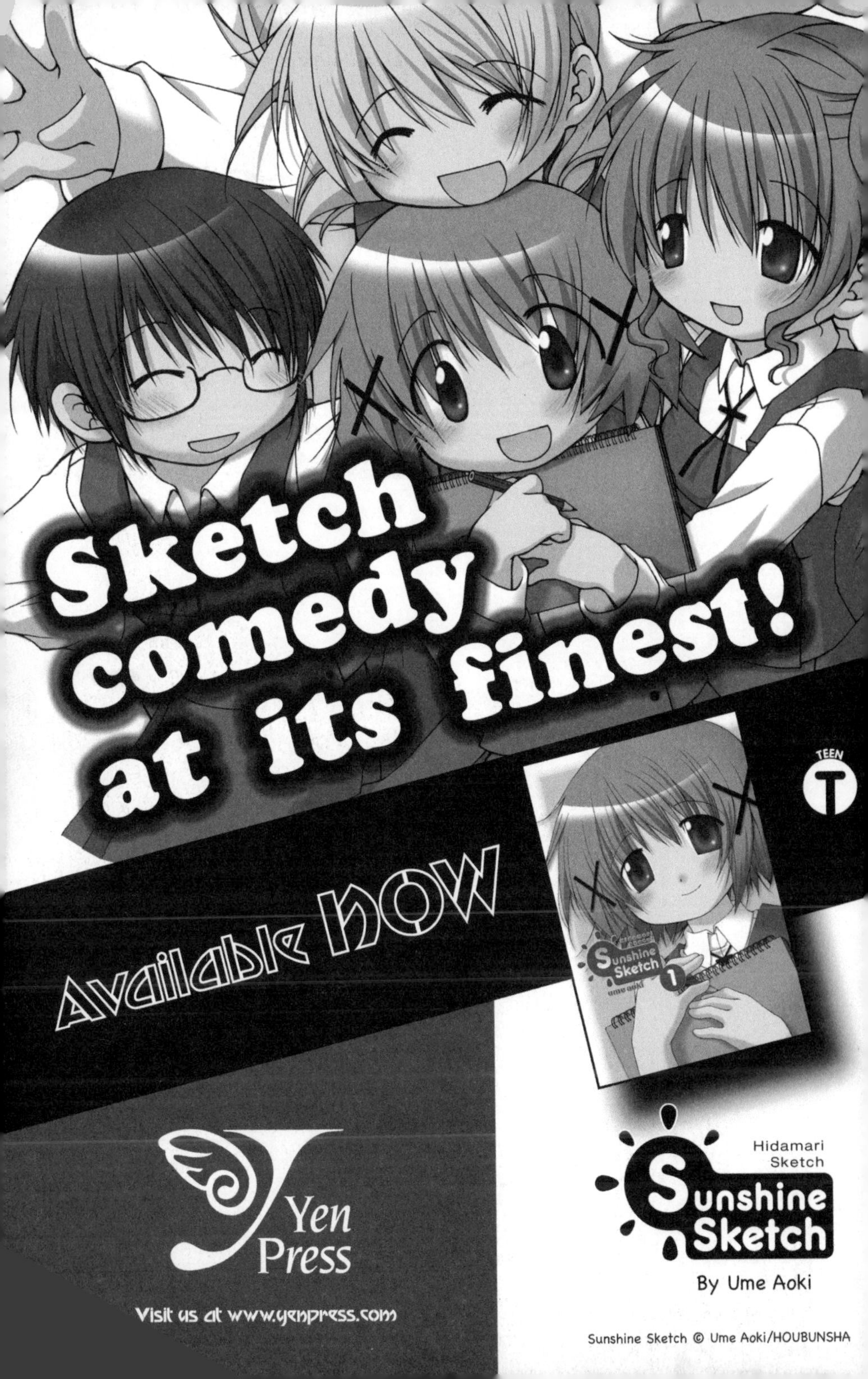
Sketch comedy at its finest!
TEEN
T
Available NOW
Sunshine Sketch 1
Yen Press
Visit us at www.yenpress.com
Hidamari Sketch
Sunshine Sketch
By Ume Aoki
Sunshine Sketch © Ume Aoki/HOUBUNSHA

SHOULDER-A-COFFIN KURO ⑤

Translation: Sheldon Drzka

HITSUGI KATSUGI NO KURO ~KAICHU TABINOWA~ Vol. 5 © 2015 Satoko Kiyuduki. All rights reserved. First published in Japan in 2015 by HOUBUNSHA CO., LTD, Tokyo. English translation rights in the United States, Canada, and the United Kingdom arranged with HOUBUNSHA CO., LTD. through Tuttle-Mori Agency, Inc., Tokyo.

Translation © 2016 by Hachette Book Group, Inc.

Yen Press
Hachette Book Group
1290 Avenue of the Americas
New York, NY 10104

www.HachetteBookGroup.com
www.YenPress.com

Yen Press is an imprint of Hachette Book Group, Inc. The Yen Press name and logo are trademarks of Hachette Book Group, Inc.

The publisher is not responsible for websites (or their content) that are not owned by the publisher.

Library of Congress Control Number: 2015956855

First Yen Press Edition: March 2016

ISBN: 978-0-316-27027-4

10 9 8 7 6 5 4 3 2 1

RRD-C

Printed in the United States of America